Personal Knowledge Management

Personal Knowledge Management

Individual, Organizational and Social Perspectives

Edited by

DAVID J. PAULEEN
Massey University, Auckland, New Zealand

and

G.E. GORMAN
Victoria University of Wellington, New Zealand

GOWER

Gower Applied Business Research
Our programme provides leaders, practitioners, scholars and researchers with thought provoking, cutting edge books that combine conceptual insights, interdisciplinary rigour and practical relevance in key areas of business and management.

Published by
Gower Publishing Limited
Wey Court East
Union Road
Farnham
Surrey, GU9 7PT
England

Ashgate Publishing Company
Suite 420
101 Cherry Street
Burlington,
VT 05401-4405
USA

www.gowerpublishing.com

British Library Cataloguing in Publication Data
Personal knowledge management : individual, organizational and social perspectives.
1. Knowledge management. 2. Knowledge workers. 3. Intellectual capital. 4. Organizational learning.
I. Pauleen, David, J. 1957- II. Gorman, G.E.
658.4'038 – dc22

Library of Congress Control Number: 2010940028

ISBN 9780566088926 (hbk)
ISBN 9781409403098 (ebk)

Printed and bound in Great Britain by the
MPG Books Group, UK

Contents

List of Figures

List of Tables

Notes on Contributors

Editors

David J. Pauleen (Ph.D.) is an Associate Professor in the School of Management at Massey University, Albany, New Zealand. Current research interests include personal knowledge management, emerging work practices, cross-cultural information and knowledge management, and virtual team leadership, dynamics, communication and technology. His work has appeared in such journals as the *Journal of Management Information Systems, Sloan Management Review, Business Insight (Wall Street Journal & Sloan Management Review), Journal of Global Information Management, Management Decision, Leadership and Organizational Development Journal, Journal of Knowledge Management, Journal of Information Technology,* and *Internet Research: Electronic Networking Applications and Policy.* He is also editor of the books *Virtual Teams: Projects, Protocols and Processes* (2004) and *Cross-Cultural Perspectives on Knowledge Management* (2007).

Professor G. E. Gorman, FCLIP, FRSA, AALIA, is Professor of Information Management at Victoria University of Wellington, New Zealand. He is once reported to have referred to knowledge management as 'the emperor's new clothes', which comment he now admits was perhaps ill-informed (a most unusual admission). In recent years he has moved into Ph.D. supervision and research in KM, and now PKM, but continues his other interests in information management curricula in Asian developing countries, information literacy education, and institutional information infrastructures. He is editor of the *Online Information Review*, Associate Editor of *Library Collections, Acquisitions and Technical Services*, and co-editor of a new initiative, *Digital Preservation Management and Technology*, to be offered by Emerald Publishing. He has published some 20 books and more than 300 peer-reviewed journal articles.

Contributors

Peter Case is Professor of Organization Studies, Bristol Business School, University of the West of England and Director of the Bristol Centre for Leadership and Organizational Ethics. He is general co-editor of *Culture & Organization* and a member of the editorial boards of *Leadership*, *Leadership & Organizational Development Journal* and the *Journal of Management, Spirituality and Religion*. His research interests encompass the ethics of leadership, organization theory and technologically mediated organization. Recent publications include *The Speed of Organization* (with S. Lilley and T. Owens, 2006) and *John Adair: the Fundamentals of Leadership* (with J. Gosling and M. Witzel, 2007).

Ricky K. F. Cheong is a DBA candidate at Southern Cross University and his research interests are in personal knowledge management and organizational learning. He is a Chartered IT Professional and Certified Information System Auditor. He has over 20 years experience in information technology and is a member of the British Computer Society and the Hong Kong Computer Society.

Paul D. Collins (Ph.D., Sociology, Rutgers University) is Associate Professor of Management, Business Administration Programme, University of Washington–Bothell, USA. He previously served on the faculty of University of Washington–Seattle and Purdue University. Paul is a recipient of several prestigious research awards, including the Academy of Management's Best Paper Award (OMT Division), the results of work conducted in his home office (disconnect) rather than his school office (connect). Paul's current research on sociotechnical connectivity in distributed project teams is a natural extension of his long-standing research emphasis on the dynamics of organizations, technology and innovation.

Jim Corner obtained his Ph.D. in operations research at the Arizona State University after completing an MBA at the University of Wyoming. Prior to joining the Department of Management Systems at the Waikato Management School, University of Waikato, he held various management positions over a period of ten years with US Steel Corp (now, USX) and Texas Instruments. His research interests include multi-attribute/multi-objective decision-making, decision analysis, decision support systems, and systems intelligence.

Jocelyn Cranefield Dr Jocelyn Cranefield is a senior lecturer in the School of Information Management at Victoria University, Wellington, New Zealand. Her areas of research interest include knowledge management and the strategic use of information systems, and her recent research investigates how online communities and social technologies can help drive professional change. Jocelyn has many years of experience as a manager and consultant in the state, educational and cultural sectors, having worked for state and local government, museums, television and in publishing.

Tom H. Davenport is the President's Distinguished Professor of Information Technology and Management at Babson College. He has led research centres at Accenture, McKinsey and Company, Ernst & Young, and CSC Index, and has taught at Harvard Business School, Dartmouth's Tuck School, the University of Texas, and the University of Chicago. Tom's newest book – co-authored with Jeanne Harris and Bob Morison – is *Analytics at Work: Smarter Decisions, Better Results*, published in February 2010. It follows the best-selling *Competing on Analytics*, which was translated into 14 languages. Prior to this, Tom wrote, co-authored or edited 13 other books, including the first books on business process re-engineering, knowledge management, attention management and enterprise systems. He has written over 100 articles for such publications as *Harvard Business Review, Sloan Management Review, California Management Review,* the *Financial Times* and many other publications, and has been a columnist for *Information Week, CIO* and *Darwin* magazines. His blog for Harvard Business Online is http://discussionleader.hbsp.com/davenport/.

Jonathan Gosling is Professor and Director of the Centre for Leadership Studies at the University of Exeter. He therefore spends much of his time as a middle manager, and also intervenes in other organizations, usually in response to an invitation to do so, with the intention of supporting greater autonomy and creativity amongst those embroiled therein. He supervises Ph.D. students, teaches on MBAs around the world, conducts masterclasses and undertakes empirical research into how people improve what matters most to them and their communities. His appreciation of these matters is informed by psychoanalysis (practical and theoretical) and platonic philosophy (ditto). He has published in scholarly and popular journals, and has written books on leadership, Lord Nelson and literary criticism (forthcoming).

Raimo Hämäläinen, Systems Analysis Laboratory, Helsinki University of Technology, is well known for his work in dynamic game theory and decision analysis. He is the author of over 180 publications and conference papers on decision-making, control and dynamic games, energy modelling and environmental decision-making and participation, and biological systems. He is also the designer of many widely used decision support systems.

As a consultant he has helped to solve problems especially in the areas of environmental policy and risk analysis. Recently he has actively worked on the new concept of systems intelligence, developed by jointly with Professor Esa Saarinen, and its introduction to different organizations.

Sally Jansen van Vuuren Sally Jansen van Vuuren is an experienced knowledge management practitioner who has worked with several New Zealand public sector organizations to introduce and embed KM as a key organizational approach. Building on a multidisciplinary background, Sally helps organizations to enhance organizational performance, improve service delivery and build capability and excel in harnessing and leveraging individual and organizational knowledge. Sally has recently completed a doctoral thesis that investigates collaboration and knowledge-sharing in public sector-based interorganizational projects and has developed a framework to guide and assist the design of initiatives in the sector. Sally also holds a Bachelor of Information Technology, and a first-class honours degree majoring in Information Systems.

Rachel Jones has a Ph.D. in English literature from Massey University, New Zealand. She is currently completing a second Ph.D. in the Management Communication department at the University of Waikato, looking at the future direction of knowledge management. Her other areas of interest include personal knowledge management, metaphor, complex responsive process theory and systems intelligence.

William Jones is a Research Associate Professor at the University of Washington where he manages the Keeping Found Things Found group (kftf.ischool. washington.edu). He has published in personal information management (PIM), human–computer interaction, information retrieval and human cognition. Professor Jones wrote the book *Keeping Found Things Found: The Study and Practice of Personal Information Management* and also edited the book *Personal Information Management*. He holds several patents relating to search and PIM from his work as a program manager at Microsoft in Office and then in MSN Search. He received his doctorate from Carnegie-Mellon University for research into human memory.

Darl G. Kolb is Associate Professor of Management and International Business at the University of Auckland Business School, New Zealand. Darl's main research interest is sociotechnical connectivity, especially as it relates to leadership and team performance and on which he and Paul Collins are conducting a large scale survey. Prior to pursuing his Ph.D. in organizational behaviour and programme evaluation at Cornell, Darl received his Masters degree at the University of Colorado, Boulder and worked for ten years as an Outward Bound instructor, wilderness guide and educator, where he learned first hand the value of separation and reflection for personal growth.

Peter Murphy is Associate Professor of Communications and Director of the Social Aesthetics Research Unit at Monash University, Australia. He is the co-author of the trilogy *Creativity and the Global Knowledge Economy* (2009), *Global Creation* (2009) and *Imagination* (2010). His other books include *Dialectic of Romanticism: A Critique of Modernism* (2004) and *Civic Justice: From Greek Antiquity to the Modern World* (2001). From 1998–2001, he worked in senior editorial roles for Australia's most successful Internet start-up company, Looksmart.

Larry Prusak is a researcher and consultant and was the founder and director of the Institute for Knowledge Management at IBM. Larry has been studying knowledge and learning in organizations for the past two decades. He has extensive experience, both within the US and internationally, in helping organizations manage their information and knowledge resources. He has worked with several US and overseas government agencies and NGOs, as well as having taught and lectured in many universities. In addition he has been widely quoted, has published several innovative and influential books and has given over 200 major speeches. He is currently a visiting professor at Copenhagen Business School, senior advisor to the World Bank on knowledge and learning and senior advisor on knowledge issues with NASA (US National Aeronautics and Space Agency).

Dave Snowden is the founder and chief scientific officer of *Cognitive Edge*. His work is international in nature and covers government and industry looking at complex issues relating to strategy, organizational decision making and decision making. He is currently leading a series of experimental programmes to create a new approach to measuring impact in public services, in the areas of health, education and social policy. This has involved the design of a new research tool to capture qualitative and quantitative data in social contexts using self-signified narrative, based on ethnographic principles. He previously worked for IBM where he was a Director of the Institution for Knowledge Management and founded the Cynefin Centre for Organizational Complexity; during that period he was selected by IBM as one of six 'on-demand' thinkers.

Eric Tsui is the Professor of Knowledge Management and Associate Director of the Knowledge Management Research Centre at the Hong Kong Polytechnic

University. He is also an editorial board member of the journals *Knowledge-Based Systems, Knowledge Management Research and Practice* and *Information and Knowledge Management.* His research interests are in knowledge management technologies, enterprise portals and e-learning. His current research projects include taxonomy–folksonomy integration for knowledge navigation, a knowledge portal for a construction organization, communities of practice and scenario-based e-learning systems. He has published in journals such as *Knowledge-Based Systems, Expert Systems with Applications* and *Information Processing and Management.* Prior to joining the university he was Chief Research Officer, Asia Pacific and Innovation Manager for CSC Australia, a large global IT consulting, outsourcing and systems integration firm.

Karl Martin Wiig is executive chair of the Knowledge Research Institute, Inc. As a technical and management consultant for more than 45 years he has supported organizations to develop systematic approaches for decision-making and effective work, has an international reputation for his work in knowledge management, applied AI and management science, and has published over 70 textbook chapters and research articles and five KM books: *Expert Systems: A Manager's Guide; Knowledge Management Foundations: Thinking about Thinking – How People and Organizations Create, Represent, and Use Knowledge; Knowledge Management: The Central Management Focus for Intelligent-Acting Organizations; Knowledge Management Methods: Practical Approaches to Managing Knowledge;* and *People-Focused Knowledge Management: How Effective Decision Making Leads to Corporate Success.*

Mark Wolfe is a senior communications consultant and lecturer based in Calgary, Alberta. Following work in print journalism and corporate communication, Mark garnered a 1994 Governor General's Gold Medal nomination – Canada's highest honour for Masters-level scholarship. Introducing knowledge management as an emerging focus for communication study, his doctoral work involved leading-edge research in broadband technology as a KM tool and the co-designing of the Masters programme in Knowledge Management at Royal Roads University in Victoria, BC. Dr Wolfe lectures in graduate and undergraduate communication and technology programmes at Mount Royal and the Universities of Calgary and Alberta.

Preface

As far as we are aware, this is the first book devoted specifically to Personal Knowledge Management (PKM), here defined broadly as an evolving set of understandings, skills and abilities that allows an individual to survive and prosper in complex and changing organizational and social environments. Such environments are not unique to the twenty-first century, but in fact have existed perhaps since *homo sapiens* began to think. The difference today is that we have begun to realize the value of PKM as a means of coping with complex environmental changes and developments.

PKM, like its parent Knowledge Management (KM), is a concept that has grown out of a combination of fields as diverse as KM itself – personal information management, cognitive psychology, philosophy, management science, education, communications and many other disciplines. This book includes chapters written from a number of these perspectives. These chapters have been commissioned from recognized scholars, consultants and expert practitioners. Together, they present an accessible, holistic and detailed understanding of PKM as it concerns the individual and individuals in relationship to organizations and society as a whole. The intention is to reach an audience ranging from academics and university students to reflective practitioners in any field.

Whilst the book covers PKM in a range of contexts – individual, organizational and social – we have not rigidly adhered to these distinctive aspects of PKM in organizing the chapters. Rather, we have sought a natural flow of ideas as a means of drawing chapters into what we hope is a coherent sequence for readers. We would like to suggest that readers consider a number of questions when reading the chapters in this collection, thereby undertaking a kind of reflexive exercise in PKM.

From the perspective of the individual interested in pursuing a PKM strategy, we suggest starting with the following three questions:

1.   How do I view my knowledge and how I have come to 'own' it?

2.   What is the role of a social network in PKM?

3.   How do I (and/or my network) maintain knowledge currency in rapidly changing environments and anticipate the inevitable changes in environmental conditions?

From the wider research and practitioner perspective, we pose three more questions:

1.   How do knowledge workers rise above the role of mere information- or knowledge-processors? Can they become knowledge forecasters, 'conglomerators', brokers and creators?

2.   Can the often seemingly clashing motivations between organizational KM and PKM be harmonized so that the 'enlightened self-interest' of both parties can be realized?

3.   What is the role of government in providing PKM skills to its citizens in times of extreme discontinuity such as we are currently experiencing?

We also recognize that many will read selectively, choosing perhaps just a handful of chapters by 'favourite' authors; therefore, we have exercised editorial prerogative to ensure that each chapter stands alone as an engaging and informative discussion of its specific topic.

In Chapter 1 the book's co-editors (from Massey University and Victoria University of Wellington respectively) introduce the principles and concepts of PKM, focusing especially on its nature and value. In particular they discuss how individuals can develop PKM strategies to remain competitive, with the focus on five practical aspects of a PKM strategy: management, lifelong learning, communication and interpersonal skills, use of technology and forecasting and anticipating. Their premise is that a PKM strategy that develops increased personal competence in these areas should assist individuals in maintaining knowledge currency and improving decision-making in relation to employment and life opportunities.

This is followed in Case and Gosling's chapter 'Where is the Wisdom We Have Lost in Knowledge? A Stoical Perspective on Personal Knowledge Management' by a philosophical grounding for PKM. Case (University of the West of England) and Gosling (University of Exeter) develop a more contextual and personalized understanding of the term 'knowledge' from both personal and organizational perspectives, in the end suggesting that Stoicism, with respect to 'philosophy as a way of life', provides practical means by which a PKM agenda might move forward.

In Chapter 3, still in a somewhat philosophical mood, Peter Murphy of Monash University investigates the links between information and imagination. Considering the vast amount of information available at our fingertips, he ponders what PKM means for the way we think, create, write and muse, specifically looking at how intuition, pattern recognition, visualization, improvisation, paradoxical thought and synchronicity shape the way that we manage personal digital libraries.

Chapter 4, by Mark Wolfe (Universities of Calgary and Alberta), offers an alternative view to Chapters 2 and 3, both of which view PKM as an established and ongoing development. Wolfe discusses his concern that technology and 'pragmatic action' may thwart PKM before it has a chance to develop. He argues that communication theory and language should be the core elements in PKM, as they form the basis of linguistic competence in individuals and organizations – but communication theory and language are not yet core concerns of PKM. This, according to Wolfe, may be a fatal flaw in PKM, because knowledge (whether KM or PKM) always occurs within a linguistic context.

While Chapters 2, 3 and 4 offer wide-ranging philosophical and critical views of PKM, Chapter 5 addresses organizational aspects of Personal Knowledge Management. Here Jones (University of Waikato), Corner (University of Waikato) and Hämäläinen (Helsinki University of Technology) discuss how PKM can assist in integrating the goals of organizations with the personal development of individual members of these organizations. They use systems intelligence as a theoretical lens for their analysis and focus on the intuitive, reflective and communicative aspects of this integration. They demonstrate how knowledge management at a personal level connects with organizations as systems, thus encouraging individuals to be aware of the systems around them, and emphasizing the potential impact of individuals' behaviour on these organizations-as-systems.

The next two chapters turn to well-known consultants for their views on aspects of PKM. Thus in Chapter 6, well-known KM author and consultant Larry Prusak and his assisting author Jocelyn Cranefield (Victoria University of Wellington) offer a personal perspective on PKM. That is, they suggest ways of actively managing personal knowledge in order to keep ideas and skills current, to inform decision-making and to remain flexible and innovative in an ever-changing world. They propose four foundational practices for personal knowledge management: scan and reinvent, vet and filter, invest in your networks, and get out of your office.

In Chapter 7 another well-known KM consultant, Dave Snowden, assisted by David Pauleen and Sally Jansen van Vuuren, suggests that the term 'personal knowledge management' may be a misnomer, as individuals are in fact part of communities and can only manage knowledge as part of a community. These authors propose the concept of social knowledge networking and suggest that with the help of technology, individuals, as part of a network, can remain current, fluid and knowledgeable in a constantly changing, complex world.

Almost as an adjunct to Chapter 7, in Chapter 8 Kolb (University of Auckland) and Collins (University of Washington) apply the lens of connectivity to PKM and introduce the concept of 'connective flow'. They acknowledge that while knowledge is socially constructed and often reliant on generative collaboration with others, a forgotten yet critical part of PKM is the need to recognize the value of 'disconnection' from our highly connected world for regenerative personal reflection. They recommend five practices that can maintain a healthy connective flow in a world of hyperconnectivity.

In Chapter 9 William Jones (University of Washington), who has written extensively on Personal Information Management (PIM) argues that it is only through information that knowledge is understood and expressed, and therefore knowledge can only be managed indirectly through the management of information. Contrary to most of the other authors in this book, he argues that PKM, whilst a predictable evolution of data and information management, is nonetheless best regarded as a subset of PIM. This is not a view that we as editors necessarily subscribe to, but it is a fairly wide-held view and deserves to be heard in a book on PKM.

In Chapter 10, another well-known KM author, academic and consultant, Tom Davenport, offers an organizational perspective on how personal information and knowledge management can improve the performance of knowledge workers and analyses the current readiness or lack thereof in today's organizations. He suggests that individuals should adopt a dual strategy of lobbying for increased attention to the issue of PKM by their organizations, and adopting better personal approaches at the same time.

In Chapter 11 Cheong (Southern Cross University) and Tsui (Hong Kong Polytechnic University) tackle an important component of PKM, personal learning, which they link to organizational learning. They argue that organizations need to align individual learning with corporate objectives and propose several PKM strategies to bridge the gap between individual learning and organizational learning. Indeed, they suggest that PKM is an enabler for effectively managing individual learning and organizational learning.

Finally, in Chapter 12 well-known KM author and consultant, Karl Wiig (Knowledge Research Institute), links the importance of PKM with the development of the much-promoted idea of the knowledge society. He argues that pursuing effective societal PKM requires in-depth understanding of societal contexts; of the nature of knowledge and intellectual capital (IC); of knowledge work; of knowledge workers; of relations between IC and strategic, tactical and operational functions; and of PKM options and opportunities. For each nation, undertaking widespread PKM becomes a necessary societal challenge.

Each chapter in this collection provides a unique and informative perspective on the evolving field of PKM – like it or not PKM is here, and has the potential to make us more effective in our personal and work lives. Organizations of all kinds should take note of this emerging phenomenon in order to better deal with their missions. Our authors discuss, argue and often disagree with one another, yet the common intention is to throw light on PKM and how it supports and affects individuals, organizations and society as a whole. As editors, we are pleased to present in one volume the views of such a distinguished set of authors; we hope that what is presented here will inform, stimulate and challenge every reader. We also accept full responsibility for any errors or omissions.

David J. Pauleen   G. E. Gorman
Massey University   Victoria University of Wellington
2010   2010

The Nature and Value of Personal Knowledge Management

G. E. Gorman and David J. Pauleen

Introduction

Mention Personal Knowledge Management (PKM) and a common reaction is, 'oh no, not another offshoot of KM!' In response, our proposition is that PKM differs significantly from Knowledge Management as currently understood, and that PKM is a form of sophisticated career and life management. We suggest that applied PKM may be one way of helping individuals survive, and prosper, through turbulent, complex and changing organizational and social environments.

PKM is a concept that has grown out of a combination of fields as diverse as knowledge management (KM), personal information management, cognitive psychology, philosophy, management science and communications as well as others (Nordin et al. 2009). However, very little empirical research or significant conceptual development has been done with PKM. A search of PKM in major databases turns up just a handful of papers, although study in the area seems to be gaining traction – *Online Information Review* 33:2 (2009) was a special issue devoted to PKM, and there are numerous websites and references to PKM, many of sound quality.

We know that PKM focuses on helping individuals become more effective in personal, organizational and social environments. The existing literature clearly points to PKM as a means of increasing individual effectiveness in work environments such as teams and organizations, and in the knowledge society generally. While the traditional view of KM focuses on managing organizational knowledge – including the knowledge that individuals possess – through combinations of technology and management processes, the core focus of PKM is 'personal enquiry': the quest to find, connect, learn and explore (Clemente and Pollara 2005). We believe that there are four essential and practical areas that an individual must 'master' to engage in effective PKM: management, learning, communication, interpersonal skills and use of technology. We suggest that a fifth area, forecasting and anticipating, would be a highly desirable, though arguably more difficult, set of skills to acquire.

In this chapter we first examine the evolving nature of knowledge work and the rapidly changing organizational and social environment that we believe necessitates an individual approach to KM. We also raise the issue of potential conflict between PKM and Organizational Knowledge Management (OKM) and how organizations might support PKM to bring greater effectiveness to OKM programmes. Then we look at how individuals can develop PKM strategies to remain competitive, and we focus on several practical aspects of KM. Finally, we discuss whether PKM might require a modicum of wisdom to be truly effective.

The World Turns and Change Occurs

In this section we highlight two aspects or problems of the evolving nature of knowledge work as it relates to environmental change (both organizational and social); both aspects, information overload and the changing nature of work, support the need for PKM.

To begin with information overload, no one doubts that individuals face the enormous problem of having access to more information than they can comfortably assimilate and manage. Information overload is a prime example of an environmental change that rapidly – and critically – affects how individuals manage and act upon their knowledge. We all know first hand the causes of information overload: large amounts of information are pushed at us through such channels as email, text messages, phone calls, radio and television, while the Internet makes available massive amounts of information of questionable veracity through websites, blogs and the like.

Equally problematic is the reality that information overload can hinder decision-making and judgment by causing stress and cognitive impediments, colloquially understood as 'paralysis by analysis'. Rooney and McKenna (2005, 316) capture the futility of always needing to know more and to have access to more information, explaining: 'More uncertainty demands more knowledge, more knowledge increases complexity, more complexity demands more abstraction, more abstraction increases uncertainty.'

While the cause of information overload is due in part to technology, the cure is also partly technology – but it is how one chooses and uses technology that is critical. One of the problems in writing about technology is the speed of change; what we refer to as current is already passé as soon as ideas are committed to print. Nevertheless, we believe technology is a tool that can assist in making PKM more effective, but in no way should the technology be viewed as an equivalent of PKM. That is, technology and its dependents such as social media are the handmaidens of PKM, nothing more.

The changing nature of work is the second environmental issue or problem affecting individuals. This problem seems to spell the end of the social compact of single career and lifetime employment, which, if not in practice, certainly existed as an ideal prior to the twenty-first century. Competitive pressures on organizations continue to grow, as does the need for greater flexibility and skill sets. As a consequence, competitive pressures on individuals are also increasing, and more diverse and unpredictable career paths are becoming common. Responsibility for self-development and lifelong learning is now in the hands of the individual, who increasingly controls the development of their career and destiny. In the world of the modern knowledge worker, it has become necessary for individuals to maintain, develop and market their skills to give them any chance of competitive advantage in the job market in both the short and long term. This conflict of priorities between individuals and organizations represents the changing contract between employees and organizations (Byrne 2001; Viedma and Enache 2008). This new reality begs the question: is there an inherent conflict between organizational KM and PKM and what, if anything, can be done to harmonize individual and organizational knowledge goals?

Organizational Knowledge Management

While an individual-focused KM approach might seem at first blush to be in conflict with conventional organization-based KM, we suggest that PKM might be a path for effectively instilling a KM ethic into the organization as a whole.

Since its inception as a field of study in the 1990s KM has focused on organizational knowledge and how it can be exploited. However, from the beginning practitioners and academics such as Davenport and Prusak (1998) forcefully pointed out that much organizational knowledge resides in the minds of individual employees working in the organization. It could be argued that PKM, with its emphasis on the communicative individual, refocuses the locus of ongoing knowledge creation on the individual (Wolfe 2010).

The traditional view of KM is centred on enabling the corporate body to be more effective by 'recording' and making available what its people know, and the emphasis in KM research has remained on how to 'prise' knowledge out of people, either by making it explicit and entering it into an information system (or knowledge management system) or, possibly more realistically, encouraging employees, as communicative individuals, to share knowledge in social and professional situations such as communities of practice. Except for adopting the negative perspective and pointing out that 'knowledge is power', and therefore individuals lack the incentive to share, little attention has been given to the perspective of the individual and their personal knowledge.

Two factors are at play here, and there is a natural tension between them. First, much, if not most, of an organization's critical knowledge resides with the employees. Of course organizational knowledge can be found in established business processes and formal patents, but creative, innovative knowledge and the kind of yet-to-be-realized knowledge critical to an organization's survival over time resides with individuals (Murphy and Pauleen 2007). There is, then, a very natural tension here between the knowledge individuals potentially offer their organization and the very personal feelings these individuals have about what they know and have experienced over the course of their lifetimes.

We do not seek to resolve this issue, but we believe that the success of organizational KM strategies ultimately rests on how well organizations value and can strengthen the individual employee's quest for personal knowledge, self-esteem and even self-realization. This is not a new idea: 3M has long allowed their most creative and innovative employees time and resources to work on projects of their own choosing. Google does much the same with their programme that allows engineers to spend 20 per cent of their time working on 'what they are passionate about' (Google Jobs 2009). In both cases organizational innovation is a direct result of allowing employees the freedom to find, connect, learn and explore (Clemente and Pollara 2005).

In view of this scenario, if organizations take PKM seriously, the 'what's in it for me?' factor is taken care of immediately, facilitating quicker individual buy-in for the whole KM concept. The difficulty is how to convince a traditional company that developing an individual employee's quest for knowledge necessarily leads to better OKM.

PKM and the Knowledge Worker

PKM is a response to the idea that knowledge workers, like all individuals, increasingly must be responsible for their own growth and learning. Recent research into an emerging class of mobile knowledge workers called 'offroaders' shows that these individuals are consciously and proactively seeking new knowledge, even knowledge not directly related to their current work (Harmer and Pauleen 2010). This is an aspect of lifelong learning related to information literacy, discussed below.

All individuals require processes and tools by which they can evaluate what they know in a given situation, and then seek ways to fill the gaps when needed. Technology can be a very helpful tool, but the fundamentals of PKM are not predicated on technology, as noted earlier. Nevertheless, there is a strong undercurrent in PKM that does emphasize its technological aspect, and we cannot deny that this is widely accepted. According to Mitchell (2004), Barth stresses that

> PKM involves a range of relatively simple and inexpensive techniques and tools that anyone can use to acquire, create and share knowledge, extend personal networks and collaborate with colleagues without having to rely on the technical or financial resources of the employer.

Indeed, later in this chapter we make passing mention of the possible uses of Facebook and Connotea as technological tools for assisting in PKM management. But we do not wish readers to assume that PKM is simply another technical process.

The history of PKM begins with the idea of the knowledge worker (Drucker 1968). In PKM one key area of interest is how people become knowledge workers, and especially how they maintain their currency as knowledge workers. Davenport and Prusak's (1998, 5) oft-cited definition of working knowledge is very much directed toward the individual and can serve as a starting point for investigating PKM: 'a fluid mix of framed experience, values, contextual information, and expert insight that provides a framework for evaluating and incorporating new experiences and information'.

To expand this definition to encompass PKM, we add that individuals need to know how to decide on and seek new and relevant information, knowledge, experiences and 'learnings'. The focus must be on the need for the constant renewal of knowledge for ever-changing environments. To facilitate this the individual is increasingly in charge of managing and anticipating career changes and challenges, as noted above.

The roots of PKM are, as previously stated, multidisciplinary. One of the more apparent antecedents is personal information management (PIM), stemming from research in library and information management and personal productivity tools and software. PIM and early PKM developed quickly in response to the technology revolution and the resulting problem of information overload (Jefferson 2006). Early work in this area focused on helping university students develop information literacy skills and use technology to organize and use information (Frand and Hixon 1999; Avery et al. 2001). Recent studies with postgraduate students have shown that there is a recursive relationship between applied PKM and PIM, with skills sets in both growing simultaneously over time (Benitez and Pauleen 2009).

The technological approach to PKM is important, but we believe it is limited. Or perhaps it would be more accurate to say that we believe it *should* be limited. As in organizational forms of KM, it is often the case that the technology is equated with a solution. We emphasize that there is much more to PKM than technology and look to other, more recent and multidisciplinary approaches. These approaches, while not always explicitly acknowledging PKM, have focused on the development of skills and attitudes that lead to more effective cognition, communication, collaboration, creativity, problem solving, lifelong learning, social networking, leadership and the like. These approaches make PKM qualitatively different from information management and can help individuals better understand information and knowledge and put them into a context that allows more effective decision-making (Dorsey 2000; Zuber-Skerritt 2005; Jefferson 2006) regarding career and life choices.

Where to Begin? The Practical Aspects of PKM

In this section we introduce the five areas we believe should be the focus of PKM strategy: management, lifelong learning, communication and interpersonal skills, use of technology and forecasting and anticipating. Rapidly changing environments present challenges for individuals who are trying to cope. We believe a PKM strategy that develops increased personal competence in these areas should assist individuals in maintaining knowledge currency and improving decision-making in relation to employment and life opportunities.

MANAGEMENT

A PKM strategy can be summarized as taking charge and developing a plan to:

$$anticipate \rightarrow explore \rightarrow find \rightarrow connect \rightarrow learn \rightarrow act.$$

Within this strategy the management aspect primarily concerns how to determine and structure a PKM strategy that meets one's personal situation and how to maintain and update it as necessary. This form of self-management requires an understanding of self, including one's strengths and weaknesses. The objective is not merely to reach goals 'out there' but to reflect continuously, to improve one's inner self and to develop a philosophy of living.

LIFELONG LEARNING

Second, lifelong learning in the form of ongoing adult education and training is likely to be an important part of any PKM strategy. Subjects of study and upgrading of skills would be determined by the changing business environment (if a job is being outsourced overseas, determine what positions are likely to remain). Personal interests and predilections are also important in determining what to study, as these will generate the most enthusiasm and may lead to unforeseen opportunities. Reading widely in a variety of subject areas may open up new horizons and lead to further study. While organizations can, and sometimes do, provide opportunities for personal development and learning, ultimate responsibility remains with the individual to determine and act on an appropriate strategy.

COMMUNICATION AND INTERPERSONAL SKILLS

Third, communication and interpersonal skills are another fundamental component of effective PKM. Here communication encompasses a variety of skills and abilities beyond giving an effective presentation or writing persuasively. As Murphy (2010) argues, perception, intuition, expression, visualization, interpretation and design are all critical forms of communication.

We also believe that cross-cultural knowledge and skills facilitate effective, empathetic communication in a globally connected world and that opportunities to meet and learn about others should be taken. Cross-cultural knowledge gleaned from cross-cultural interactions has significant value in an inter-connected global world. Whilst Murphy (2010) refers to 'perception' as a component in effective communication, there is yet a more fundamental aspect to cross-cultural competence. This is the ability to engage in 'perspective-taking', defined by Holden (2002) as the ability to understand other worldviews that underpin insight and knowledge generated by other communities. We suggest that perspective-taking, and understanding other worldviews, underpins all effective communication and therefore significantly affects PKM, which by definition includes communication in some form or other.

Another vital communication skill is the ability to network with others. Effective networking can provide access to those with special knowledge, rare competencies, sources of finance and forms of influence (Holden 2002). Snowden et al. (2010) call this Social Knowledge Networking; it is a potential source of local and global knowledge, but it can only be effective if one possesses effective communication and networking skills.

A critical part of networking is the ability to collaborate, coordinate and synchronize efforts and motivations with others. This implies a robust matrix of social networking synapses or ties between individual or organizational actors (sometimes termed 'nodes'). If we tried to map the social networks that support an individual's PKM, the result would be an intensely complex series of matrices or webs: between individuals, between individual and groups, between individuals and families, between individuals and formal organizations (including workplaces), as well as informal organizations – and perhaps many more nodes.

As yet untested in any thorough manner is the way in which social networking tools such as Facebook (http://www.facebook.com/), or social bookmarking tools such as Connotea (http://www.connotea.org/), might assist an individual in better controlling or organizing their social knowledge networking, and thereby achieving better PKM control. Social bookmarking is a useful tool for locating, classifying and sharing Internet resources through the use of shared lists of user-created bookmarks. It also allows users to create tags for bookmarks, which are organized so that other users can search and browse the tags as well as the bookmarks of other people (Godwin-Jones 2006). Current work by Chu et al. (2009) suggests that Connotea is a quick and easy way to create, save and share bookmarks for both personal information management and group information management. This begs the question, what organizing and distributing role might a service such as Connotea have for PKM?

USE OF TECHNOLOGY

The fourth component, and one related to tools such as Connotea, is being able to use technology effectively. This is clearly a *sine qua non* in today's world, and we do not contest this. However, it should be treated as a tool that serves a PKM strategy, not as a substitute for the strategy. Technology, in the form of the Internet, certainly makes information more easily available, but, as discussed above, too much information is a curse of its own. To deal with information overload and to use the Internet more effectively, information literacy and personal library skills – the ability to categorize information and create taxonomies in personally meaningful ways – should be a part of any PKM skill set. Information management skills will help individuals make better use of the growing number of personal productivity tools. Communication technologies, such as broadband, 3G networks and Web 2.0 are valuable in, for example, letting us connect to global knowledge networks, but again one needs the management and communication skills to use these networks effectively.

FORECASTING AND ANTICIPATING

The fifth and final area we believe is critical to PKM strategy is forecasting and anticipating, and this is a challenging skill to develop. Unless one has extrasensory powers, one is unlikely to be able to forecast the future with any degree of accuracy. Nevertheless, it may be argued that high-quality information, carefully considered, may indeed allow us to better understand the possible development of trends. The key skill here, perhaps, is to be able to entertain various possibilities, prepare in appropriate ways and be ready to act as necessary. If the possibilities do not eventuate, then it is just a matter of nothing ventured, nothing gained. In any case the skills needed in forecasting and anticipating and the information and knowledge accrued are likely to prove valuable in a PKM strategy.

We believe that fundamental to effective forecasting are research skills including reading, canvassing, observation, paying attention, interviewing and reflecting. Using our senses to gather information about the present may allow us to visualize patterns that help us to understand where events are heading. Once we become skilled in recognizing patterns in the people and events around us, we are practising sense-making, the process of creating situational awareness and understanding in situations of high complexity or uncertainty in order to make decisions (Klein et al. 2006). The value of sense-making in forecasting and PKM is clarified by Klein and colleagues, who explain that sense-making is a deliberate effort to understand connections among people, places and events in order to predict their 'trajectories' and act accordingly.

Capitalising on Synergies

The five areas that we have discussed as the focus for a PKM strategy are in fact tightly intertwined. It is difficult to think about improving communication skills without also being up to date with communications technology. Social knowledge networks can provide one with the information and knowledge to engage in sense-making and provide leads on environmental changes. Prusak and Cranefield, in 'Managing Your Own Knowledge' (2010), get to the heart of the interconnectedness of these areas with their foundational practices of PKM:

- scan and reinvent,

- vet and filter,

- invest in your networks, and

- get out of your office.

In a sense these four foundational practices appear somewhat related to what Chilton (2008) refers to as the 'seven information skills':

1. retrieve information,

2. evaluate information,

3. organize information,

4. collaborate around information,

5. analyse information,

6. present information, and

7. secure information.

In fact these are precisely those same skills iterated earlier by Dorsey (2000), although in a slightly different sequence, so it seems that we have at least some agreement on the information skills needed for effective PKM.

That is, what Prusak and Cranefield refer to as scanning, reinventing, vetting, filtering and investing require the specific information skills which Chilton and Dorsey discuss. In our view there is a nexus between knowledge and specific skill sets. As Chilton (2008) suggests, it is important to educate knowledge workers 'to effectively use these skills in the context of their personal responsibility for managing knowledge'.

This leads naturally to the field of information literacy, to which we have alluded previously. When we hear the words 'information literacy' there is a tendency to think of a schoolroom or an academic library, yet information literacy is part of lifelong learning and the development of professional self-management, including PKM. Information literacy is for everyone, at any stage in life, whether individuals (reflective practitioners), groups or organizations (what we might refer to as the learning organization).

Following Dorner and Gorman (2006, 284), we use their definition of information literacy, with added italics to suggest the most relevant synergies with PKM:

- To be aware of why, how and by whom information is created, communicated and controlled, and how it contributes to the *construction of knowledge.*

- To understand when information can be used to improve their daily living or to *contribute to the resolution of needs* related to specific situations, such as at work or school.

- To know how to locate information and to *critique its relevance and appropriateness* to their context.

- To understand how to *integrate relevant and appropriate information with what they already know to construct new knowledge* that increases their capacity to improve their daily living or to resolve needs related to specific situations that have arisen.

Looking closely at this definition of information literacy, it is clear that effective PKM requires its practitioners to be information-literate. Specifically the information-literate PKM practitioner certainly is engaged in the construction of knowledge, uses KM and PKM to solve problems and resolve needs, critiques information before committing it to affective and effective personal knowledge, and absolutely creates new knowledge through the information-seeking and knowledge acquisition process. Therefore, information literacy can be viewed as an essential process and set of skills for PKM.

Wisdom: The Final Frontier?

How will individuals cope with increasing environmental and personal complexity? We have explored a number of areas in this chapter, and the other chapters in this book also tackle these questions. What we may be seeing is that the 'higher' level skills and knowledge characteristics of PKM have traditionally been referred to as wisdom.

Perhaps it is not too early to raise the possibility of personal wisdom management. Although it may make a great number of people in the business world uncomfortable, exposition on wisdom and wisdom practices have been with us at least from the time of the Greek philosophers, and wisdom does seem to provide a framework for managing a number of the issues we have raised here, including inexorable environmental change, information overload and practical decision-making. Indeed, wisdom principles, characterized by flexibility and intuition, have been described as especially appropriate for our times (Vaill 1998; Weick 2004). For example, fundamental to wise practice, and as we discussed in relation to PKM, is the ability to engage in 'reflexive thought'. According to Rooney and McKenna (2005, 314) reflexivity can be defined as an aspect of wise practice that:

- acknowledges the ambiguous, fragmented and contested nature of knowledge, but does not prevent a determination of the understood 'facts' in a matter,

- acknowledges that there are multiple perspectives to any phenomenon, each with their own vocabularies, theories, interpretations and frames, and

- understands as far as possible one's own subject position individually and as a member of a community of practice, and that this will influence the perception of the object.

Arguably then, to master PKM a form of practical wisdom may be necessary. But, to end on a provocative note, we may well ask, with apologies to T.S. Eliot, if knowledge leads to loss of wisdom, can wisdom of any kind help us to master any form of knowledge?

Conclusion

The world of knowledge work is intensifying. While success in work, both organizational and individual, may still be about what we know and who we know, ever-growing expectations require increasingly rapid connections to knowledge sources, human and digital. Until now, knowledge management has clearly evolved in service to the organization. KM provides both the rationale and practices to assist organizations to make the greatest use of their resources, the most important of which are their employees. The perception, genuine or otherwise, is that employees are a resource to be exploited. Not surprisingly, many knowledge workers will resist this paradigm. As we have indicated, we believe PKM not only empowers individuals to take control of their own career paths as the nature of work continues to change, but it also gives organizations an opportunity to link their KM strategies with those of their employees, thus making success more likely.

But we have also emphasized that PKM can help individuals manage more than just their careers: it also serves as the impetus to consider lifelong learning and the development of skills and networks to extend one's horizons – to become not only more knowledgeable about 'things', but to become more reflective and ultimately wiser about life. From this perspective, PKM can be seen to serve the individual, the organization and society as a whole. And this, we believe, makes PKM much more than just another KM offshoot.

References

Avery, S. et al. (2001), 'Personal Knowledge Management: Framework for Integration and Partnerships', *Association of Small Computer Users in Education 2001 Conference Proceedings*, http://fits.depauw.edu/ascue/Proceedings/2001/avery.html, accessed 3 November 2009.

Barth, S. (2004), 'Self-organization: Taking a Personal Approach to KM', in M. Rao (ed.) *Knowledge Management Tools and Techniques: Practitioners and Experts Evaluate KM Solutions* (Burlington: Elsevier Butterworth-Heinemann).

Benitez, E. and Pauleen, D. (2009), 'Brainfiltering: The Missing Link Between PKM and PIM?', *AMCIS 2009 Americas Conference on Information Systems Proceedings,* http://aisel.aisnet.org/amcis2009/13/, accessed 3 November 2009.

Byrne, R. (2001), 'Employees: Capital or Commodity?', *The Learning Organization* 8:1, 44–9.

Chilton, K. (2008), 'Personal Knowledge Management: Educational Framework for Global Business', *Work Literacy: Web 2.0 for Learning Professionals* http://workliteracy.ning.com/profiles/blogs/personal-knowledge-management, accessed 9 November 2009.

Chu, S. K.W. et al. (2009), 'Social Bookmarking Services: An Empirical Analysis of Connotea – Users' Perspective', paper presented at The Sixth International Conference on Knowledge Management/The Tenth International Symposium on Knowledge and Systems Sciences, Hong Kong, 3–4 December 2009 Proceedings.

Clemente, B. and Pollara, V. (2005), 'Mapping the Course, Marking the Trail', *IT Professional* 7:6, 10–15.

Davenport, T. and Prusak, L. (1998), *Working Knowledge* (Boston: Harvard Business School Press).

Dorner, D. and Gorman, G. (2006), 'Information Literacy Education in Asian Developing Countries: Cultural Factors Affecting Curriculum Development and Programme Delivery', *IFLA Journal* 32:4, 281–93, http://ifl.sagepub.com/cgi/reprint/32/4/281, accessed 3 November 2009.

Dorsey, P. (2000), 'Personal Knowledge Management: Educational Framework for Global Business', Millikin University, www.millikin.edu/pkm/pkm_istanbul.html, accessed 15 October 2009.

Drucker, P. (1968), *The Age of Discontinuity* (New York: Harper & Brothers).

Frand, J. and Hixon, C. (1999), 'Personal Knowledge Management: Who, What, Why, When, Where, How?'. Working Paper, http://www.anderson.ucla.edu/faculty/jason.frand/researcher/speeches/PKM.htm, accessed 3 November 2009.

Godwin-Jones, R. (2006), 'Tag Clouds in the Blogosphere: Electronic Literacy and Social Networking', *Language Learning & Technology*, 10:2, 8–15.

Google Jobs (2009), 'The Engineer's Life at Google', http://www.google.com/support/jobs/bin/static.py?page=about.html&about=eng, accessed 15 October 2009.

Harmer, Brian M. and Pauleen, David J. (2010) 'Attitude, aptitude, ability and autonomy: the emergence of "offroaders", a special class of nomadic worker', *Behaviour & Information Technology* 15 July 2010, http://www.informaworld.com/smpp/content~content=a922667777

Holden, N. (2002), *Cross-cultural Management: A Knowledge Management Perspective* (Harlow: Financial Times/Prentice Hall).

Jefferson, T. (2006), 'Taking it Personally: Personal Knowledge Management', *VINE* 36:1, 35–7.

Klein, G. et al. (2006), 'Making Sense of Sense-making 1: Alternative Perspectives', *IEEE Intelligent Systems* 21:4, 70–3.

Mitchell, E. (2004), 'Technologies for Personal Knowledge Management', Knowledge Board, https://secure.knowledgeboard.com/cgi-bin/profile.cgi?page=1, accessed 11 November 2009.

Murphy, P. (2010), 'From Information to Imagination: Multivalent Logic and System Creation in Personal Knowledge Management', Chapter 3 this volume.

—— and Pauleen, D. (2007), 'Managing Paradox in a World of Global Knowledge', *Management Decision* 45:6, 1008–22.

Nordin, M. et al. (2009), 'Investigating KM Antecedents: KM in the Criminal Justice System', *Journal of Knowledge Management* 13:2, 4–20.

Prusak, L. and Cranefield, J. (2010), 'Managing Your Own Knowledge: A Personal Perspective', Chapter 6 this volume.

Rooney, D. and McKenna, B. (2005), 'Should the Knowledge-based Economy be a Savant or a Sage? Wisdom and Socially Intelligent Innovation', *Prometheus* 23:3, 307–23.

Snowdon, D. et al. (2010), 'KM and the Individual: It's Nothing Personal', Chapter 7 this volume.

Vaill, P. (1998), 'The Unspeakable Texture of Process Wisdom', in S. Srivastva and D. Cooperrider (eds) , *Organizational Wisdom and Executive Courage* (San Francisco: The New Lexington Press).

Viedma, M. and Enache, M. (2008), 'Managing Personal Human Capital for Professional Excellence: an Attempt to Design a Practical Methodology', *Knowledge Management Research & Practice* 6:1, 52–61.

Weick, K. (2004), 'Mundane Poetics: Searching for Wisdom in Organization Studies', *Organization Studies* 25:4, 653–68.

Wolfe, M. (2010), 'Recovering the Individual as the Locus of Knowledge: Communication and PKM', Chapter 4 this volume.

Zuber-Skerritt, O. (2005), 'A Model of Values and Actions for Personal Knowledge Management', *Journal of Workplace Learning* 17:1/2, 49–64.

2

Where is the Wisdom we Have Lost in Knowledge? A Stoical Perspective on Personal Knowledge Management

Peter Case and Jonathan Gosling

Introduction

> *Where is the Life we have lost in living?*
> *Where is the wisdom we have lost in knowledge?*
> *Where is the knowledge we have lost in information?*
>
> Eliot (1985 [1934], 7)

This extract from the chorus of T.S. Eliot's *The Rock* captures rather elegantly the *problematic* that we wish to address in this chapter. For developed and developing economies alike, *information* seems to have been elevated to a status that has no historical precedent. Continuing an exponential trend facilitated by innovations in information and communications technology (ICT) that began in the latter part of the twentieth century, the information revolution continues apace. Information saturates our lives. It proliferates at speeds and in quantities that quite literally boggle the individual and collective mind, invading every sphere of activity in an inexorable colonization of private and public spaces. These trends have tempted some authors, quite reasonably it might seem, to view information as a defining characteristic of emerging 'information societies' (Castells 2000) populated by 'knowledge workers' (Drucker 1999) who occupy roles in 'infomated organizations' (Zuboff 1988). Quite often, as in the case of the authors just cited, the information revolution is understood as heralding liberating potential for individuals, organizations and societies. It offers new freedoms and possibilities for personal exploration, reflection, education and collective organization (through virtual interaction, virtual teamwork, virtual organization, and so on). Proponents of the liberating possibilities of the Internet and World Wide Web also point to the prospect of a collective ICT-mediated politics, with promises of enhanced participative democracy, shared decision-making, mass involvement and so forth.

While we would certainly not deny the reality of information's ascendancy in contemporary societies, we would suggest – following Eliot's prescient poetic insight – that the lived reality of an information-saturated life may detract from the optimistic promises of its enthusiastic proponents. If we take the case of organizational roles, for example, many individuals and groups struggle to cope with the sheer deluge of information which ICTs facilitate on a daily (if not moment by moment) basis. Electronic mail is a particular culprit in this respect. From our experience as educators and consultants working with managers and leaders, there seems to be a common desire to escape the perceived tyranny of the email 'Inbox'. In the information and knowledge-managed economy, many lives are now shackled by email communication and the demands of instantaneous responses every bit as much as they were chained, in previous generations, by the relentless pace of the assembly line. Although, of course, the external conditions of employment may well have improved considerably, the stress of being regulated by others' technologically meditated expectations is there for all to experience.

What, then, might be the implications for *personal* knowledge management (PKM) of the postmodern privileging of information? To gain some perspective on the question, we suggest, it will be useful to mount a brief historical critique – in the space available – of the development of knowledge and information. First, it is necessary, we contend, to be able to discriminate between 'information', 'knowledge' and 'wisdom' in order to explore the possibilities and dynamics represented by PKM. As part of this definitional work, we review the development of knowledge, first, in a post-Enlightenment context (which has witnessed the privileging of cognition and rationality over other forms of 'knowing' and 'being'); and, secondly, in a premodern context within which wisdom, intuition and virtue played as important a part of the 'knowledge' alembic as cognition.

The French classicist Pierre Hadot has traced a genealogy of monastic Christian philosophy and practice back through neoplatonist transition to origins in the classical schools of Ancient Greece (Hadot 1995, 2006). He demonstrates that monastic scholasticism led to a bifurcation of philosophy and theology which paved the way for modern conceptions of knowledge which privilege *ratio* over intuitive wisdom and other forms of contemplative understanding. This bifurcation made possible the occlusion of mystical knowledge that characterized the Enlightenment quest for secular scientific knowledge and is a legacy which, of course, remains with us to the present day. In the pre-Renaissance world, *intellectus* – the notion that understanding could come from direct intuitive insight – was balanced by the faculty of *ratio*, or what we might now take to be discursive *reason* (Brient 2001). There was an appreciation of how virtue and wisdom, which had at its core a relatively unselfish or other-directed disposition, could arise out of *contemplation* of truth. Virtue and faith came from *simplex intuitus*, that is the direct intuition or apprehension of the moral good obtained from understanding the principles of a natural order ordained by God. In this sense *ratio* was in the service of *intellectus*, virtue, faith and wisdom.

Our contention is that the wisdom which was fundamental to pre-classical understandings of knowledge and virtue has been lost in the post-Enlightenment drive to reveal and represent rational truth. We seek in the first few sections of this chapter to indicate how this loss occurred before proceeding to develop a more *contextual* and personalized understanding of the term 'knowledge'. With respect to organizational life, we suggest that it might be helpful to construe knowledge as finding the 'person-in-role' rather than simply as a free-floating resource or possession of autonomous individual occupants of roles. The chapter concludes with a discussion of Stoicism and suggests that its prescriptions with respect to 'philosophy as a way of life' (Hadot 1995) contain practical means by which a PKM agenda might be taken forward.

Knowledge and Personal Knowledge

To attempt a full critique of knowledge in one brief contribution such as this would be, at best, overly ambitious and, at worst, absurdly ostentatious. Nonetheless, to advance the argument we want to make with respect to PKM we must give some attention, albeit cursory, to the modern understanding of knowledge. Studies of epistemology, of course, constitute one of the major branches of philosophy and it will not be possible to survey the entirety of this tradition. Suffice it to say that within post-Enlightenment philosophy knowledge is generally equated with an exclusively *rational* and cognitive conception of 'justified true belief'. This notion underpins the search for true propositional statements and much of Western philosophy has been preoccupied with attempting to derive rational criteria, principles and methods for establishing truth and justification. Yet the central notion of 'belief' restricts any resulting conception of knowledge to the domain of cognition, however sophisticated the reasoning that supports 'justification' and 'truth'.

If we turn to definitions of knowledge within the social sciences, we find, perhaps unsurprisingly, a similar dependency on rationality and cognition. To take one seminal epistemological contribution as illustration, in his book *The Coming of the Post-Industrial Society* Daniel Bell defines knowledge as 'a set of organized statements of facts or ideas, presenting a *reasoned judgement* or an experimental result, which is transmitted to others through some communication medium in some systematic form' (Bell 1999, 175, added emphases). Modern social scientific definitions, of which Bell's is typical, thus draw on a post-Kantian philosophical tradition that prioritizes reason and judgement with respect to knowledge. If our beliefs are founded upon reason, itself supported by evidence, we are justified in treating them as true and sharing the resulting knowledge. Bell's definition of knowledge is broadly representative of the rational consensus within social science which we shall be at pains to challenge in this chapter. His interrogation of epistemology, nonetheless, does acknowledge the role of the 'personal' in knowledge creation. This aspect of his study is particularly germane to our discussion of PKM. Bell (1999, lxi–lxiv) distinguishes between *data*, considered to be an ordered sequence of items or events; *information* which introduces more context into the arrangement of data and indicates the relationships between elements; and *knowledge* which involves personal judgement concerning the significance of the information within a given context. Hence, data, information and knowledge may be arranged along a continuum according to the degree to which there is *personal* human involvement with, and interpretation of, reality.

Bell's admission of the part played by personal judgement with respect to the interpretation of data and information bears a family resemblance to the more or less contemporaneous views of Michael Polanyi (Polanyi 1958, 1966, 1975). As the editors of the current volume acknowledge, the field of PKM is yet to flourish in its own right but its embryonic emergence must surely owe a great debt to Polanyi's intellectual tour de force *Personal Knowledge* (Polanyi 1958). Michael Polanyi was a highly successful natural scientist before his mid-career migration to the social sciences. This talented polymath was able to bring his intellectual powers to bear, with great effect, on epistemological issues faced within social science. Somewhat surprisingly for a thinker schooled and expert in natural scientific method, Polanyi made a strident case for acknowledging the part played by *personal judgement* in the formation of both individual and collective knowledge. Rather than advance the idea of value-neutral science and social science, Polanyi claimed that all knowledge is inevitably pervaded by personal values, commitments and contextually conditioned understanding. Moreover, he challenged the received wisdom which simply equated knowledge with post-Enlightenment notions of 'justified true belief', an intellectual project which is roundly rejected in the following assertion:

> *Tearing away the paper screen of graphs, equations and computations, I have tried to lay bare the* **inarticulate manifestations of intelligence** *by which we know things in a purely personal manner. I have entered on an analysis of the arts of* **skilful doing** *and* **skilful knowing***, the exercise of which guides and accredits the use of scientific formulae, and which ranges far further afield, unassisted by any formalism, in shaping our fundamental notions of most things which make our world.*
>
> Polanyi (1958, 64, added emphases)

In one sense, as we shall see shortly, Polanyi can be viewed as having rediscovered or re-intuited certain classical forms of knowledge that had, to that point, been relatively neglected within the Western epistemological tradition. For Polanyi, human judgement may be inscribed or embodied in collective human forms but, nonetheless, has to find expression in personal interpretations of signification at the individual level. Humans participate in, or, to use Polanyi's term, *indwell* complex socio-material contexts. To this extent, therefore: '*All* knowing is personal knowing – participation through indwelling' (Polanyi 1975, 44, original emphasis). This leads to a recognition and acknowledgement of the 'artful' nature of doing and knowing. If it is accepted that personal participation is a 'universal principle of knowing' (Polanyi 1975, 44), then knowledge – a noun which Polanyi prefers to render actively as 'knowing' – will always be a skilful, context-based, accomplishment. An important dimension of Polanyi's work is dedicated to a phenomenological enquiry into the foundation of human knowing. In this respect, his project is not dissimilar to that of the philosophical explorations of Heidegger (see Heidegger 1962). Indeed, in Polanyi's attempt to differentiate between *explicit* cognitive and *tacit* non-cognitive dimensions of knowing, he uses examples, such as the use of a hammer, which directly parallel those employed in Heidegger's magnum opus *Being and Time*. Tacit knowledge is akin to Aristotle's intellectual virtue *technē*. It is, as it were, an embodied form of knowledge; a skill, such as riding a bicycle or playing a musical instrument, which has passed the threshold of rational cognition and become established at a deeper, bodily and subconscious, level. Indeed, if such embodied skills get questioned by the thinking function, the result can be quite disastrous for the person performing a given task. The introduction of rational self-consciousness can easily cause the pianist to stumble clumsily over notes, the rider to fall off a bicycle, or the artisan to strike their own thumb as they attempt to strike a nail. The encroachment of the rationally explicit into the domain of the tacit results in a form of paralysing 'stage fright' (Polanyi 1958, 56).

Knowledge Management and Organizational Knowledge

Having suggested that it is important to appreciate the tacit, embodied and participative dimensions of knowledge, we turn now to the question of how knowledge is treated in contemporary organizational discourse and practice. This will necessitate some analysis of theories associated with 'knowledge management' (KM) and 'organizational knowledge'. If we are concerned to advance a PKM agenda, how might the 'personal' augment or articulate with KM? In order to answer this question, we shall need, paradoxically, to suspend consideration of the *personal* dimension of PKM in order to focus on approaches that *de*personalize knowledge in the interests of supra-personal organizational ends.

KM defies simple definition, but appears to consist in a network of principles, methods and practices that, mediated by ICT, are intended to facilitate the instrumental exploitation of knowledge within organizations (Scarborough and Swan 2001). Nonaka, one of the most well-known architects of KM, outlines a programme of 'encoding' knowledge in order that it can be readily shared and disseminated throughout organizational networks (Nonaka 1994). Within Nonaka's scheme, knowledge is not restricted exclusively to ideas (explicit knowledge) since it seeks consciously to embrace differing forms of organizational skills (tacit knowledge). Despite acknowledging the role of tacit knowledge, Nonaka's emphasis is still on the *codification* (externalization) and communication (socialization and internalization) of such knowledge. In practice, this has been widely interpreted as involving the use of information technologies to facilitate objective and objectifying shared understandings.

Several critics of Nonaka's and related technology-led approaches to KM have pointed to the limitations of seeking to codify tacit knowledge and constraints which ICTs, owing to their calculative configuration, invariably introduce (Blackler 1995; Tsoukas and Vladimirou 2001; Cabrera and Cabrera 2002; Thompson and Walsham 2004). In short, naive resource-based understandings of organizational knowledge upon which KM is predicated carry certain risks. They may simply be ineffective and unable to deliver on their promises thus representing a waste of capital investment on ICT equipment and training, or, in more serious cases, result in counterproductive interventions that actually damage extant practices. Thompson and Walsham, for example, provide a graphic case study account of a software development company which dismantled what had been an effective informal process of knowledge sharing in favour of a KM system designed to objectify these processes using ICT (Thompson and Walsham 2004). They describe how the former 'Bardic' tradition, which propagated and sustained organizational knowledge through relationships that were sensitive to the *social context*, was destroyed by the KM system.

This cautionary tale speaks to various concerns about resource-based, instrumental and narrowly utilitarian conceptions of organizational knowledge and KM. In their comprehensive and critical appraisal of discourse and practice, for example, Scarbrough and Swan conclude that KM:

> has helped IS [information systems] specialists to legitimate and mobilize management support for organizational change programmes aimed at using IT to capture and codify knowledge. The 'softer' side of KM – that which focuses on the accumulation of intellectual capital through the development of skills and competencies – has often been lost in these initiatives.
>
> *Scarbrough and Swan (2001, 10)*

This observation, of course, invites questions as to just what practices the euphemistic 'softer side' of KM might involve and, moreover, what alternatives there might be to disembodied, apolitical and timeless conceptions of knowledge represented within KM of the instrumental variety.

One set of answers to such questions would entail following Polanyi's lead and reintroducing both the *personal* and the *contextual* into conceptions of knowledge and KM. Examples of more sophisticated interpretations of organizational knowledge would include the work of Blackler and Tsoukas and Vladimirou (Blackler 1995; Tsoukas and Vladimirou 2001). Blackler, for instance, offers a typology of knowledge that views collective understanding – itself predicated on the interpenetration of multiple personal understandings –

as being *culturally* embedded in firms or other forms of organization, enabling them to deploy resources in particular ways. By acknowledging both an individual and collective dimension of knowledge, Blackler identifies four classes of knowledge thus: individual-explicit (embrained), individual-tacit (embodied), collective-explicit (encoded) and collective-tacit (encultured or embedded). A similar degree of complexity and interdependency between the personal and the collective is acknowledged by Tsoukas and Vladimirou in their characterization of organizational knowledge as

> the capability members of an organization have developed to **draw distinctions** in the process of carrying out their work, in particular **concrete contexts**, by enacting sets of generalizations (**propositional statements**) whose application depends on historically evolved **collective understandings** and experiences.
>
>   Tsoukas and Vladimirou (2001, 983, original emphases)

Thompson and Walsham take the critique of KM further than Tsoukas and Vladimirou by claiming that the subjective nature of personal knowledge inevitably resists instrumental management within *relational* social contexts. Indeed, the implication of Thompson and Walsham's argument seems to be that the search for KM based on unitarist notions of 'shared knowledge' must inexorably flounder on the sands of organizational complexity. As they put it,

> **the meaning of any objective 'knowledge' will always remain the subjective product of the person in whose mind this is constituted, always relationally defined, and therefore does not transfer easily to others in a form which may be operationalized to the benefit of the organization.**
>
>   Thompson and Walsham (2001, 726, original emphases)

A common thread to the critique of instrumental forms of KM is the accusation that, in their idealistic efforts to instantiate objective forms of shareable knowledge within organizations, they neglect sufficiently to account for personal and social *contexts*. It follows that if we are to integrate the 'personal' within 'knowledge management' to produce a hybrid PKM, we should seek to establish an indexical understanding of these three terms. In other words, we must have a rounded appreciation of PKM's possibilities within organizational contexts. It is to the question of what that appreciation might entail that we now turn.

Personal Knowledge: Role and Discipline

The heuristic of 'person-in-role' attained a central position in open-systems theory, alongside those of 'primary task' and 'boundary' (Miller and Rice, 1967) when extended from the original socio-technical systems work of Trist and Bamforth (1951). Open systems theory considers organized work as a conversion of inputs to outputs. The conversion process is the primary task of the system, for which roles are defined and allocated to role-holders (persons-in-roles). One of the responsibilities of those in managerial roles is to regulate the transfer of inputs into the system, and outputs from the system; this is one aspect of boundary management – the other being the responsibility of every role-holder to manage the boundary between self and role.

This could appear a very mechanistic model of human work and organization, but, of course, the intellectual influence of open systems theory has been significant precisely because of its ability to accommodate cultural, social and political forces, inter- and intra-psychic dynamics as well as the transformation of material goods and services. For example, the primary task of the hospice as a system is to care for the dying, and the task of managers is to organize roles and sub-tasks to this end. To do so, managers must find ways to cope with the immaterial and uninvited inputs of anxiety, hope, and so on, as well as the formal and intended inputs. In a hospice as an open system, the outputs include cadavers, reassured relatives and various waste products. Inputs include terminally ill patients, trained staff and material resources such as medicines, food, funding, and so on; in addition to these more obvious inputs, the system must cope with anxiety about death amongst patients and relatives, anxiety about the ability to care on behalf of staff, social attitudes towards death, hope for a blessed relief from suffering and guilt associated with abandoning the dying to an institution; and many other unconscious or partially acknowledged projections and introjections. Often, systems evolve ways of working that are adapted to handle high levels of anxiety even at the expense of what might on paper appear to be more efficient modes of organizing: an insight which gave rise to the term 'social systems as a defence against anxiety' (Menzies, 1975).

Another source of inputs to an open system is the people who take up roles within it. In addition to the skills, attitudes, behaviours, contacts, symbolic referents and competences for which any of us might be formally appointed to a role, we bring our personal propensities, emotions, prejudices, anxieties; and also conscious and unconscious knowledge associated with other aspects of our social life – race, gender and age are just some of the more obvious factors. A role is not a fixed entity, and will always flex to a certain extent to accommodate the person who fills it – less so for commoditized labour than for bourgeois or entrepreneurial roles. Managing oneself in role therefore involves managing the possible developments of the role in relation to other roles and to the primary task of the system. Managers of a system regulate this role flexibility, and provide the conditions in which role-holders manage themselves and all that they bring with them into the role. Figure 2.1 provides an indication of how we are conceiving this.

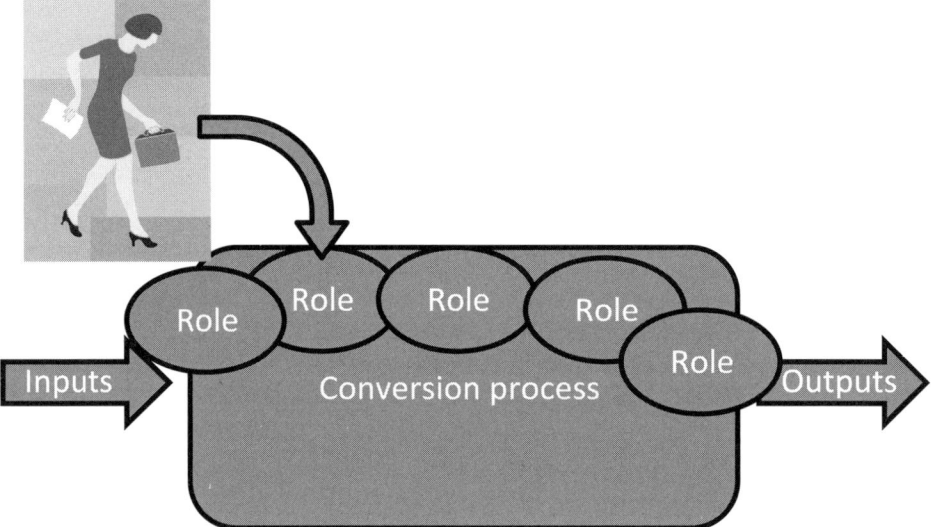

Figure 2.1   **Person in role (within an open system conceived as a process of converting diverse inputs to outputs)**

Conceived in this way, 'managing oneself in role' is a collaborative venture shared by the person-in-role, other role holders, the managers of the system, and the embedded systems and informal processes that have evolved to handle both the formal and unconscious inputs to the system. In open systems theory the *personal knowledge* required to undertake the work of 'managing oneself in role' is usually framed as consciousness raising (Lawrence 1979) and informed by methodologies such as 'process consultancy', group psychodynamics or (with more of an engineering bias) soft systems methodology (Checkland 1981), explicitly drawing on the politics of workplace democracy that played a formative role in the development of this body of theory.

As we argued above, the employability of knowledge is problematic. Not all knowledge exists ready for the taking; in addition to that which is tacit, much of it is dynamically active in the unconscious of individuals and collectives, so that people and institutions unknowingly 'act out'. This might include anxieties raised by anomie, uncertainty or social fixedness, for example; as well as other forms of tacit knowledge about how to do things. Further, some knowledge touches the unknowable, or bleeds seamlessly into the inscrutable – such as knowledge of death, of love, of wholeness and of dependency.

Thus a person taking up a role in an organization must deal with various kinds of knowledge that goes with that role. For example, someone taking a role in the front line of a pro-democracy demonstration in Myanmar will have to manage knowledge of fear and mortality, along with all the other aspects of the role. Such a person is likely to manage this awareness by mobilizing sentiments of bravura, solidarity, group enthusiasm and so forth, all of which may be mobilized as if automatically and subconsciously (Chapman and Long, 2008).

So when we consider the relatedness of person to role, we are constructing these two entities for purely heuristic reasons – to try to appreciate a nexus of knowledge management between social and political forces on one hand, and intimate personal dynamics on the other. Personal knowledge cannot be understood if we concern ourselves only with what is the conscious possession of the individual; we must also consider the awareness or knowingness that comes into being through the availability of a person in a role. In other words, we are concerned with *contextual* knowledge in search of a knower, just as much as with intelligent individuals in search of knowledge.

Wisdom in Context

We began the chapter by suggesting that the privilege afforded to rationally and instrumentally circumscribed notions of knowledge and information means that contemporary organizational actors have lost touch with wisdom. Indeed, we would go so far as to suggest that Western civilization has, in very large measure, rejected wisdom in favour of data, information and knowledge. That 'wisdom' is conspicuous by its absence in managerial and organizational discourses which dominate the workplace is symptomatic of a much wider malaise (Case and Gosling 2007; Rooney and McKenna 2007). Western philosophy, for example, gives very little heed or space to any conception of wisdom. As illustration of the eschewal of the term, we note that *The Oxford Companion to Philosophy* devotes only two relatively short paragraphs to its entry on 'wisdom' (Honderich 1995, 912). In confessional tone, its author Professor John Kekes, observes:

> *Although wisdom is what philosophy is meant to be a love of, little attention has been paid to this essential component of good lives in post-classical Western philosophy. It is perhaps for this reason that those in search of it often turn to the obscurities of oriental religions for enlightenment.*
>
> *Honderich (1995, 912)*

The implication of this rather sorry admission is at least twofold. First, if we are to understand the wisdom tradition within Western civilization we shall need, more or less, to bypass '*post*-classical philosophy' in favour of *classical* or pre-modern approaches to the topic. Secondly, as Kekes suggests, we may find enlightenment (with a small 'e') in oriental, that is, *non-modern* philosophies. As to the supposed 'obscurities' of such perspectives, we contend that they only remain obscure to those who refuse staunchly to investigate them systematically. By pursuing lines of enquiry that follow from this twofold implication we shall be able to advance an argument that re-establishes the role of wisdom within a Western tradition of 'knowledge', albeit a classical one. Furthermore, by approaching wisdom from *both* classical Western and oriental perspectives we shall be able to highlight its *contextual* nature and come to an understanding of PKM that addresses some of the concerns expressed by critics of KM.

The English word 'context' derives from the Latin verbs *texere*, meaning 'to weave', and *contexere*, denoting 'to join together', 'knit together' and 'to connect'.[1] This etymology thus evokes active images of interconnectedness, which is precisely the semantic investment that we would want to make when using the term *context*. When considering knowledge and practices in context, therefore, we are moved to think of interrelationships between various actants (human and non-human) in a given domain at any given moment in time. We need to think in terms of the holism implied by Polanyi's conceptions of *participation* and *indwelling*, for example, both of which carry a sense of interweaving processes

---

1   *Oxford English Dictionary Online*, http://dictionary.oed.com/entrance.dtl, accessed 4 November 2008.

with respect to knowledge and action. There are also other exemplars of this emphasis on *context*. Within contemporary social science, actor network theory (ANT) has sought to expose and explore interconnectedness, particularly when examining complex organizational processes, such as computer design and applications, public policy decisions and so forth (Callon 1986; Latour 2005, Woolgar 1991). Yet considered from a philosophical standpoint, ANT has, in one important sense, simply rediscovered premodern and non-modern modes of explanation and understanding. Indeed, one of ANTs leading proponents, Bruno Latour, has admitted as much in his bold claim that 'we have never been modern' (Latour 1993).

Latour puts forward nothing less than a moral and political programme for rediscovering what he considers to be the excluded middle of modernity. A false dichotomy has been created by the moderns between 'transcendent Nature', on the one hand, and 'immanent Society' on the other, he suggests. Since the Enlightenment, the moderns pursued a programme of ontological 'purification' that denied acts of human mediation between the two respective provinces of society and nature and attempted to ensure that the 'things' of nature remained uncontaminated by the social constructions of apperceiving minds. It is therefore imperative, Latour maintains, to expose the networked nature of both 'things' and 'social order' and hence dissolve the false duality that modernity has imposed. Ontology is always already a matter of networked processes: of mediation, delegation, distribution, mandate and utterance. And yet, in the acts of purification necessary for the stabilization of modern objects and modern conceptualizations of 'humanity', 'society', 'knowledge' and so forth, the a priori fact of mediation has to be occluded or consigned to a kind of 'modern unconsciousness' (Latour 1993, 37). In effect, Latour and other ANT colleagues have alighted upon a form of philosophical holism which resonates strongly with premodern and non-modern cosmologies. ANT owes a debt to the unwillingness on the part of premoderns to differentiate 'durably' between nature and society and mirrors their persistent attempts to find and expose hybridized human/non-human connections within the universe.

Knowledge and Wisdom in Aristotelian Philosophy

We would want to go further than ANT, however, in trying not only to revitalize new forms of philosophical holism but also to reintroduce a vocabulary of *wisdom* with respect to human efficacy. ANT may well provide a most valuable analytical tool for considering organizational complexity but, as a programme, it seems scrupulously to have avoided a close consideration of ethics. In order to reinvent the language of wisdom for the contemporary organizational world, it is instructive to look – within the Western knowledge tradition – to classical schools of philosophy. Certain aspects of debate in the fields of leadership and management studies are already inclining toward an exploration of the premodern. Keith Grint, for example, has considered how the first three elements of Aristotle's fourfold typology of intellectual virtue might be mobilized to improve our understanding of leadership practice (Grint 2007). He takes the divisions of *technē* (know-how), *episteme* (intellectual knowledge) and *phronesis* (practical wisdom) and demonstrates how these offer mutually complimentary dimensions of assessing problems and dilemmas faced by leaders. While this is a commendable contribution in many respects, it nonetheless overlooks certain important aspects of Aristotle's philosophy. As Morrell (2007) has pointed out, for instance, Grint takes no account of the *aesthetic* dimension of Aristotle's thinking but, more importantly from our point of view, the fourth and final element of the typology set out in the *Nichomachean Ethics*, namely, *theoria* (contemplation), gets no mention at all (Aristotle 1955).

Phronesis requires, according to Aristotle, the power of deliberation, beyond scientific deduction, because it must deal with situations and contingencies of which the causes are too diverse to arrest. Its chief function is to consider 'what matters', which can be accomplished only in collective deliberation amongst those who share a concern for a shared polity. Moving beyond the secular confines of the first three intellectual virtues, however, Aristotle posits *theoria* as the fourth, describing it as:

> the only [intellectual virtue] that is praised on its own account, because nothing comes of it beyond the act of contemplation ... Such a life will be too high for **human** attainment. It will not be lived by us in our merely human capacity but in virtue of something divine within us.
>
> Aristotle (1955, 304–5, original emphasis)

The fundamental significance of *theoria* in Aristotle's schema is often ignored because it is taken to be too immaterial, unreasonable or literally theoretical to have much application in modern times (for example, Grint 2007; Stamp et al. 2007). However, to do so is to miss the possibility that Aristotle's premodern conceptualization of a continuity between the human and divine, with human reason at the hyparxis, might have contemporary relevance.

Aristotle's four intellectual virtues help explicitly chart the territory between between self, role and organization (or *polis*). It is traditional to describe the intellectual virtues as if from the bottom up, an ascending scale from *technē* (embodied skill) to *episteme* (cognitive abstract knowledge), thence to *phronesis* (practical intelligence, wise judgement or circumspection) and on to *theoria* (contemplative participation with divine reality). However, we shall approach things from the opposite direction. *The Nichomachean Ethics* in which these intellectual virtues are laid out most directly is a collection of lecture notes suggesting a basis for ethical conduct. Although not made explicit, Aristotle's assumptions about the nature of the world are clearly important, because these assumptions – his theory of being, knowledge and intellect – underpin all that he says is virtuous, and his concept of a good life. So while *The Nichomachean Ethics*, and most modern commentators, give an account of the ascent of human virtue from *technē* through *episteme* to *phronesis*, we will get a better sense of where all this is coming from, as it were, by commencing with *theoria*, the participatory contemplation of 'wholenesses', from whence intellectual energy (*nous* or knowingness) descends into the discursive meditations and deliberations required of *phronesis*. The concepts that coagulate, as it were, from these intuitive meditations, are the stuff of *epistemic* knowledge, while *technē* is their manifestation in skills and habits of the body (and in related tools and technologies).

This downward or involutionary arc of ideas is thus logically prior to the evolutionary arc of intellectual virtues. Although the ascent of the virtues charts the growth of each individual, it is a growth into something – into our inheritance of ideas. Each stage of the developmental ascent mirrors and represents a stage in the prior descent of ideas into more concrete, objective and personalized knowledge (see Figure 2.2). So by approaching the intellectual virtues as just that – powers of the intellect exercised in the manipulation of different phases of knowledge – we discern the nature of the knowledge (and ideas) at each stage. As we show below, this notion of ideas available to be known is precisely what we imply in the concept of knowledge that is indigent to a role, realized by a person-in-role through the act of managing themselves in that role. The role itself 'calls forth', as it were, *a priori* role-specific knowledge in the role holder, uniting perceptions indigent of the role with the capacity for apperception in the person.

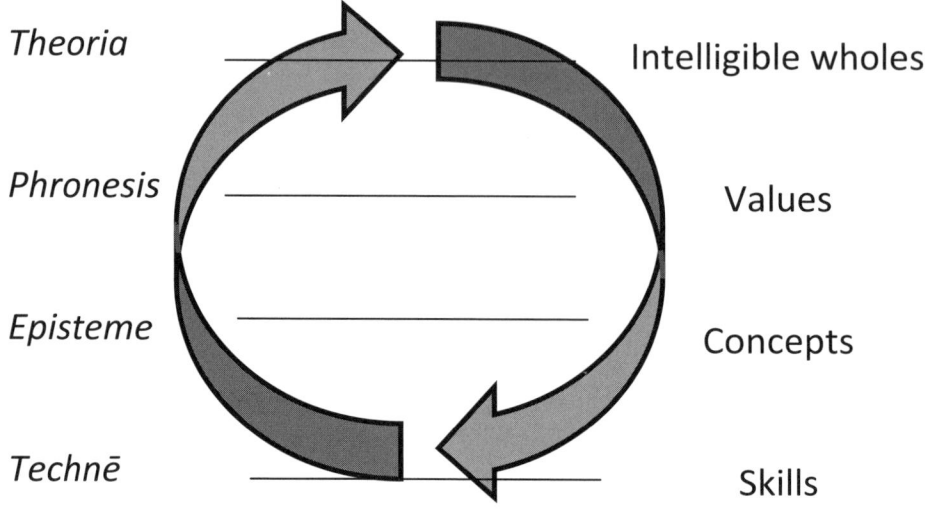

Theoria — Intelligible wholes

Phronesis — Values

Episteme — Concepts

Technē — Skills

Figure 2.2   Involutionary arc of potential knowledge and evolutionary arc of actual or realized knowledge

In *The Nichomachean Ethics*, Aristotle eschews detailed comment on *theoria*, on the grounds that it deals with knowledge that will be lived by us 'in virtue of something divine within us' (Aristotle 1955, 305). This is knowledge awaiting a knower, intelligible wholeness in which human intellect participates, to which extent knower and known are inseparable, and so 'more divine than human'. Divine knowledge is necessarily eternal and un-indigent of anything logically posterior to it; it must therefore be the context within which personal knowledge exists, and in a Platonic sense, the 'stuff' of which personal knowledge is made. Relating to our earlier comments about context, ideas are the 'text' of which knowledge is woven. (In this sense – if not in others – Aristotle concurs with Plato's model of the intellectual universe of Ideas; it is in the subsequent working out of the implications that he differs, as well as in the motivating role of the idea of the Good.)

Phronesis is the ability to make judgements about 'what matters'; not something that can be decided once and for all, because what matters at any given time, for any given group of people or collective venture, depends on the circumstances and how these circumstances are perceived and understood. *Phronesis* is therefore realized collectively and requires people able to perceive and consider the social, political and cultural aspects of knowledge referred to above. This requires a degree of maturity, insight and common interest.

The latter is crucial, because the consideration of what matters is always situated in a particular community: it is what matters *to us*. In fact Aristotle asserts that *phronesis* can be properly exercised only amongst friends, who have each others' best interests at heart; this is so important that he dedicates two of the ten sections of *The Nichomachean Ethics* to friendship. French et al. (2009) argue that in classical times friendship was thus defined as a social, even a political quality; the personalization of friendship responds to the modern emergence of the person. The same might be said of *phronesis*, which in many modern accounts is described as an individual attribute or attainment, almost an ornament of the wise (Grint 2007); but in our account, *phronesis* might better be translated as *circumspection*, following Heidegger's 1924 translation of *phronesis* as *umsicht*. As the etymology reveals, *phronesis* as *circumspection* implies the apperception of wholeness, deriving as it does from a composite of the Latin *specere*, 'to see' and *circum*, 'around' or 'complete'. Circumspection (*phronesis*) is thus collective deliberation about a political system as a whole; philosophically, it is the search to contain the multiplicity of factors in a universal idea (Aristotle 1955, 1141b–1142a); the concept of universals – that is, the idea of this intellectual project, considering all things in one idea – derives from the participative contemplation of wholes, as practised in *theoria*.

Of course any community or *polis* is imbued with its values, even if no one is deliberating about them. The knowledge is potentially there, to be actualized by those able to take up the role of *phronimoi*. In such circumstance collective values might be somewhat attenuated, locked into customs and unarticulated assumptions. Contemplation would be of little use in making these explicit; such is rather the role of critical reflection, a rigorous observation and interpretation of the life of the *polis*. This would be impossible without the ability to analyse, assess and manipulate cognitive abstractions. Yet such intellectual abstractions are mediated by language, comprising what Blackler (1995) calls 'encoded knowledge'. As an intellectual virtue *episteme* requires mental training and also a common codification of knowledge, categories and language games. While *phronesis* requires friendly deliberation amongst wise members of the *polis*, *episteme* requires a common system of language and meaning. As an intellectual virtue it is not identical with such a semantic system, but cannot be realized without it (in the same way as phronesis is not identical with a political process, but cannot be realized without it [Aristotle 1955, 1141b]). Taking up a role of 'thinker' within a linguistic culture is to inherit the wealth of its meanings, to think the thoughts that are available, as if in search of a thinker (Bion 1984 [1967]); and also to contribute new meanings and possibilities to the culture, insofar as one engages with others. An organized body of concepts and theories about any *polis* is an ideology, and is the intellectual basis for action.

By *technē* Aristotle refers to all manner of skilful know-how, in which category we must include actions that follow from circumspect deliberation and conceptual analysis. Ideologies thus find expression in political activity and other social engagements. At the most complex level, *technē* includes organizational and political know-how, constructing and sustaining the conditions for *phronesis*. At more simple levels, technical skill is the embodiment of social and material relations of production. Of course from the perspective of the individual, it appears that skills are learnt first at the most personal and simple level, developing along with more complex intellectual abilities as one grows towards the capacity for *phronesis*, circumspect deliberation on what matters to the community. However, as we have sought to demonstrate, this focus on the individual obscures the context of ideas and knowledge that always precedes the individual, and is the material from which each one of us weaves a place in the world.

Aristotle's exposition of intellectual virtue, we contend, offers a much richer account of knowledge than that provided by contemporary theories of KM. It not only expands and contextualizes our understanding of the personal in relation to knowledge and wisdom but also enables us to show how germane classical philosophy is to dilemmas and issues faced in today's organizations. Before concluding the chapter, however, we would like to consider how wisdom might be pursued *in practice* within everyday human settings, including those encountered in the workplace. This will enable us to re-examine, recontextualize and, perhaps, revitalize the concept of 'management' in relation to personal knowledge.

Stoicism and the 'Management' of Personal Knowledge

'Do not try to make things happen the way you want, but want what happens to happen the way it happens and you will be happy' (Epictetus, cited in Hadot 2004a, 133). One of the most pragmatic approaches to developing wisdom within the Western tradition arguably comes from classical Stoicism. The Stoic school was founded by Zeno toward the end of the fourth century BC, was given further impetus under the influence of Chrysippus in the third century and, following a sectarian split, continued to flourish during the Roman period until the second century AD (Hadot 2004a, 126–39). Important protagonists and practitioners of Stoicism during the Roman era were Seneca, Musonius, Epictetus and Marcus Aurelius (Hadot 2004b) and, as little remains of the founding texts of Zeno and Chrysippus, it is in these Greco-Roman writings that the principles of Stoical philosophy have been preserved. In this philosophy one discovers a practical and gentle approach to the art of living which, we suggest, has much to offer contemporary role holders in organizations. As with our discussion of Aristotle, the focus of this section will again be on *virtue*.

As Hadot (1995, 2004a, 2004b) is at pains to emphasize, it is crucial to understand the difference between Stoical conceptions of *philosophical discourse* and *philosophy as a way of life* in order to understand this tradition. To the extent that love of wisdom has to be taught by those that live philosophically to those who aspire to do so, the Stoics developed abstract *theories* of knowledge with respect to the three core virtues of physics, logic and ethics. The true *purpose* of such discourse, however, was to enable aspirants to enter into a philosophical life within which all the virtues combined to produce a way of *being in the world*. That way of being, moreover, was governed by an overarching principle that required philosophers to pursue the good, which, in turn, entailed directing their actions toward the benefit of others. The pursuit of the good and avoidance of evil instantiated in Stoical ethics followed inexorably and necessarily from the need to act in accordance with universal Reason. Stoics strove to live in harmony with Nature; a concept that represented the myriad complex processes of the cosmos including, of course, human consciousness, thought and action. Stoicism was predicated on an axiomatic truth of the cosmic interconnection between human and non-human realms such that the world was understood to be 'one single living being which [was] likewise in tune with itself and self-coherent' (Hadot 2004a, 128–9). The spiritual practices which were central to living the Stoical life were all directed toward helping individuals realize this truth by way of abandoning the conceit of 'individuality' and, through a form of personal surrender, bringing intentions, thoughts and actions into line with Nature.

Thus, for the Stoics, wisdom is to be realized by refraining from thinking, speaking or acting in ways that contradict Reality. As the opening words to this section by Epictetus convey, the route to happiness lies in not wanting things to be different than they actually are. The philosophical discourse and spiritual exercises of Stoicism are all directed at bringing about a transformation in consciousness that will lead to such wisdom. As noted in earlier work (Case and Gosling 2007), Stoical methods parallel the elements of the famous Christian prayer attributed to the philosopher of religion, Reinhold Niebuhr,[2] 'God, grant me the serenity to accept the things I cannot change, the courage to change the things I can, and the wisdom to know the difference', each clause of which can be related, respectively, to Stoical notions of physics, ethics and logic. With respect to physics, for example, it is necessary to understand the sphere of one's own action and influence. There are many aspects of Nature over which mere human will has no power whatsoever. In the last analysis, we have no control over the metabolism of the bodies we conventionally consider to be 'our own'. No individual can anticipate or control the precise circumstances of their own death (even, ultimately, that of the suicide), or will not to suffer from illness, loss of loved ones and so forth. Similarly, we neither have ultimate control of the thoughts, decisions and actions of others nor over the more macro supporting conditions of our lives, such as the parents we are born to and the society that we grow up in and so forth. Everything from the weather to current geopolitics are totally out of our hands and, from a Stoical viewpoint, we are like so much flotsam and jetsam in the great ocean of life. For the Stoic, such exogenous conditions result from the workings of Fate. The wise way to respond to any causally conditioned circumstances over which we have no control, moreover, is to accept them with equanimity. The idea of *volitional response* implicit in this attitude brings us to the second Stoic virtue, namely, ethics.

Within Stoic philosophical discourse, the fact that Nature is in large measure determined by an unfathomably complex set of causal conditions does not mean that there is no possibility for free will and moral action. On the contrary, the cultivation of good intention and good action is central to Stoic philosophy as a way of life. Accordingly, the Stoics – Epictetus in particular – developed a detailed and elaborate theory of *duty*. Fate may well dictate the circumstances of our lives but, unlike the Sceptics who resigned themselves to worldly indifference, or the Epicureans who chose to withdraw from the world of suffering in order to find happiness, Stoics sought wisdom through engagement with the *polis*. Stoicism does not provide an excuse for 'indifference', in a pejorative sense, and a commensurate backing down from responsibility to oneself and others. The Stoic is quite likely to lead a family life, have children,

---

2   Niebuhr (1892–1971) held a chair in ethics and the philosophy of religion at Union Theological Seminary, New York City from 1928 to 1960 but is best remembered for his popular prayer. Niebuhr's claim to have composed the prayer has not gone uncontested. There is some evidence to suggest that the prayer is apocryphal and may even have originated in Indian or Greek antiquity. There is a chance, therefore, that the prayer's Stoical qualities result directly from Stoical influence; in which case, the comparison we make here reduces to pure tautology. For a discussion of the prayer's origins, see http://www.aahistory.com/prayer.html (accessed 30 October 2008).

work, pursue a career and engage fully in the political life of the city. But all this needs to be done *ethically*, that is, with a mind to the welfare of others; both those near to one and those within the wider community. Such attitudes and obligations are dictated by Nature and universal Reason themselves which have, in effect, endowed humans with moral choice and determined that it is *good* to care for oneself and others.

This brings us to a consideration of logic, the third and final Stoic virtue. As with physics and ethics, there is a philosophical discourse which supports the spiritual exercises of logic in the form of training in uses of dialectic and syllogism, but it is the *practice* of logic that distinguishes Stoicism from other Hellenic schools of philosophy. Logic as spiritual exercise entails paying close attention (*prosokē*) to physical sense perception and mental representations in order to become skilful in judgement of, or assent to, the Real. Our senses and mental representations are real enough in themselves and are, in large measure, conditioned by physics or Fate. Responses to those perceptions, however, involve choices which involve skilful or unskilful judgements. Logic entails the development of awareness and reasoned response to the world which pre-empts or 'defuses' actions based on passionate responses. To use an example given by Epictetus by way of illustration, if one is on a boat in stormy weather and hears a terrifying clap of thunder, logic can be invoked to maintain equanimity in the face of apparent adversity. Attention to experience informs one that the perception of the clap of thunder is real, so, too, the experience of terror. Thus far, one's training in awareness alerts one to a set of physical and mental preconditions. In the absence of attention, one might fall unconsciously into a conditioned habit pattern – say, a tendency to panic – and act unwisely; to ponder one's imminent demise, for example, or to worry about all the possible unpleasant consequences of being at the mercy of the storm. To fall unreflectively into such a passionate response would be unwise ('evil') from a Stoical perspective. Training in the spiritual exercise of logic and *attention* enables one to accept the reality of the frightening situation without falling into redundant fantasy and worry. One simply does not give 'assent' to the fantasies. Instead, equanimity is maintained in the face of such circumstances permitting one to respond with reason and efficacy rather than blind panic.

Stoical spiritual exercises of the sort set out in detail by Marcus Aurelius in his *Meditations* (2003 [167 AD]) throw a completely different complexion on the notion of personal knowledge management. 'Management' of knowledge is clearly possible within the Stoic philosophy but in a sense that differs considerably from the KM of contemporary organization theory and practice.

What is at stake here is a far more subjective and contextual 'management' through the careful development of personal awareness, skilful judgement in relation to mental representations and restraint of unwise action.

Conclusion

Our conclusions are in two parts: first, we draw together the theoretical understandings of PKM developed in this chapter; secondly, we consider implications of our argument for those taking up leadership and management roles in organizational and political systems, and for leadership and management development in general.

An appreciation of premodern ways of knowing and being are, we maintain, highly pertinent to the postmodern context. These philosophies and their associated practices, if taken seriously, can also help inform a radical conceptualization of *personal knowledge management*. We have argued in this chapter that in an age that has lost its wisdom in knowledge, and its knowledge in information, it may be timely to reconsider the role that virtue can play in the quest for PKM. There are many contemporary leadership and management contexts where *wise action*, as opposed to rational utilitarian judgement, would be extremely valuable. If understood and enacted, for example, the virtues of Aristotelian and Stoic philosophy could help individuals and groups mediate between cognitive knowledge and practice in ways that, arguably, have been lost to the present generation. We might even go so far as to define the Stoic 'spiritual exercises' (*askesis*) as providing the practical route to 'personal knowledge'. There is also a 'managerial' dimension to *askesis* if we casuistically stretch its meaning a little. The self-managing aspects of Stoic exercises that accompany the development of the skills of attention, selective assent to mental representations, discernment of truthfulness and 'care of the self' more broadly, for example, constitute a form of *personal knowledge management*. Yet, in such a definition, we need carefully to reappraise and amend our contemporary understanding of the three terms: 'personal', 'knowledge' and 'management'.

We have argued that PKM involves disciplining intra-psychic processes, disciplinary practices that might take Stoic spiritual exercises as their source of inspiration. Furthermore, PKM also involves perceiving, internalizing and working with knowledge that becomes available through taking up a role, including conscious and unconscious aspects of knowledge. This we have characterized as a boundary-management task, encompassing the boundaries between self and role, between the specific role and other roles, and system-level boundaries. In particular, we have drawn attention to the processes by which certain kinds of knowledge are brought into being by the confluence of person and role, which we characterize as a knowledge nexus. Epistemologically, we claim that roles are so closely associated with some forms of knowledge that they might, indeed, be defined *by the knowledge to which they give access*; and further, that it makes sense to think of this knowledge as a potential awaiting actualization by a person taking up and managing themselves in that role. We thus propose a theory of knowledge that refers to ideas as wholes, rendered particular and 'known' by role-holders exercising the intellectual virtues as described by Aristotle. We are aware of the Platonic roots of this epistemological position, and propose further research on the implications for constructionist and critical realist accounts of PKM.

We believe the implications of our account are both relevant and challenging for people in leadership and management roles. The Stoic spiritual exercises as described by Epictetus and practised by Marcus Aurelius provide a profound and valuable guide for managing oneself in role. Our account of *phronesis* emphasizes both its collective realization and its rootedness in contemplative intuition of wholes (rather than the simple accretion and manipulation of epistemic concepts: a distinction between cleverness and wisdom, perhaps). This promises new insight into the function of *reflectiveness* in leadership and management development. All too often, reflection is described as learning from past events and sometimes as reflexive awareness of the here and now. *Theoria*, however, is qualitatively different, arising from participation in intellectual wholenesses, described as 'divine', and thus transcending purposive agency of human effort. Here we enter the domain of spiritual practices, beyond reflective practices, though quite possibly enabled or enhanced by reflectiveness. We suggest that this goes some way to explaining the continuing (and perhaps increasing) commitment to religious adherence in otherwise secular working environments – because religions may offer the opportunity to contemplate symbolic representations of ideal wholenesses, an intellectual contribution that is vital to the practice of *phronesis*. This contemplative union is quite distinct from the personal disciplinary benefits of reflection or the Stoic virtues, though it may be partially a fruit thereof. We suggest that further research into contemplative engagement, in religious or philosophical terms, would offer valuable insights into the basis for ethical leadership and organizational process.

References

Aristotle (1955), *The Nichomachean Ethics*, trans. J. Thomson (Harmondsworth: Penguin).

Aurelius, Marcus (2003 [167 AD]), *Meditations*, trans. M. Staniforth (Harmondsworth: Penguin).

Bell, D. (1999), *The Coming of the Post-Industrial Society* (New York: Basic Books).

Bion, W. (1984 [1967]), *Second Thoughts* (London: Karnac).

Blackler, F. (1995), 'Knowledge Work and Organizations: An Overview', *Organizations Studies* 16:6, 1020–46.

Brient E. (2001), 'From Vita Contemplativa to Vita Activa: Modern Instrumentalization of Theory and the Problem of Measure', *International Journal of Philosophical Studies* 9:1, 19–40.

Cabrera, A. and Cabrera, E. (2002), 'Knowledge-sharing Dilemmas', *Organization Studies* 23:5, 687–710.

Callon, M. (1986), 'Some Elements of a Sociology of Translation: Domestication of the Scallops and the Fishermen of St Brieuc Bay' in J. Law (ed.), *Power, Action and Belief: A New Sociology of Knowledge* (London: Routledge & Kegan Paul).

Case, P. and Gosling, J. (2007), 'Wisdom of the Moment: Pre-modern Perspectives on Organizational Action', *Social Epistemology* 21:2, 87–111.

Castells, M. (2000), *The Information Age: Economy, Society and Culture, Vol. 1, The Rise of the Networked Society*, 2nd edn (Oxford: Blackwell).

Chapman, J. and Long, S. (2008), 'Role Contamination', *Organizations and People* 15:3, 40–45.

Checkland, P. (1981), *Systems Thinking, Systems Practice* (Chichester: Wiley).

Drucker, P. (1999), *Management Challenges for the 21st Century* (Oxford: Butterworth-Heinemann).

Eliot, T. (1985 [1935]), *Plays* (London: Macmillan).

French, R. et al. (2009), 'Friendship and Betrayal', *Society and Business Review* 4:2, 146–58.

Grint, K. (2007), 'Learning to Lead: Can Aristotle Help Us to Find the Road to Wisdom?', *Leadership* 3:2, 231–46.

Hadot, P. (1995), *Philosophy as a Way of Life* (Oxford: Blackwell).

—— (2004a), *What Is Ancient Philosophy?* trans. Michael Chase (London: Harvard University Press).

—— (2004b), *The Inner Citadel: The* Meditations *of Marcus Aurelius* (London: Harvard University Press).

—— (2006), *The Veil of Isis*, trans. Michael Chase (London: Harvard University Press).

Heidegger, M. (1962), *Being and Time* (Oxford: Blackwell).

Honderich, T. (1995), *The Oxford Companion to Philosophy* (Oxford: Oxford University Press).

Latour, B. (1993), *We Have Never Been Modern* (Cambridge: Harvard University Press).

—— (2005), *Reassembling the Social: an Introduction to Actor-Network-Theory* (Oxford: Oxford University Press).

Lawrence, W. (1979), 'The Management of Oneself in Role', in W. Lawrence (ed.), *Exploring Individual and Organizational Boundaries* (Chichester: Wiley).

Menzies, I. (1975), 'A Case Study in the Functioning of Social Systems as a Defence Against Anxiety' in A. Colman and W. Bexton (eds) , *Group Relations Reader Vol. 1* (Washington: A.K. Rice Institute).

Miller, E. and Rice, A. (1967), *Systems of Organization* (London: Tavistock).

Morrell, K. (2007), 'Aesthetics and Learning in Aristotle: A Note on Grint's "Learning to Lead"', *Leadership*, 3:4 497–500.

Nonaka, I. (1994), 'A Dynamic Theory of Organizational Knowledge Creation', *Organization Science* 5, 14–37.

Polanyi, M. (1958), *Personal Knowledge: Toward a Post-Critical Philosophy* (Chicago: University of Chicago Press).

—— (1966), *The Tacit Dimension* (Garden City: Doubleday).

—— (1975), 'Personal Knowledge' in M. Polanyi and H. Prosch (eds), *Meaning* (Chicago: Chicago University Press).

Rooney, D. and McKenna, B. (2007), 'Wisdom in Organizations: Whence and Whither', *Social Epistemology* 21:2, 113–38.

Scarbrough, H. and Swan, J. (2001), 'Explaining the Diffusion of Knowledge Management: The Role of Fashion', *British Journal of Management* 12:1, 3–12.

Stamp, G. et al. (2007), 'Strategic Leadership: an Exchange of Letters', *Leadership* 3:4, 479–96.

Thompson, M. and Walsham, G. (2004), 'Placing Knowledge Management in Context', *Journal of Management Studies* 41:5, 725–47.

Trist, E. and Bamforth, K. (1951), 'Some Social and Psychological Consequences of the Longwall Method of Coal-getting', *Human Relations* 4, 3–38.

Tsoukas, H. and Vladimirou, E. (2001), 'What is Organizational Knowledge?', *Journal of Management Studies* 38:7, 973–92.

Woolgar, S. (1991), 'Configuring the User: the Case of Usability Trials', in J. Law (ed.), *A Sociology of Monsters: Essays on Power, Technology and Domination* (London: Routledge).

Zuboff, S. (1988), *In the Age of the Smart Machine* (London: Heinemann).

3

From Information to Imagination: Multivalent Logic and System Creation in Personal Knowledge Management

Peter Murphy

Introduction

What does personal knowledge management mean for the way that we think, create, write and muse? How does it impact and alter the process of creation? Inversely, how do the media of creation – intuition, pattern recognition, visualization, improvisation, paradoxical thought and synchronicity – shape the way that we manage personal digital libraries? The following explores the role of personal knowledge management in bridging between the shallows of our data streams and the depths of our creative imagination.

Information

It is increasingly common today for researchers, artists or writers to possess a 180GB computer hard drive and a 500GB external drive. As movie and image collections expand, personal terabyte drives will grow in popularity. At a person's fingertips, then, is a larger universe of information than in early versions of inter-networked computing. So what do we do with all the bytes that we now store in our personal digital libraries on mobile phones, PDAs, iPods, personal computers and flash drives? On one level we treat them as information objects – data to be retrieved. First of all we accumulate and archive it. Then we browse and search the amassed information capital, seeking useful items.

Information retrieval is the most elementary relationship we have with the mountains of data on our machines and devices. In this simple state, we find ourselves a little like the child who goes to the information desk at the local library seeking to find out the birth date of the 42nd President of the United States. Each one of the actors in this story begins by hoping that an all-knowing automaton will serve up the required information. The child looks expectantly at the seemingly omniscient librarian, while the seasoned PC-user fires up their desktop search tools. However, as even the child in the library soon discovers, information is never unmediated. There are catalogues, indexes and classification systems to master before anyone can effectively retrieve information. Extracting granular information requires a grasp of high-level information architectures. Automated search tools may appear to sidestep this but, in reality, command of those tools requires the ability to match search terms with correct guesses about their indexing assumptions. Such matching is intuitive and often resists explicit description. Nonetheless, it is real – and it rests on long-term learning of the relation between low-level units of data and high-level cognitive architectures.

This learning begins young. With the aid of teachers, parents and librarians, the amorphous mass of information in a library and the world at large gradually acquires a legible shape in the mind of the child. This happens through the interaction of classificatory systems and data elements. Children learn to move back and forward between parts (fragmentary data) and the whole (ontology and taxonomies). They learn about elements and they learn about frames. They learn to match one with the other. Users of personal digital libraries find themselves in the same position. They are both retrievers and classifiers of information. They access data and they catalogue it. They tag it, group it and bunch it in clusters. Yet, in one respect at least, these do-it-yourself cataloguers find themselves in a yet more complicated position. For they not only have to juggle their need for data with an understanding of its systematic arrangement by means of taxonomies, cataloguing, indexing, nomenclature, tagging, labelling, grouping, classing, sorting and categorization – sometime users of personal digital libraries and archives also have to be creators of their own systems of classification.

This is an odd situation to be in. Most users in an everyday setting just want to find information on their machine or device. Yet to do that effectively, they have to catalogue and file documents and media objects. This cataloguing and filing, admittedly, is often not very good. It is the work of an amateur – in this case, the 'prosumer'. The prosumer by definition is not an expert – and yet this agent is not simply a user or consumer of information systems either. Nor is the cataloguing and filing that the prosumer does on a computer automatically predefined or prestructured. The prosumer in fact has license to create all kinds of information architectures, given the power and flexibility of the software on personal computing devices. At the same time, this is a necessity. Even if the user hates filing, it has to be done. Most prosumers of information do not experiment very far with their information architecture. Typically they use the stock information tree hierarchy that comes built-in with the standard operating system, and will store files on that tree alphanumerically. The tree hierarchy is the most common of all taxonomies. While the technology offers enormous latitude for users to create artful classification systems, that latitude is rarely explored in any great depth or rigour. Nonetheless the fact that it exists is interesting. Even in avoiding the challenges that technology presents, the prosumer has to confront some of the very peculiar issues that the process of 'creating systems' presents.

Information management is a form of architecture. It involves both the design and building of structures. Users typically find the granular data they want by paying attention to the clues provided by the taxonomic structure underpinning the information system. There is a good chance users will find the data they are looking for as long as there is a legible fit between the data sought and the enveloping information structure. Political science books are in the '300' Section of the Dewey Decimal Classification system. If I walk into a library and want a politics book, I look for the '300' signs. Numeric sequence is a structuring principle. The crux of information management – whether it is on a personal computer or in the setting of an institutional library – is the systematic arrangement of information. If data is deposited by one person in a system or structure, there is a good chance that another person can find that data as long as they understand the underlying principle of systemic order that has been used. No information system is infallible. This is so for very good reasons. The Dewey system draws the distinction between politics books and engineering books, but a book on the politics of engineering might be classified as a politics, engineering or management book. Distinctions create clarity. They also create ambiguity. Both are inherent in systems – though at different levels of systems. Clarity is a premise of the everyday operation of systems. If a system does not generate legibility, it will be self-defeating. On the other hand, in order to create a system, ambiguity is necessary.

A comparison can usefully be made with the conduct of research. Dissemination of knowledge is very effectively done through the systemic drawing of distinctions between knowledge fields, for instance by the development of distinctive teaching disciplines. Creation of new knowledge, in contrast, requires the blurring of boundaries between established fields of knowledge and the breaking down of distinctions between them. New knowledge most often is generated at the intersection of such fields. The classic driver of research is 'interdisciplinary' work. Conversely, once knowledge has been created, and validated, the openness of boundaries closes, and the porous relations between researchers and their organizations is replaced by the strong boundaries of a teaching discipline that functions to propagate the knowledge thus created. The difference between knowledge creation and knowledge dissemination broadly parallels the difference between the design of a system and the building of a system. The method of creating a system is substantially at odds with the way a system is subsequently developed and made operational.

Let us put to one side for the moment the question of the creation of a new system. We will return to that matter shortly. Let us focus for now on the issue of an operational system. To operate well, a system needs to engender clarity. Clarity is the epistemological face of efficiency. Systems that operate well are efficient. Efficiency is central to information retrieval because information is always 'urgent' in some sense. Think how few people on a website use the browse function, and how many people use the search function. Indeed, think how few people use advanced search, and how many people use the basic search function. This is because they are 'in a hurry'. Commentators have often assumed that this is a function of the computer medium. Somehow magically it turns us all into speed freaks. But I doubt that this is true. More like it, we are always in a state of hurrying when looking for information. We browse luxury catalogues at our leisure, day dreaming. But when we need a hammer, because the one we were using is broken, its handle has sheared right in the midst of repairing the roof, and it looks like a storm is brewing, we want to find the address of the local hardware supplier as quickly as possible. So we grab the phone book and quickly flick through it searching for the right classification under which we will find the address we need. We expect the telephone book and its classificatory system to be as clear as possible. We are all intuitive Cartesians when it comes to information searching. Ambiguity, complexity and lack of clarity stand in the way of quick information retrieval.

If that all sounds mundane, then it is. The emotional excitement surrounding information is generated by the frenetic search for it. That is why the Internet has been so appealing. Its speed is seductive. It engages us when we are bolting through a task, animated by one of the endless minor urgencies that seem to define human life. But swiftness requires a clear pathway to the information we need, even if it is only to find out the birthday of the 42nd President. To a child that task is urgent as well – 'because Miss Salisbury told us that we have to find out'. For a ten year old, Miss Salisbury is a daunting authority, so the one charged with the task had better get on with it. The child approaches the librarian, another of these seemingly infallible authorities, with a sense that 'all shall be revealed'. And indeed it shall, but only through the effort of the child guided by the keeper of the books who gently instructs the youngster in the mysteries of classification. What the child eventually learns are the basic functions of taxonomies, ontologies, indexes, tags, labels, sets, classes, clusters, frames, lists and categories.

Users retain enough sense of classificatory systems not only to use them regularly throughout their lives but also to build classificatory systems themselves irregularly. As we store larger and larger amounts of data on our machines and devices, we find increasing need to categorize and organize that data, but truth be told, our personal information management is suspect. We are not very good at it. We have no real system. We are not good auto-librarians. Our taxonomies are idiosyncratic. If it was not for fast desktop search technologies, in many ways the most useful generic software application of the past decade, we would be lost. We have been saved by the search index from being buried in the vastness of our personal information stores.

Yet none of that takes us much beyond the horizon of the child who entered the library searching for the vital answer to Miss Salisbury's question. At a certain age, a child learns to use the library catalogue's subject index, follow the numeric classification, get a book down from the shelf, turn to its index or table of contents, and scan the entries – until some likely trail to the requisite birth date is found. That is no trivial achievement, and some of us will repeat similar tasks every day for the rest of our lives, but those who do this also realize that the function of a library is more than this. There is more to books than their indexes or the numbers on their spines – or their reference, almanac and encyclopedic functions.

Knowledge

This is where the distinction between information and knowledge comes into play. A book may be used to store information – and some books are filled with information. But most books contain more than information.[1] Most of them contain knowledge – and knowledge is not the same thing as information. Sometimes knowledge is mistaken for information, but we ought not to perpetuate that confusion. Knowledge occupies the continuum – or spectrum – between information and imagination. Knowledge is a halfway house between information and imagination. The more demanding knowledge is, the more it is characterized by imagination, and the more difficult it is to systematize and manage.

As we shall see later on, high-end knowledge – knowledge that is suffused with imagination – demonstrates something that is double-edged. It shows both how information systems are constructed and the enormous strain system building places on the predicates of those systems. This reminds us that often the best way to make a system is to break a system, and this will be considered later on. But we are not at that point quite yet. For the moment, let us content ourselves with the distinction between information and knowledge. Let us suppose the obvious – that a library is more than an information desk, and that its users spend a fair portion of their time at the library in the quest for something that is more than information. It does not matter whether the library is in a building, online, or on a hard-disk on a personal computer.

To clarify this, let us consider what else a book does apart from carry information. In brief – books tell stories and provide explanations. Stories and explanations make the world meaningful. We manage and order the world by telling stories and by giving explanations. This applies to information systems as it does to all of the domains of human life. One of the ways we arrange the holdings in a library is by 'telling a story'. National museums in the late twentieth century, for instance, moved away from taxonomy as a basis for displays. They adopted narrative as a structuring principle. Many popular library exhibitions these days do something similar. They tell a story. Digital storytelling, a subset of narrative techniques, took off as a key tool for online and in-house representations of libraries and museums in the early 2000s.

The extension of this into the world of PC-based personal knowledge management is entirely conceivable. The hard disk of a computer, no less than the servers that support the Internet, is an archive of data. An archive has to be structured in order to be accessible and legible. Narration is one way of creating such a structure. This is especially applicable to data that has a personal significance. Human beings like to tell stories about themselves.

---

1   What applies to a book applies equally to film, music and visual artworks.

The practical obstacle to this in a digital setting is the time involved in doing it well. Yet it is plausible that narrative, in the form of prepackaged narrative lines, one day might become the structural principle for hard-disk archiving of document and image files. We ought not to assume that the standard information tree hierarchy of today's computer operating systems will continue to dominate personal archiving strategies.[2] For the moment, though, most people rely on the default node-and-branch cascading tree hierarchies of computer operating systems.

These hierarchies are so familiar that we almost forget they exist. This should not surprise us. Successful structures are always invisible. Invisibility is a sign of their success. The more we need to discuss a structure, the more this is a sign that it is failing to function properly. Human beings do not much discuss the viability of their skeletons because skeletal structure is, for the most part, very well adapted to human functioning. Skeletons don't need much fixing. The pragmatic criterion ('does it work?') is always important when we are considering systems. This is because systems need to be efficient. They need to reduce the use of time and energy. Yet there is an expansive range of structural principles deployed in human and non-human domains. So, while branching tree hierarchies may serve many purposes very adequately, it is a reasonable assumption to make that they will not serve all purposes equally well. Thus in building knowledge systems, especially in pioneering areas where we are building experimentally, it is useful to be able to step back from the subset of familiar 'taken for granted structures' and explore the much larger, encompassing set of 'efficient structures' in their entirety.

For the purposes of knowledge systems in general, narration and explanation, as has already been suggested, are key structuring principles. Explanations in general are more abstract than stories – or at least they lend themselves to greater abstraction. From the impulse to explain arises science.[3] While explanations are usually more abstract than stories, explanation and narration nevertheless share in common the structuring element of time. They share a sense of 'before and after'. Science prominently employs explanations involving prior causation. *If* one thing occurs, *then* another follows sequentially

2   The work of David Gelernter, Professor of Computer Science at Yale University, and his company Mirror Worlds Technologies, to produce indexing software that operates on the principle of 'life streams' or electronic life stories is a case in point. See for example Heiss (2003).

3   Generally causation is distinguishable from magic. The child thinks of the power of their teacher or parent as magical. Adults can think magically as well. Computer-user neophytes sometimes think that computers 'cause' knowledge. This enchanted or magical belief is soon brought undone, just as the child comes to realize that Santa Claus does not exist.

in time. Scientific explanation refers to sequences of events in time that occur either without exception or else probabilistically. In human conduct, 'before and after' refers to sequences of motive and consequence, intention and result. The latter are less predictable than those reported by science. Yet they may still bear the weight of necessity. The fateful and tragic decisions of human beings can have all the baleful force of nature at its most unrelenting.

Just as time is a fundamental category of explanation, so also is space. When we explain matters in spatial terms, we identify how one thing 'stands' in a spatial relationship to another thing – and the effects and meanings that flow from that relationship. The spatial relationship may be hierarchical, lateral, vertical, horizontal or skeletal. It may be modelled after an intersection of axes, webbing or networks, sponges and lattices. Its principal features may mimic cracking and erosion patterns, polygonal and hexagonal symmetries, spirals and slalom curvatures, highlights and accents, grades and ranks. There is a large set of standard spatial (spatial-kinetic, spatial-visual, spatial-auditory) structures that can be deployed to build systems, be they cognitive or social systems – or models of natural systems. Even the stock-standard tree hierarchy is a subset of spatial-visual explanation. Hierarchy has long been employed in the explanation and formation of a wide range of cognitive and social systems, and equally pervasively in the explanation and formation of natural systems.

Another way of thinking about explanation as a structural principle of knowledge systems is to think about the 'four categories of causes' that Aristotle identified (1960, Alpha. 3). These are parts, beginnings, ends and forms. Or – to put it more exactly – Aristotle invented the very useful schema of material, efficient, final and formal causes. We owe him much. Many of the common ways that we organize knowledge assume 'beginnings and endings'. This is true of knowledge right across the spectrum between information and imagination. Classic information trees, for example, have a root node which is 'where we begin'. We click down the hierarchy of subsidiary nodes till we reach the bottom-most node. Having a beginning and an ending is one of the key ways that human beings make the world around them meaningful and create order out of chaos. Both stories and explanations, irrespective of whether they are simple or sophisticated kinds, suppose beginnings and endings. The start and conclusion of an information trail is the equivalent of the motive and the goal of human conduct. 'Home' is the ubiquitous sign of a web page. Leaving home and returning home is the animating force of much of the great corpus of human literature.

If start and finish – motive and teleology – are repeatedly found in system architecture, so also are 'parts and wholes'. All structure, including cognitive structure, involves a relationship between parts and the whole. Every structure has constituents or elements. The millions of media objects on a terabyte hard disk are elements. We have to compose, combine and structure those elements – and find an efficient and elegant relationship between the parts and the whole. But at this point, in doing this, we discover something startling. We began with the distinction that Aristotle made between parts, beginnings, ends and forms. This is an excellent typology of the structures involved in system building. However, as we begin to build systems, we start to realize that in doing so these distinctions begin to break down. As we will see shortly, they break down as we move across the spectrum of knowledge away from information and toward imagination. In the case of the structuring principle that says that parts or elements have to be composed or combined together in a whole – which is a very sound principle – we find that in fact one of the best ways of doing that is with the aid of what Aristotle called formal causes. We combine parts into brilliant wholes through patterns and shapes – that is through the medium of forms. A book, for instance, is a form. Through the form of the book, we compose words into sentences, sentences into paragraphs, paragraphs into sections, sections into chapters and chapters into books. Each one of these parts composed into a whole is a form enacted within a larger form. Each form permits or effects a combination of elements.

The form of anything is its shape. The form of the human face gives us an impression of beauty or lack of beauty. That is equally true of an information system or an archive. We are impressed by its elegance or irritated by its lack of the same. Beautiful systems give us great pleasure. The pleasure that we get from virtually 'walking though' an information space – or browsing the shelves of a traditional library – derives from the tacit structures of these spaces. Even when we do not expect a system to arouse in us pleasure, it may do so. Note how computer users will often tell us that 'time disappears' when they are working to screen. This experience is the result of the operation of a formal cause. Formal causes turn our actions into ends in themselves. Thus even relentless clicking through web pages or a database can become seductively pleasurable. Routine work of this kind can even become mildly addictive. This is explicable in musical terms. The tap-tap-tapping of the keyboard – and the click-click-clicking from one web page to the next – sets up a rhythm. Rhythms seduce us. They bathe us in pleasures. In the case of rhythm, this is the uncanny pleasure of 'repetition and change' – or 'same and difference'. Rhythms repeat,

repeat, then they change on the beat. We don't notice this subtle union when we work. We don't think about it.

All successful systems work best when we are least aware of them. We focus instead on the problems that we have to solve. Building systems should be the exception, not the rule. Good knowledge systems help us solve problems by having in place a facilitating order – a framework of knowledge. Such frameworks operate like the organization of musical tones in melodies, chords, or rhythms. We organize information 'musically' all of the time. This is because we have a large stock of forms that we draw on, usually tacitly, when we build systems. These are forms such as ratio, right proportion, symmetry and rhythm. Each of these represents key ways in which we can put together the parts of a whole. Crucially such forms give us the capacity to create a union of contrary qualities. In this manner, we create unions of large and small, hard and soft, same and different, up and down, major and minor, light and dark. As in the Dewey Classification system, science co-exists with literature, and engineering with philosophy. The best – the most audacious – systems are like Bach's music. They are built on a kind of structural counterpoint. Counterpoint is a contradiction in terms. It is the union of two independent, contrasting melody lines that are harmonically interdependent. A child learns to play a melody, a young adult learns to compose a melody – but all of that is still far removed from the composer who works effortlessly in counterpoint.

Imagination

The systemic aspect of a system invariably comes up against an ultimate limit. This is the limit of creation itself, and the limit of creation is the challenge of the imagination. Every functioning system has to be invented. When we invent things, we do so first by adapting what is close to hand. Invention is as much a function of what is old as what is new, but the converse is equally true so that invention is never simply a function of precedent either.

When digital computers were created, there were pre-existing calculating machines. The digital computer also interpolated a pre-existing system distinction. Literally the operating system of a digital computer is built on the distinction between true and false. The bivalent value is hard wired into the logic chip of the digital computer's central processing unit. 'True and false' is a powerful system-building distinction. Any system builder would be foolish to ignore a distinction like this when it is close to hand. The architects of the digital computer adapted the terminology of George Boole's logic and its animating distinction between true and false. In Boolean logic, a set of elements can contain only two possible values – 'true' and/or 'false'. These two axiomatic values can be given a variety of alternative names. They can be called yes and no, one and zero, on and off – and so on. Digital computing is two-valued. It is built on electrical circuits that can be in either of one of two states – defined by high or low voltage. The voltage of the current cannot be high and low simultaneously. In figurative terms, a Boolean switch cannot signify 'true and false' ('one and zero') *at the same time*. Anyone who has ever experienced the unforgiving nature of a machine spellchecker knows what this means. There is no room for fuzziness or ambiguity – or multivalent logic – in the central processing unit of a digital computer.

Yet all system builders who embrace the true-false distinction, which is a very powerful and very useful distinction, will at some stage have some doubts about doing so. Such doubts are inscribed in the very act of system creation or system design. A system may be built on the true-false distinction, but to conceive – or imagine – the distinction in the first instance requires the person doing so to suspend the distinction. The act of imagination occurs in a medium that is constituted by three or more values. Its logic – if that is a word that is applicable to the imagination – is multivalent. Human beings *think* – as opposed to *reason* – in multivalent terms. The principal media of thought are analogy and paradox.[4] Thinking means connecting the unconnected and making the dissimilar similar. This may be summarized thus: paradox is contradiction. At the core of difference is likeness. Analogy brings disparate things together.

Analogy and paradox create agreement between disagreeing terms, but that is not their only role. For, before we can draw a distinction between two terms, we must first of all draw an analogy between them. Creation is the third term that binds together two contrary terms which it posits in the act of creation. Think for example of the most influential of all classification systems, Carl Linnaeus's taxonomy of living things. Linnaean taxonomy classifies the animal and plant world using social terms like 'domain', 'kingdom', 'family', 'tribe', 'class' and 'legion'. The agreement of terms precedes their distinction. In the act of creation, no distinction is drawn between axiomatic pairs (such as the biological and the social) without an implied analogy or connecting thread between them –

---

4   An elegant introduction to the topic of analogy and paradox is Hugh Kenner's short book on the work of G. K. Chesterton, *Paradox in Chesterton* (1947). Kenner was a prominent associate of Marshall McLuhan, who was himself an artful master of analogy and paradox. On McLuhan's use of paradox, see the study by McLuhan's student – Theall (2001).

no matter how polarized they may appear to be when looked at from certain vantage points. No axiomatic polarity – no twinning of ultimate truth-values – occurs outside an implied system that binds them together: a priori and in unison. This is the paradox of system creation. The system provides the third term that unites polarities – the 'middle' of the story unites the 'beginning' and the 'end'. The Boolean true-false distinction can be hardwired into a machine, but at some point, out of necessity, the designer of the machine will have had to have thought in terms that suppose not the bivalent logic of George Boole but the multivalent logic of Jan Łukasiewicz and Hans Reichenbach.[5] This is an odd state that all creators find themselves in from time to time.

Multivalent logic can be thought of as a formalized description of how the imagination or intuition works. The imagination connects the unconnected. This imaginative ability – to make the 'dissimilar similar' – lies at the core of system creation. This is not a universal view. The mathematician George Spencer-Brown, in his influential work *Laws of Form* (1969), in contrast emphasizes the importance of drawing a distinction.[6] A distinction is a line or boundary that separates something from everything else. Drawing a distinction is akin to the act of a demi-urge that creates something from the chaos of the void. It is tempting to think of system building in this sense. But system creation in fact rests on a paradox: to draw a distinction the designer must first erase the distinction. The implication of this is that it is not the sharpening of the distinction (say) between 'major and minor' or 'inside and outside' that matters in the act of system creation, but rather the coalescence of 'major and minor' or 'inside and outside'. The medium of creation is an analogical or paradoxical super-positional entity, rather than two distinct counter-positional entities. This is a strange matter, doubtless, but then so is system creation.

In practical settings, it is just as likely to be the amateur as the expert who notices this strange quality. The expert acquires expertise through familiarity with distinctions. The most commonplace distinction is represented by the boundary of the expert's discipline. Knowledge in general is erected on system distinctions. This is very apt. Yet sometimes it is useful to look at things not as

---

5   A short account of multi-valued logic is presented in Hans Reichenbach (1951, 225–7). Notably the starting point of this discussion is the failure of classical two-valued logic to account for antinomies and paradoxes.

6   The system theory of Niklas Luhmann (1995), for example, emphasizes the drawing of the boundary between system and environment, and Spencer-Brown is cited as key support for the system–environment distinction that permeates Luhmann's work. The criticism of this from the standpoint of TPA – the theory of paradox and analogy – is that every system is an environment, and every environment has systemic characteristics.

the expert does 'from the inside' but as the little boy who viewed the emperor did – 'from the outside looking inside'. While the royal tailors are busy dressing the naked king in nothing at all, the little boy declares 'the king has no clothes'. So let us consider the problem of knowledge system building not from the standpoint of the expert, but from the standpoint of the amateur.

Personal computing has led to the wide diffusion of tools to build knowledge and information systems. The technology is inexpensive. Consequently the barriers of entry into the world of knowledge system building are low. This is not to say that there are not other barriers, aside from the cost of technology. Most people with a computer are not going to build a personal knowledge management system from scratch. Rather they are going to make an ad hoc adaptation of structures that are already built into their computer. But even adaptive behaviour is a kind of invention. It is the inventiveness of everyday life. It may not lead to the development of a formal system, but it will expose substantial numbers of people incidentally to experiences that formal system builders face in a more exacting fashion. Two experiences are of especial note.

First a system builder must 'choose the distinction' on which to begin to build a knowledge system. Truth and falsity, beginning and end, material and formal cause, part and whole, space and time, arrival and departure – all of these are powerful distinctions on which systems can be raised up. Secondly a system builder will encounter moments of intuition when these powerful distinctions begin to break down. This is an uncanny, even vertiginous, experience. Personal knowledge management highlights these experiences because it is a 'wild west'. Nobody is around to tell the amateur designer what to do. Most amateur designers will not do very much. Nonetheless the relative openness of the terrain of 'working with your own computer on your own time' means that there are also not the built-in institutional resistances to those surreal moments of having to 'choose the system of distinction' or – even worse – having to cope with the breakdown of all systems of distinction (at least momentarily) as the amateur comes face-to-face with what it really means to 'compose in counterpoint'. Most, sensibly, will give up at such a point because they realize it is too difficult. But, in a way, giving up is better than having been an institutionalized drudge and not having even noticed that there is a counterpoint moment in system design.

The amateur designer will have a modest ambition: to build an archive in which to store the family photos. But often the seemingly simplest things are the most difficult. For the designer begins with a tricky choice: on which distinction shall the design be based? Will it be the distinction between ending and beginning, matter and form, truth and falsity? Let us pursue this further via a thought experiment. We'll begin by supposing that a choice is made. Our amateur designer decides to create an information architecture on an 'historical' principle. The reason is that three generations ago there was a famous family member. The family story circulates around this person. The information architecture is designed to mimic this order of events. The images of this person must have prominence. Perhaps that person's image file is created as the node of the family file hierarchy, or the famous predecessor's images are chosen as the start of a slide show, or a Flash movie is created with a narration that casts the predecessor as the family icon, or a website is created with the family icon prominent on the home page and subsidiary pages devoted both to the illustrious figure and to other family members. The point of such design is seemingly clear. Yet it also poses some tricky issues for the designer. For the system assumptions that seemed evident at one point are liable to become more ambiguous later on.

Nagging questions start to arise. Is the architectonic apex of this design, that is, 'the beginning' – the illustrious ancestor or the present-day family? Will the fixation on the famous predecessor remain, or will focus move to the precursors of the predecessor? The 'historical principle' of organization begins to slide around under these forces. The 'origin' of the system is pushed back or forward in time. In a practical sense the creator will create and delete, move and rearrange files and file structures as the niggling questions emerge. Files that were expected to be large will not fill up. Files that were intended to be subsidiary will become primary. What began as an apparently certain nod to the axiom of 'the beginning' ends in confusion. Is the beginning something that is in the present or the past? Does the beginning have earlier beginnings? If so, does anything really begin or is it already started before it begins? Can something not yet begun – the future – be the beginning of something?

System designers deal with such questions not articulately but intuitively. They get a flickering sense that either their structures are built on firm distinctions – or not. Sometimes in a project firmness gives way. The plunging sensation that follows is not an intimation of chaos. It is rather a graphic apprehension of the paradox of system creation. Systems are built on distinctions. To create a distinction, distinctions must be collapsed. Here we confront the paradox of creation 'in the first instance'. We are looking in on the 'moment of gestation' of a system. That our creator in this case is an amateur is all the more interesting because the naivety of the amateur makes the puzzle of gestation all the more evident. The amateur designer is trying to think structurally about how the images of a family shall be arranged and presented. The outcome of this process is likely to be idiosyncratic. There is no settled formula for how this might be done. It may produce results that no one, not even the creator, is interested in. Yet the questions posed by such experimentalism are questions that system creation always poses – sometimes on infinitely grander scales.

What this discussion points to is the counterpoint moment of creation. The child who was sent by Miss Salisbury to the local library is on a quest for certainty. The information desk is a beacon of salvation. The poor kid is faced with a world that is filled with information that sounds mostly unintelligible. The child has the aggravating task of making sense of things, many of which are difficult to make sense of. At ten years old, the youngster understands birthdays, but as for Presidents, or America, or States – what are those things? The child needs clarity, in the same way that a child goes through a long phase where the world is divided into 'good children' and 'bad children'. That is necessary in order to learn morality. We all have to learn to distinguish between good and bad. But when children become adults they come to understand that sometimes bad people do good things and sometimes good people do terrible things. In the world of the adult, there is ambiguity, paradox and irony. The great art of the world teaches us this. This is the lesson of comedy and tragedy – and counterpoint. In a parallel sense, an information provider like Wikipedia frequently offers us disambiguation pages – when you searched on 'president' did you mean a political leader or the chief executive officer of a company? When we deal with information, we want clarity. We do not want a long debate about whether the President of the United States is a leader first and foremost or an executive figure charged with implementing the laws of the country. Once we are past the childish state of learning, though, we realize that the American President is *both* – and at the same time. We start to grasp that this is a deeply ambivalent office, one that is difficult to get a handle on, let alone occupy. We don't expect a child to grasp that. They first have to understand what a leader is. Then they have to understand what an executor does. Then, if they have the nous, they will figure out that there is an ambiguous state in which someone can 'lead and execute', 'initiate and serve' at the same time.

Conclusion

What such ambiguity does is to undermine distinctions between true and false, beginning and end, matter and form. At a certain stage we come to realize that gestation is both a start and an end. It is both past and future combined.

What we start to appreciate is that at least some aspects of the world that we inhabit have a super-positional or 'quantum' nature. We also start to understand that some parts of our own selves have a 'quantum' nature as well. This is especially so when we have to deal with the question of creation.

At the moment of creation, systemic distinctions between true and false, matter and form, ending and beginning collapse. They do not collapse into chaos, though. Quite the contrary – nothing is less chaotic than counterpoint. The distinctions collapse by folding into each other. Through the media of analogy and paradox they enter into each other seamlessly. Axiomatic system distinctions do not give rise to themselves. Taxonomic pairs are not their own unconditional presuppositions. Thus the collapsing of distinctions – or more exactly their super-positioning – is a matter of necessity. The creation of distinctions, and systems based on them, requires that those distinctions are inoperative. All pivotal system distinctions – all axiomatic values – in the moment that they are posited are conditioned by a supervening state. In this state, system distinctions are not distinct but rather exist in the symbiosis of analogy and paradox. In the act of system creation, we see – as William Blake saw – the world in a grain of sand and eternity in an hour.[7]

References

Aristotle (1960), *Metaphysics* (Ann Arbor: University of Michigan Press).

Heiss, J. (2003), 'Computer Visions: A Conversation with David Gelernter', *Sun Developer Network*, July, accessed 4 October 2008. http://java.sun.com/developer/technicalArticles/Interviews/gelernter_qa.html

Kenner, H. (1947), *Paradox in Chesterton* (New York: Sheed and Ward).

Luhmann, N. (1995), *Social Systems* (Stanford: Stanford University Press).

Reichenbach, H. (1951), *The Rise of Scientific Philosophy* (Berkeley: University of California Press).

Spencer-Brown, G. (1969), *Laws of Form* (London: Allen and Unwin).

Theall, D. (2001), *The Virtual Marshall McLuhan* (Montreal: McGill-Queen's University Press).

---

7   From Blake's *Auguries of Innocence* (Composition date: *c*.1800–1803)

   To see a World in a Grain of Sand
   And a Heaven in a Wild Flower,
   Hold Infinity in the palm of your hand
   And Eternity in an hour.

4

Recovering the Individual as the Locus of Knowledge: Communication and Personal Knowledge Management

Mark Wolfe

Introduction

Communication is the critical component in knowledge management (KM) undertakings but the theory at the core of communication study remains ignored within the KM domain. KM-related approaches such as organizational narratives, storytelling and sense-making implicate communication but bypass this core theory in much the way KM itself has typically bracketed out a theory of knowledge in favour of more 'hands-on' approaches. This has allowed KM to get on with its business but also has resulted in KM theories and commentary ranging widely over disparate conceptual domains that are contentious and lack a core orientation. Further, the constant state of reinvention within KM has not only generated volumes of academic and industry commentary that do little to ground the field, but the sheer weight of this uncoordinated discourse has helped suppress its adoption (Wolfe 2003). The matter is now further complicated with the emergence of Web 2.0 and its foreseeable iterations (Web n.0) that present a double-edged sword: on the one hand, the inherently participatory nature of Web 2.0 already recovers the individual as the locus of knowledge due to the emphasis on communications and information self-management that network work entails; on the other hand, Web 2.0 also comes associated with cultures of use that critics and employers perceive as narcissistic at best, and therefore counterproductive. Yet it is precisely this attribute of self-managing communications agency that behooves us to take another look at communication itself and its relation to knowledge in a deeper way.

In this essay, I contend communication is not only the theoretical and pragmatic but also the ethical grounding long lacking in KM, and that Personal Knowledge Management (PKM) in particular – with its recovery of the communicative individual as the primary locus of ongoing knowledge creation – is a timely and appropriate domain in which to make the case. After a brief historical scan of the communication–knowledge connection in Western philosophy, the work of Maturana and Varela will be enlisted as the first in a two-prong central argument. First, that because it precedes and is the basis of *all* subsequent symbolic mediation and sense-making of the world as undertaken by individuals and collectives, communication *is* and needs to be seen as *the* ontological substrate of all organizational activity, including and especially knowledge creation. Here, 'ontological substrate' means its dynamics and place in the human make-up are not just fundamentally prior to all other organizational experience but are often at the root of organizational dysfunction itself. The second prong of the argument comprises a review of the study of communication pragmatics by Jürgen Habermas that will be posited as the core theory of communication and therefore core to a theory of knowledge itself. Because all effective communication necessarily invokes assumptions of truth – where claims made are also always open to contestation by interlocutors – speakers thereby need to own what they say, raising fundamental issues of transparency and accountability in a time when the world is suffering from an egregious lack of both in our organizations and social (viz. governing) institutions. Practical suggestions for ways in which a recovered focus on communication can ameliorate common organizational pitfalls will be offered.

Communication, Knowledge and the Third Linguistic Turn

The conceptual and thematic connection between language-based communication and knowledge stems from the original musings of the ancient Greeks, but the substantial work in understanding human knowledge has occurred over the last 125 years – much of it based in what could be called a tri-fold 'linguistic turn' in contemporary thought.

The first turn stemmed from the efforts by Peirce and Frege in the late 1800s to expand and systematize logic, and then those by Whitehead and Russell in the early twentieth century to ground mathematics as a closed logical system. The former aimed at widening the conceptual approaches and successes of analytical philosophy in general by bringing to the domain of human language use a rigour that had not been entertained since Leibniz. Along with his discovery of calculus, Leibniz conceived of a language calculator that would 'crunch' arguments the way he had designed his seventeenth-century 'stepped reckoner' to compute basic arithmetic formulae beyond simple addition and subtraction. The latter succeeded in entrenching symbolic logic as a core subdiscipline within academic philosophy and laid the groundwork for further attempts to demystify knowledge by establishing the logical definitions and conditions under which any claim to knowledge could be said to have obtained. While aimed primarily at overcoming the previous centuries' grand systems theories of knowledge and human experience – particularly those proposed by Kant and then Hegel – this 'analytic turn' most fundamentally signalled an important break from the influential Freudian analysis of consciousness based on subjectivism. However, it set the stage for investigating natural language in the form of abstract, symbolic computation – the dominant conceptual framework that not only gave rise to cybernetics and cognitive science prior to and following the Second World War but for many scholars accounts for the enduring bias in organizations towards technology solutions to managing knowledge.

Somewhat in parallel but to lesser effect within the organizational domain, a second turn can be conceived as grounded in the work of Lev Vygotsky 1962) and Jean Piaget (1971), whose investigations of language in social and biological terms respectively helped recast the notion of language and knowledge as progressively developmental. Here, knowledge was seen as a function of individuals building up both their conceptual and practical awareness of the world by successfully engaging their meaning-laden natural and social environments over time – the test for which being simply, and following the later Wittgenstein, the extent to which individuals can communicate by using those concepts to appropriate effect. While this signalled an important break from associationism and behaviourism as approaches to studying human knowledge based on patterns of observed human activity, the notion that knowledge falls exclusively in the domain of social language use failed to take hold in the organizational environment per se. Instead, the organizational arena became dominated by the cybernetic paradigms just discussed, with the emergence of Human Resources and theories of administration embracing these computation-inspired and prescriptive-functional approaches (Simon 1947 [1997]) – an era brought into sharp relief through early studies of technology-based systems keyed to automating inherently social processes (Zuboff 1988).

Indeed, had the social/biological paradigm of knowledge and communication prevailed over its logico-computational rivals, it is debatable whether a phrase like knowledge management, let alone personal knowledge management, would even have come about.

THE THIRD LINGUISTIC TURN – MATURANA AND VARELA

Against this backdrop, a third linguistic turn can be postulated as having emerged in the last decade, coinciding with the historical rise in popularity of knowledge management itself, but perhaps more importantly driven and shaped primarily by complexity theory – the recent movement across the disciplines to help account for evolutionary dynamics in their domains of study. With mathematical roots in chaos theory, complexity theory also reflects a computational bias but it is precisely in fields like biology (Kauffman 1993, 1995), social theory (Luhmann 1982, 1984, 1989) and communication (Krippendorff 1999; Leydesdorff 2001) where researchers and theorists, consciously or otherwise, have made good on elements of complexity theory in conceptually productive ways. This has shown promise of translating into new approaches to knowledge management because concepts like 'emergence' and 'self-organization' have at least retrained our focus on human communicative interaction as the critical ways and means of knowledge production – a focus taken up to good effect by practitioners such as Dave Snowden, even if the deeper theoretical foundations of the communication–knowledge nexus remain largely unexplored or unarticulated in that work.

One body of work, however, that does stand out as redressing the communication–knowledge equation comes from Maturana and Varela. Their theoretical and methodological differences notwithstanding, Maturana and Varela in particular have been exemplary in making accessible Piaget's original goal of anchoring knowledge in a biological understanding of language and communication (Maturana 1980; Maturana and Varela 1987 [1998]). Decrying the penchant in Western culture for valuing action over reflection, Maturana and Varela describe our long-standing avoidance of the question how do we know that we know? – a question explicitly avoided in the KM literature itself (see for example Davenport and Prusak 1998) – as one of our most 'shameful ignorances'. That is because implicit in the avoidance of this question is the equating of knowledge with human states, and consequently with our make-up and actions as abstract processes. Instead, they argue we should see knowledge as continually *arising* from these processes as concrete, everyday responses to a world:

Therefore, underlying everything we shall say is this constant awareness that the phenomenon of knowing cannot be taken as though there were 'facts' or objects out there that we grasp and store in our head. The experience of anything out there is validated in a special way by the human structure, which makes possible 'the thing' that arises in the description.

Maturana and Varela (1987 [1998], 25)

This passage stresses a necessary circularity between action and experience that grounds knowledge as dynamic in evolutionary ways: viz. it is not the environment that determines responses in the individual but the human structure itself that selects from a variety of possible responses to physical and mental events that act as mere triggers in the environment – hence the authors' fondness for the aphorism 'all doing is knowing, and all knowing is doing'. This is already a key lesson for traditional command-and-control managers and the training and compliance-based information systems typically designed and deployed in their service. But Maturana and Varela go further in ways that resonate even more deeply in the (P)KM context:

When we speak here of action and experience, we mean something different from what occurs only in relation to the surrounding world, on the 'purely' physical level. This feature of human activity applies to all the dimensions of our life, in particular, it applies to what we – the reader and the writer – are doing right here and now. And what are we doing? We are dealing in language, breezing along in a distinctive way of conversing in an imagined dialogue. Every reflection, including one on the foundation of human knowledge, invariably takes place in language, which is our distinctive way of being human and being humanly active. For this reason, language is also our starting point, our cognitive instrument, and our sticking point ... Every reflection brings forth a world. As such, it is a human action by someone in particular in a particular place.

(1987 [1998], 26)

Viewed from a biological perspective, then, we might propose another aphorism of relevance to the domain of management and knowledge management in particular: *knowledge is where you find it*. This effects good alignment with the notion that personal knowledge management recovers the significance of the individual as the locus of knowledge but also does it one better: by re-conceiving knowledge as a set of complex responses built into every (viz. conscious, deliberate) action, including the action of reflecting on knowledge itself, knowledge can be seen as a system-level property arising from the raw cognitive capacities, skills, values, attitudes and inclinations that are already engaged in bringing forth worlds that comprise knowledge in the first place. Skills, values, capacities and inclinations/habits are therefore no more add-ons to knowledge than cylinders are an add-on to the concept of an internal combustion engine. Indeed, most of what passes for KM 'theory' is couched in traditional management terms that at best comprise a kind of second-order analysis – viz. the perceived need on a more abstract and reflective level of control and predictability for managing what has already been managed on a lower (viz. individual) level.[1] In the context of knowledge as fundamental human communicative process, the very phrase 'personal knowledge management' comes off at best as misleadingly redundant and logically bemusing – somewhat like referring to an 'electric' iPod.

If knowledge is not something out there to which people need to be invited, or to acquire and consume, but instead is core to human communicative experience and action as such, this does not yet explain *how* communication succeeds and, more importantly, what the ramifications for individuals and the organization are when it does not. The matter is of chief concern. On the one hand, individuals cultured, counselled and/or marketed into believing they are *solely* responsible for managing the information resources backstopping their knowledge are apt to become even more disconnected from the organization than what is already being commonly effected by a workplace generation gap that is further split along values and technology lines. On the other hand, senior managers retreating into command-and-control mode in reaction to these emerging dynamics of self-reliance are very likely to *create* disconnects with the very people they rely on to survive as an organization. This is particularly relevant and timely in light of Web 2.0 applications that, aimed primarily at a specific demographic, risk further propagating 'all about me' cultures – a development making communication across organizational boundaries of department, job classifications, gender and generational lines more important and challenging than ever.

---

1   This is not to suggest the individual's place in the organization is not holonic – a whole that is also part of a larger whole requiring rational coordination and guidance on a different structural level. The worry is that consistently skipping over the more fundamental components and dynamics of knowledge creation as grounded in human communication will keep KM on the treadmill of writing that to some degree and in one way or another mirrors Davenport et al.'s (1998, 44) description of KM projects as 'attempts "to do something useful" with knowledge, to accomplish organizational objectives through the structuring of people, technology and knowledge content' – as if both, knowledge is an unproblematic given that is separate from people and it is not already doing something useful.

Communications Pragmatics

The good news is, communication pragmatics are universal (Habermas 1979, 1998), meaning they are implicated in the human use of any language in a normal way in some social context (two or more people) – regardless of whether the second party in a communication is physically present, as in a public address or face-to-face communication, or remote, as in the case of distributed context received through books, articles, web sites and the like.[2] In principle, communications practitioners and managers in the organizational environment up on this core theory are well-deployed to adapt to changes and challenges often brought on by new technology and applications. The bad news is that a disturbingly low number of communications and management educators and therefore practitioners are trained in this area or at this level of communication theory – a sorry state of affairs that accounts in large part for why communications is still handled by lower management public relations departments that function mostly as senior management mouthpieces. It is also why senior management itself, good intentions aside, still spends prodigious consulting dollars on generating mission statements that too often merely pay lip service to values, and training programmes too often driven by a technology 'solution', instead of applying resources and talent toward developing individual capacity and communication programmes in the first place to action those values.

On the one hand, communication suffers a fate similar to knowledge itself when those responsible for it – namely all of us – assume that because we all already communicate and know stuff, there is little value in picking apart how these human ways of being actually work. On the other hand, the low uptake of fundamental communication theory even amongst communication professionals can be seen as due largely to the source of this core theory. As described above, part of its lineage stems from early twentieth-century philosophy of language that was part of a linguistic turn inspired and shaped primarily by advances in mathematics and formal logic. Subsequent discipline territorialities, especially within linguistics itself, as well as a well-entrenched members-only mentality in professional philosophy in particular, have ensured little curriculum-based

---

2   Although there are grounds to question whether the subject need be human, as suggested by the case of Kanji – the bonobo under primate expert Sue Savage-Rumbaugh's charge and on whose mother the attempts to teach American Sign Language (ASL) largely failed but who spontaneously acquired the ability to sign through incidental exposure as the primary subject's ever-present offspring (Savage-Rumbaugh et al. 1998). The case is similar with Washoe and Nim Chimpsky – two chimpanzees from separate trials reported as having acquired the rudiments of ASL and used it to ask questions and express declarative thoughts in a testable way.

uptake beyond philosophy departments per se. The other part of its lineage, however, is its more recent and more socially grounded instantiation in the form of 'universal pragmatics' – a phrase still new to many readers. This seam of the theory stems from the work of Jürgen Habermas, who himself presents something of a perfect storm in terms of the potential uptake of theory in the English-speaking domain: the writer is German; the level of abstraction and impenetrability of the larger social critique embedded in the theory follows in the tradition of Heidegger and Luhmann and is legendary even for native German readers; and because Habermas himself was the youngest member of the so-called Frankfurt School of critical theory that, following the Second World War, agitated for radical social change by challenging the increasing reliance in society on scientific methodologies.

The paradox is that, while Habermas' larger social/critical theory based on universal pragmatics is almost overwhelmingly comprehensive – to a point of 'grand theory' in the traditional of sociologist Talcott Parsons – his analysis of speech acts is quite accessible, where the ethical dimensions built into it pertain to power dynamics with striking similarity to what organizations face today. The paradox is only underscored by the legions of communications and management graduates entering the workforce with either only a passing understanding of this theory, or no familiarity with it at all. Little wonder, then, that many public affairs departments languish near the bottom of their corporate totem poles when their members can and should be guiding the organization in strategic areas such as cultures of use of technology, sustainable development and corporate responsibility where increasingly savvy and connected employees and publics demand transparency and accountabilities in these areas.

For Habermas, all attempts at speaking or writing aimed at mutual understanding necessarily involve making claims that are meant to validate the communication as: intelligible to the receiver; about something that is true in the world;[3] well-formed – that is, stated in a understandable, credible way; and appropriate to the matter at hand. Or, as Habermas himself summarizes:

> *The aim of reaching understanding is to bring about an agreement that terminates in the intersubjective mutuality of reciprocal comprehension, shared knowledge, mutual trust and accord with one another. Agreement is based on recognition of the four corresponding validity claims:*

---

3   Including, of course, existing fictions – Homer Simpson is not a real person but his depiction as a cartoon character is real.

comprehensibility, truth, truthfulness and rightness. In its narrowest meaning, it indicates that two subjects understand a linguistic expression in the same way; in its broadest meaning, it indicates that an accord exists between two subjects concerning the rightness of an utterance in relation to a mutually recognized normative background.

(1998, 23)

Not all communication goes smoothly, of course, or there would be no need for a theory of communication in the first place. The myriad shades of grey between understanding and not, between intentional and unintentional deception, and between motives for striking accord (or not), mean for Habermas that the process for reaching understanding is always a dynamic bringing about of agreement. In other words, understanding based on agreement is always necessarily a negotiation using the validity claims as the universally and mutually accepted ground on which communication proceeds at all:

*Reaching understanding is a process of bringing about an agreement on the presupposed basis of validity claims that are mutually recognized. In everyday life, we start from a background of consensus pertaining to those interpretations taken for granted among participants. **As soon as this consensus is shaken, and as soon as the presupposition that the validity claims are satisfied (or could be vindicated) is suspended in the case of at least one of the four claims, communicative action cannot be continued.***

(1998, 23 – my emphasis)

IMPLICATIONS FOR KM

The implications of a theory of communicative action that analyses speech acts (utterances) in terms of mutually recognized[4] and universal validity claims should be fairly apparent to those interested or working in knowledge management. For instance, one is tempted to assume that most communication in evolved domains like that of established organizations is intelligible and relevant to its own or client/customers' needs, but this is in no way a given – especially in the case of front-line functions like reception and helpdesks.

---

4   Precisely *how* these claims come to be mutually recognized is the subject of the earlier linguistic-based knowledge theories of Piaget and Vygotsky. For the former, linguistic competence is a stage in the development of the individual contingent upon the acquisition of concepts through physical and social action in the world. For the latter, linguistic competence was likewise developed but, unlike Piaget, Vygotsky denied these stages of development were fixed but rather iterated throughout the life of the individual.

The blunt reality is that, with more foreign-speaking and younger workers entering the workforce at these levels, intelligibility and the ability to anticipate and then address relevant customer needs – not to mention establish credibility and accord with them – will become increasingly problematic. Further, the situation is only made worse when protocol-based and case-based training initiatives are simply thrown at the problem, often aided and abetted by technology, and with little regard to the communication barrier(s) giving rise to these problems in the first place. The result too often is employees who internalize responses to situations algorithmically and based on common symptoms, instead of being trained holistically to recognize context-based instances of fundamental communication impasse, assess options for overcoming the impasse and then implement strategies for doing so. Emphasis on the latter would result in fewer frustrated and/or flight-risk workers and less unproductive corporate expense.

The larger implication for knowledge management, though, stems from the latter two validity claims – those involving credibility and the overall 'rightness' of the communication. This is where an ethical dimension comes into play, since built into communication is the notion that one is making claims that are testable and so the speaker is accountable for the claims raised. Moreover, by attempting to effect agreement about something, one is also responsible for setting the stage for further bringing about of agreement and/or action toward some greater good or purpose[5] – not unlike what is being attempted right here in this chapter and the book at large.

In the organizational context, that greater good comprises at very least the enduring survival of the company in such a way that its growth and contribution go beyond the balance sheets to include increased welfare for both its own employees and the jurisdictions that allow it to operate. That much is intuitive. But the ethical dimension to Habermas' theory of communicative action in the organizational context implicates managers most directly, since it falls to anyone charged with the supervision of others to ensure that goals, values, strategies, tactics, rules of engagement, internal cultural codes and

---

5   Indeed, this is central to Habermas' larger social critique, where the whole point of critical theory is to overcome the tendency in society of ruling elites to systematically distort communication in favour of preferred discourses. In the post-war historical context in which Habermas grew up and wrote, the theory of communicative action cashes out as a theory of 'emancipatory knowledge' in contradistinction to the dominance of scientific rationalism that, in its coldest form, was instrumental in the technological brutality of the Second World War. Further, the notion of emancipatory knowledge is hardly alien to knowledge management, with its roots in empowerment and self-organized team movements, and its original message that people bring a lot more to their work than what is ultimately utilized.

mores and so on are understood, monitored, evaluated and promoted. This is increasingly a tall order: as mentioned above, organizations significantly split along generational lines face increased pressure in a personal knowledge management domain where the potential exists for the technology to rend these divisions further asunder; however, the theory of communicative action based on universal pragmatics of speech acts implicates managers also because we live in a time when society is increasingly intolerant of old-world models that have become monologic (even monolithic) in their unfolding. Indeed, writers like Don Tapscott (2006) argue the industrial models of the old world are already well past their due dates in terms of what is demanded by way of long-term thinking and full-cost accountability – where 'full-cost accountability' implicates social, ethical and environmental considerations holistically and strategically, not just as old-world tropes pumped out by marketing and investor relations departments.

In short, the validity claims implicated in any speech act aimed at understanding require speakers to *own* what they say, otherwise the consensus, in Habermas' words, is 'shaken' and the communication fails. The classic case of this on the organizational level is the tobacco industry's persistent attempts to dissuade consumers of the dangers of smoking. ExxonMobil's long-standing denial of human-based climate change is another. Concerted efforts like these to mislead or deny growing consensus elsewhere in society Habermas refers to as 'systematically distorted communication' from which a society needs to be emancipated, if balance is to be struck between the natural level of solidarity that arises among its people through everyday communication, and the level of responsibility that unfolds in communication at the higher structural level of management (Habermas 1984).

The issue of balance also resonates in the context of knowledge management: because a primary driver of the KM movement in the early 1990s was precisely the emancipation of people within the organization who had come to be seen as always bringing a lot more to the party than what their job descriptions called or allowed for, KM was seen as approaches to encourage the fuller engagement of people in innovative/creative and self-sustaining ways that would ultimately benefit the organization by affording it more resources with which to weather environmental perturbation. Indeed, the myriad frustrations KM historically has experienced in striking a balance between employee capacity and management control – a key tension behind the constant reinvention in the field that proponents indulge in precisely for lack of a base theory – has usually sourced from a reluctance of senior management to let go of the reins.

With the advent of personal knowledge management, with its technology-abetted promotion of self-management, the potential for exacerbating this imbalance seems greater than ever.

Communication and (Personal) Knowledge Management

It is in the context of technology-enabled self-management described above that PKM becomes a useful move in the overall knowledge management game. That is because it recovers the person implicated in any knowledge process. To recap, knowledge of something always takes place in language, which is our distinct way of being and acting human. In turn, language assumes linguistic competence that necessarily implicates mutually recognized conditions for truth, credibility and purpose of a communication that further imply an ethical requirement that speakers own what they say – in other words, be ready and available to back it up and otherwise be accountable for deceptions and the like. In the traditional organizational context, the onus for productively managing knowledge falls first and foremost to managers who need to bring their charges into agreement with the realities of the organization from its myriad cultural, operational and legal perspectives. In an ideal world, these realities are articulated at the senior management level and then cascaded throughout the organization, through training, example and just good culture at work in the work.

We never have and never will live in a perfect world. Anyone who has worked in an organization knows from experience that communication is fraught with difficulties at every step along the way: senior management relies on information that is often not the best available and they remain communicatively distant from most of the organization's employees; rivalries and personal agendas proliferate; departments often hoard the best of their work; and many employees just do not care about their jobs or the organization itself. It is little wonder, then, that knowledge management has faced uphill battles in even establishing itself as a discipline (Wolfe 2003) when the obstacles in its way on a theoretical and practical level are formidable.

In other words, it is relatively easy to see why most KM programmes fall short or fail outright since it is either not clear from the start what knowledge is or how it is created and/or it is construed simply as information, and the project becomes merely an exercise in technology. Worse, lacking a theory of knowledge automatically discounts communication as adding anything strategic or valuable in a fundamental way and so communication is construed merely as information *exchange*, and the project further becomes one of technology training and compliance. Worse still, lacking a culture of dialogic communication in Habermas' sense between members of the organization means fewer and fewer people having to own what they say, and the organization lapses further into localized solidarities (silos) and loose-tie networks at best (with an increasing number of nodes in the network being outside the organization).

With its focus, then, on enhanced individual capacity based on next-generation information management tools and better understanding of learning styles, personal knowledge management comes at a timely juncture but here too we must be careful. While much of the hype around social networking and information management applications conveys a sense of broadened participation in internal and external matters of relevance to the organization, many of these applications derive from or promote usage within very narrow demographics. In the same way that parents are not really invited into the world of Facebook, senior management – already estranged from both technology and technology-enabled solidarities – have little access and even less inclination to take these technologies up. Further, the counter argument that this is a temporary situation based on a soon-to-be-passing older generation is a shaky one. For one thing, the rate of technological innovation today reduces the traditional concept of generational change based on the biological cycle of about twenty years (roughly the time it normally takes an individual to reach maturity) to a new technology-driven cycle of about five years where entire social codes, mores, attitudes and Gestalts seem to shift with the emergence of dominant applications (the MSN 'generation' of five years ago giving way to the Facebook 'generation' of today and so forth). This suggests even today's tech-savvy employees are apt to be tomorrow's out-of-sync/style managers.

Recovering the Individual

None of which, though, means there are not relatively simple things that can be done to ameliorate such situations. I have been drawing on my background as a communication lecturer, researcher and curriculum designer to argue that communication *is* the core theory for knowledge management. As a senior communication practitioner with executive experience in the corporate and institutional setting, though, I can offer one simple overriding directive: communicate more and merely exchange information less. This means designing and deploying a number of tactical and strategic foci for the organization that re-emphasize the individual.

REACH OUT AND TALK TO SOMEBODY

The president of a large Canadian advertising firm getting blowback from staff unhappy with his decision to fire a favourite and valued colleague was flummoxed to learn his email notification of the 'termination' seemed to make matters worse. It never occurred to him to simply walk the halls and gather up the troops for quick face-to-face briefings on the event and the unavoidable reasons behind it. Getting out and talking to your charges and owning your communication may not always be sufficient for bringing about agreement on key matters but is one of the most effective ways of achieving it.

(DE-)HUMAN(-IZING) RESOURCES

Most HR departments are basically in the communications stone age when it comes to how they recruit and select individuals for employment. Increasing dependence on automated keyword filters and alleged matching algorithms that reduces the individual to a specialized skill sets (or lack thereof) serves to discount communication as the fundamental capacity for not only acquiring these skills in the first place but also for effectively deploying them in the organizational setting that is, after all, a *cultural* environment. Further, how individuals are recruited and selected only teaches employees that communications is at best an after-thought. The increasing number of HR departments that do not even have a human answering their main telephone number only further signals that communication is a low priority.

COMMUNICATIONS DEPARTMENTS

Public Relations and Public Affairs departments must come up in the world and take their rightful place as the logical home for strategizing, designing and implementing organizational communication effectiveness and knowledge-based programming – planning that is usually outsourced to high-priced consultants because communications itself remains at best in a reactive role, as in the case of emergency response and crisis communication, and at worst mired in a functional role of writing what other people (viz. managers) do not have the time and/or skill to write themselves(!). However, in order to prepare communications graduates for the task, core communication theory and the ability to speak and write well need to be stressed *above all else* in first-year college and university courses, with failure rates approaching that of engineering and medicine – a major lacking in many communications programmes. The result has been individuals ill-trained to conceptualize and negotiate organizational complexity, and hence Communications and PR departments ill-equipped to take on higher-level strategic functions, such as information technology assessment and design, corporate strategies research and sustainability planning.

MANAGEMENT TRAINING

Perhaps the best solution to the myriad disconnects stemming back to communication, however, is to reinvent management from the ground up. This follows Mintzberg (2004), who describes as 'obsessive' the focus in MBA programmes on financial analysis that transpires at the expense of leadership and management training that (a) necessarily go together, and (b) involve developing individuals capable of engendering 'communityship' – where people care about the organization and each other. Not surprisingly, informal communication tops the list of configurations in Mintzberg's own theory of organizational forms. Although not motivated by critical theory like Habermas, Mintzberg has publicly decried the threat to management itself as a credible discipline and sector of society at a time when we need leadership most – particularly in light of recent world events involving questionable foreign policies, major corporate scandals, implosion of the global financial sector and ongoing filibustering over climate change (regardless of its causes). Management trained in a theory of knowledge based in communication pragmatics would eliminate a good deal of the pinch points in organizations in terms of their ability to coordinate and culturally cohere along the directions it takes that arise in part from the input of empowered employees – not just technologically enhanced self-reliant workers.

K-12

Arguably, much of the obsession in our schools with testing as the only measure of student progress and capacity is an extension of what is going on in contemporary management. This partly accounts for the armies of undergraduate students interested far more in grade point averages than in the longer-term objective of learning for the sake of personal development. Teaching ancient Greek history and thought that emphasizes their contribution to communication – such as rhetoric and the social impact of the invention of the phonetic alphabet – would go far in driving appreciation for the value of social history and knowledge in general. And while this would better prepare individuals for social sciences as careers, it would also better prepare those in the natural sciences, medicine, engineering and management where interdisciplinarity is critical to the sort of long-term thinking and leadership that society now demands.

Conclusion – Whither KM in a Web 2.0 World?

Personal knowledge management, then, presents something of a double-edged sword: it recovers the person as the locus of knowledge in a timely way that draws attention to communication in its pragmatic and ethical dimensions. This offers a theory of knowledge in terms of a theory of communication and is meaningful for a world seeking transition from older 'industrial' models of leadership and management to something requiring more holistic and accountable action. On the other hand, the time and skill required to personally manage the prodigious amounts of information generated in a Web 2.0 world actually risks demoting interpersonal communication as a primary means of creating and managing knowledge. This not only threatens to further split the organization along lines based on technology and generation but could serve to undercut the very pragmatic and ethical dimensions to communication as advocated in this chapter – the more emphasis being placed on supporting applications like social networking that encourage self-management, the more *solipsistic* the workplace becomes.

That is, the workplace increasingly becomes similar to the kind of world depicted by Michael Heim (1993) in relation to virtual reality: an ontologically deep cultural domain of technology in which users become like Leibniz's monads – disembodied substances that relate to other monads only by virtue of the interface, thereby effecting qualities of anonymity already legendary in social networking and online gaming environments for their rupture of social norms and behaviours. This also extends the critical perspective of writers like Andrew Keen who perceive Web 2.0 applications as fatally narcissistic. It even implicates Web 'n.0' hopefuls like Tim O'Reilly (2009), who see future iterations of the network as becoming more cognitive and stimulus responsive to the world and us in it. This takes knowledge creation and work to next levels, the spin being the network as a cognitive assistant ultimately would augment human knowledge capacity by forcing us to raise our game with technology.

Despite these critical, dystopian and utopian perspectives, however, we remain essentially embodied and social beings dependent upon interpersonal interaction for fundamental concept creation and development to the higher orders of mental capacity that equip us for using technology in the first place. It is too easy, then, to get sidetracked by the very kinds of commentaries the critics themselves complain of and forget that communication and knowledge are the very substrate of human interaction as such, wherever and however it unfolds. The central argument of this chapter is simply that better understanding of these core attributes of human being and behaviour would go some distance in effecting better management of individual capacity for addressing change and challenge, and therefore better organizational resilience in the aggregate to environmental perturbance.

A QUESTION OF RISK AND TRUST

The foregoing is also of value in underscoring the shortcomings of traditional management approaches that proceed under industrial-world models of input–output designs, command-and-control managing, and information technology as the baseline for understanding knowledge that are no longer sustainable. It raises questions about risk and trust on the part of those managers who remain content with well-defined organizational hierarchies, the unambiguous ways and means of communication it inculcates, and the deployment of readily measurable IT systems to that end. One question for the traditional manager becomes: why should I risk the uncertainty and upheaval to the status quo that might well be produced in a Web n.0-enabled domain?

In an important sense, it is however not a question of whether a manager can afford to risk the upheaval of empowerment but rather if they can afford *not* to risk empowerment of the type described above, given increasing demands for organizational resilience of the kind requiring collective and expansive rather than singular and constrained expertise. This implicates trust as a critical feature of organizational design, culture and practice but in order have a culture of trust, one must already be engaged in trusting.

Giddens (1990, 34) defines trust as a type of confidence 'in the reliability of a person or system'. However, for Giddens trust is not 'bound up' with risk but rather with contingency: 'reliability in the face of contingent outcomes, whether these concern the actions of individuals or the operation of systems'. This can be seen as imploring managers to seek warrants for trust based not on loyalty and obedience but rather on confidence in employees to carry out tasks and to respond to challenges in a given context – confidence of the kind often associated with the liberating and empowering attributes of Web n.0 applications.

This also underscores why we still need a theory of knowledge management in the first place and why our core understanding of communication is that theory. I have argued that an instrumental approach to knowledge is largely a function of post-war technology proliferation that reflects our historical faith in calculative reasoning over the holistic capacity of individuals to engage reality symbolically. How misplaced that faith in technical approaches to knowledge is can be seen in light of the anti-climax of Y2K, or in the case of organizations not only not replacing the knowledge they lost in the downsizing of the early 1990s but investing in inflexible IT systems. But with the power over information and communication technology now having largely shifted from management to staff, the challenge now falls to new-world managers to be oriented toward rewarding focused self-management and self-aware communication that makes a difference.

References

Davenport, T. et al. (1998), 'Successful Knowledge Management Projects', *Sloan Management Review* 39:2, 43–57.

Davenport, T. and Prusak, L. (1998), *Working Knowledge: How Organizations Manage What They Know* (Boston: Harvard Business School Press).

Giddens, A. (1990) *The Consequences of Modernity* (Stanford: Stanford University Press).

Habermas, J. (1979), *Communication and the Evolution of Society* (Boston: Beacon Press).

—— (1984), *The Theory of Communicative Action: Reason and the Rationalization of Society* (Boston: Beacon Press).

—— (1998), *On the Pragmatics of Communication* (Cambridge: MIT Press).

Heim, M. (1993) *The Metaphysics of Virtual Reality* (New York: Oxford University Press).

Kauffman, S. (1993), *The Origins of Order* (New York: University of Pennsylvania and the Santa Fe Institute).

—— (1995), *At Home in the Universe: The Search for Laws of Self-Organization and Complexity* (New York, Oxford University Press).

Krippendorff, K. (1999), 'Beyond Coherence', *Management Communication Quarterly* 13:1, 135–45.

Leydesdorff, L. (2001), *A Sociological Theory of Communication: The Self-Organization of the Knowledge-based Society*. Internet download, Universal Publishers, http://www.universal-publishers.com/book.php?method=ISBN &book=1581126956

Luhmann, N. (1982), *The Differentiation of Society* (New York: Columbia University).

—— (1984), *Social Systems* (Stanford: Stanford University Press).

—— (1989), *Ecological Communication* (Chicago: University of Chicago Press).

Maturana, H. (1980), *Biology of Cognition. Autopoiesis and Cognition: The Realization of the Living* (Dordecht: D. Reidel Publishing Co.).

Maturana, H. and Varela, F. (1987 [1998]), *The Tree of Knowledge: The Biological Roots of Human Understanding* (Boston: Shambhala).

Mintzberg, H. (2004), *Managers, not MBAs: A Hard Look at the Soft Practice of Managing and Management Development* (San Francisco: Berrett-Koehler Publishers).

O'Reilly, T. (2009), 'Tim O'Reilly Talks Web 2.0', http://fora.tv/2009/04/02/Tim_OReilly_Talks_Web_20

Piaget, J. (1971), *Biology and Knowledge: An Essay on the Relations between Organic Regulations and Cognitive Processes* (Chicago: University of Chicago Press).

Savage-Rumbaugh, S. et al. (1998), *Apes, Language, and the Human Mind* (Oxford: Oxford University Press).

Tapscott, D. and Williams, A. (2006), *Wikinomics: How Mass Collaboration Changes Everything* (New York: Portfolio).

Simon, H. (1947 [1997]), *Administrative Behavior*, 4th edn (New York: The Free Press).

Vygotsky, L. (1962), *Thought and Language* (Cambridge: MIT Press).

Wolfe, M. (2003), 'Mapping the Field: Knowledge Management', *Canadian Journal of Communication* 28:1, 1–29.

Zuboff, S. (1988), *In the Age of the Smart Machine: The Future of Work and Power* (New York: Basic Books).

5

Systems Intelligence as a Lens for Managing Personal Knowledge

Rachel Jones, Jim Corner and Raimo Hämäläinen

Introduction

Knowledge management (KM) has become well established as a field of research since it first gained momentum with the 1995 publication of Nonaka and Takeuchi's *The Knowledge Creating Company* (1995). It is not a uniform field, however, and has been described as being informed by two competing perspectives (Hazlett et al. 2005). Due largely to KM's emergence from information sciences, the computational or technological paradigm has clearly dominated the field. The assumptions of this paradigm typically lead to a reification of knowledge and a focus on hard systems, technology and modelling. In contrast, those who subscribe to the organic or socio-organizational paradigm, see the computational emphasis as neglecting social, contextual and communication issues except as peripheral to the goal of optimizing organizational KM through the use of technology. Interest in communities of practice, social networking and creativity is heavily informed by this paradigm (Hazlett et al. 2005).

Perhaps partly because of the existence of these two conflicting outlooks, KM as a field continues to expand and increase in complexity. In addition, its growth is also at least partly fuelled by the increasing recognition that the concerns of KM cross-disciplinary boundaries and thus many disciplines contribute to research on KM topics (Jones 2008). However, this multidisciplinarity means that KM research draws from many theories and methodologies, further resulting in a multitude of competing definitions and perspectives. Scholars worry about the fragmentation and the impact of the apparent inability to define key terms like 'knowledge' and 'knowledge management' (Firestone 2008; Lloria 2008) with some calling for an end to debate (Stankosky 2005) while others encourage pluralism (Jackson 2005). At the same time, more and more subcategories, such as knowledge transfer, knowledge auditing and competitive intelligence are burgeoning under the KM canopy (Henczel 2001; Parent et al. 2007; Wang and Wang 2008). KM is a complex, unsettled and dynamic field for academics.

For practitioners, KM is a field that is often noted to have fallen short of its promise (Gueldenberg and Helting 2007; Sinclair 2007). One area of disillusionment with KM in terms of practice has been the association of KM with expensive but only partially successful information technology (IT) deployments. KM has become linked with high costs, the need for user training, the implementation of unwieldy organization-wide structures, and ongoing support and maintenance (Sinclair 2007). As a result, where historically KM has focused heavily on the 'top-down, systematic management of existing knowledge using information technology' (Jackson 2005, 189), there is now increasing recognition that the emphasis might be better placed on user-driven technology managed by communities and individuals (Sinclair 2007).

Thus there is some practical interest in the role of organizational members in KM, and how individuals might interact with IT in a way that enhances organizational management of knowledge. A subcategory of KM that potentially addresses this interest is Personal Knowledge Management (PKM). Organizations generally have formal sets of rules that govern their functioning as a system. Where KM tends to address the flow of knowledge within that legitimated system, PKM shifts the focus from the management of knowledge across an organization to the management of knowledge by an individual. Such an approach, however, risks confining PKM to the technological perspective of KM. The discussion that follows takes a multidisciplinary approach by applying a theory developed in the area of Systems Research – Systems Intelligence (SI) – to PKM. In doing so it also attempts to bridge the division between the technological and organic perspectives of KM, by illustrating that PKM is as much concerned with social and communication skills as it is with interacting with technological systems.

SI is a theoretical perspective that provides an opportunity to integrate KM perspectives because it is concerned with the characteristics of both formal systems and individual people. It offers insight into PKM's attempt to integrate the concerns of organizational knowledge management with the development of the abilities and skills of the individual. PKM has been developed in part due to the recognition that the knowledge goals and skills of individuals and organizations may not always coincide. Rather than adopt typical 'bipolar subject–object thinking' where a 'person either perceives him or herself to be a subject that acts upon an external system, seeking to cause an impact, or else the environment as a subject acts upon him/her as an object' (Hämäläinen and Saarinen 2004, 21), SI takes into account the individual, subjective and emotional aspects of systemic life.

An SI approach to PKM reminds us that individuals are governed by emotion, the ability to break rules, self-interest, and the competing demands of the multiple social systems to which they belong (Houchin and MacLean 2005), as well as the needs and expectations of their workplace. By focusing on the intuitive, reflective and communicative aspects of PKM through the perspective of SI, we can gain an understanding of how knowledge management at a personal level connects with organizations as systems. Research on PKM, then, can begin to address the intricacies of human behaviour that are unaccounted for by a traditional KM approach, as well as study how individuals function within the formal organizational structure. The main premise of SI considers that people have an intuitive ability to operate effectively within systems and that highly systems intelligent people are able to instigate systemic change. As Houchin and MacLean note, the 'rules that determine the interactions in social systems are socially constructed, and are not fixed by the laws of nature' (2005, 160). Approaching PKM through SI emphasizes the broader competencies such as the ability to use intuition, critically reflect, develop relationships and so on, that support the micro skills of finding, storing and retrieving information that are more often the subject of research and the focus of practice.

PKM and Systems Intelligence

The divisions that have weighed down KM as a field are also potential pitfalls for PKM. PKM's stressing of the individual over the organization would seem to inherently avoid KM's top-down systemic issues, but early efforts in PKM mirror KM's early concern with technologically driven rather than organically driven issues. There has been significant focus on how individuals use technology to manage information (Miller 2005) rather than how people develop and enact knowledge in interaction with one another, for example. As one practitioner has noted, if organizations 'stopped spending so much time and money on process and technology solutions and uncovered the latent potential in employees, then real value and differentiation would be harnessed through PKM' (Higgison 2004, para. 5).

Also, like KM, PKM is struggling to define its core concepts. Miller notes that PKM 'is a difficult concept to nail down because it involves many different types of information as well as approaches and methodologies' and that PKM 'is interpreted differently by different people', with some seeing personal *information* management as quite different from personal *knowledge* management and others regarding the two as interchangeable (2005, 38). When the focus is on knowledge management rather than information management, the definition of PKM becomes very expansive. According to Gao et al. personal knowledge is owned by individuals and involves a mix of 'theory, technique, learning, capacity and skill' but also 'ethics and morals' (2002, 12). Wright (2005) proposes that PKM involves a combination of cognitive, information, social, learning and development competencies, which individuals draw on to function effectively in the workplace. According to Higgison (2004), its core issues include the accessibility and meaningfulness of information and knowledge, the maintenance of social networks, and effective engagement with personal capital. Without consensus about what PKM is, it will be difficult to evaluate 'its effects, its successes, its failures, and its future' (Firestone 2008, 13).

It seems important for the development of PKM that it does not construct the artificial dichotomies between individuals and organizations, and technology and people that have characterized KM. Encouragingly, recent studies are emphasizing the role of a dynamic work environment in motivating employees to manage their personal knowledge in a way that combines it with organizational needs (Hasgall and Shoham 2008). Indeed, PKM invites an approach to KM that encourages organizations to facilitate workers taking responsibility, managing information, and increasing their own productivity, through a variety of tools and techniques (Jefferson 2006). The practices of problem solving, learning, and inquiry central to individuals constantly interacting with their information-rich environment are dynamic, non-linear, adaptive processes that require feedback and reflection (Avery et al. 2003; Wright 2005). Consequently, rather than focusing on the tools, such as particular technologies likely to quickly become obsolete, PKM could be said to be more usefully concerned with techniques such as learning how to learn (Avery et al. 2003) or developing a range of competencies (Wright 2005).

Thus, a broad working definition of PKM could be an individual's ability to develop, acquire and utilize skills that will support their learning in an information-abundant, ever-changing and system-based environment, that is, an organization. PKM affords an opportunity to merge the two paradigms of KM (the technological and the organic) at the individual level. Though Avery and colleagues (2003) concentrate on developing the concept of PKM with regard to improving students' experiences of higher education, their understanding of teaching PKM as entailing 'sharing both intelligent practices that guide the use of tools as well as intelligent and efficient use of the tools themselves' (Avery et al. 2003, Overview of PKM, para. 1) applies equally well to individual workers' experiences of organizational life. Effective organizations combine the personal knowledge needs of employees with the company's needs, and employees having the freedom and ability to make independent decisions that may vary from accepted routine is instrumental to those organizations' success (Hasgall and Shoham 2008). The dynamic work environment needed to successfully utilize personal and organizational knowledge comes from striking a balance between how individual workers participate in the organization and how the organizational system functions. SI is a theory that combines these elements.

SI draws from and extends notions of intelligence (Gardner 1993; Goleman 1995, 2006), combining it with the structure of systems thinking (Senge 1992). Like PKM, it is concerned with individuals in context with others and the systems to which they belong, with SI proposing that people operate within a given systemic context with a greater or lesser degree of intelligence. One goal of PKM is not just to encourage individuals to increase their knowledge and information management skills, but for them to put those into practice in the social context of organizations (Avery et al. 2003), and SI both accounts for and encourages individuals' ability to function successfully within the complex world of continually emergent systems in which they live (Hämäläinen and Saarinen 2004, 2006, 2007; Jones and Corner 2007). Though there is an increasing body of literature introducing systems and complexity thinking to KM (see Gao et al. 2002, 2003; Jackson 2005; Wierzbicki 2007), very little directly addresses the contribution of individuals, tending instead to examine theoretical overlap or organizational knowledge systems. The strength of SI as a theory lies in its combining of the structure and holistic perspective of systems thinking with an emphasis on the abilities and responsibilities of a person. It thus provides a particularly useful lens through which to consider PKM.

Another strength of an SI approach to PKM is that rather than just seeking to account for the way things are as individuals interact with their complex environments, SI is a theory that looks to actually drive and foster positive change. That is, it is a theory that can be actioned. Similarly, PKM is concerned with assisting individuals to at least survive, if not prosper, in dynamic organizational settings. It is a field that focuses on the actions of individuals and the enacting of their knowledge. While the focus of PKM can be on technology and organization processes, intuitive abilities, the ability to reflect and communicative competence are all part of the skill set that allow people to effectively manage their growth and learning. SI provides a theoretical but pragmatic framework which helps people account for and develop their intuition, reflectiveness and communicative abilities. Considering personal knowledge through SI provides a holistic perspective of the individual in their environment, and gives impetus for individuals to convert knowledge into action. In addition, approaching PKM through SI removes the artificial binary opposition between individual and organization.

One of the core beliefs of SI is that while people usually perceive themselves as separate individuals, existing independently from one another, they are in fact part of a series of complex systems. As with other systems theories, in SI a system is built as much by the interconnectedness of its individual elements as the individual elements themselves. The system has the power to generate, and to generate beyond what its individual elements can produce. It has its own emergent features, which cannot be reduced merely to the features of its individual elements. However, though the system has primacy over its components, those components can influence the nature of the system. Though systems can be merely mechanical, individuals belong to a range of socially constructed systems with flexible boundaries. SI particularly emphasizes the personal, subjective elements of systems. 'Systems Intelligence is a capacity in the human being that involves instinctual, intuitive, tacit, subconscious and unconscious and inarticulate aspects that cannot be straightforwardly reduced to a full-fledged and transparent cognitive dimension' (Hämäläinen and Saarinen 2004, 16).

PKM as a field needs to avoid being reduced to the study of the practical and objective skills of information retrieval, storage and analysis at the expense of the less tangible and more subjective individual attributes such as intuition, personal awareness and communication. Rather, it needs to consider individuals as holistic beings and like SI simultaneously emphasize the personal and the systemic, viewing people and their environment as interconnected and interdependent. The following discussion considers how SI might lead to action in the three PKM skills of intuition, reflectiveness and communication.

INTUITIVE ABILITIES

While traditional systems-thinking issues like explicit problem structuring and solving skills, interconnectivity and intervention management matter to SI,

SI equally emphasizes implicit knowing or intuitive abilities (Leppänen et al. 2007). This is because, unlike traditional systems thinking, SI does not advocate stepping outside the system to analyse the best way to move forward. Rather, it maintains that as systems are complex and emergent, individuals cannot ever remove themselves from them and study them separately and objectively. Instead, people must manage to go on in life with partial knowledge of the contexts within which they are placed. SI explains and explores how people use intuition, one aspect of systemic intelligence, to make decisions as they move into an unknown future.

Individuals always have to act into the unknown as the future is simultaneously predictable (from previous patterns) and unpredictable (able to be changed). That is, the future is perpetually under construction in the processes of relating to one another and the environment (Stacey 2001). While individuals are constantly called on to act based on only partial information, some are able to act more successfully than others. The ability to intuitively, tacitly and non-verbally interact with the physical and human environment is a key aspect of SI (Hämäläinen and Saarinen 2006). An understanding of such actions is also important to developing PKM. Hasgall and Shoham (2008), for example, found that individual workers' personal knowledge was important but so was their ability to use processes, adapt, and change to emerging situations. 'The level at which systems intelligence takes place in the human mind is for a large part semiconscious, rather than the conscious level that systems thinking based action settles on' (Leppänen et al. 2007, 5). Systems-intelligent individuals may not be able to articulate or reason through why they behave in certain ways, but they are able to act instinctively.

SI posits that individuals have a greater or lesser innate ability to foresee the impact of their behaviour on the system as a whole, to take into account the effect of actions beyond their immediate impact and realize their eventual benefit. Systems-intelligent individuals are capable of acknowledging the invisible parts of a system, are adaptive and sensitive to changes in their behaviour, are capable of understanding changes in the structures of the system and are then able to revise their behaviour accordingly (Hämäläinen and Saarinen 2004). SI is themed around 'know-how' rather than 'know that' in that it is an instinctual competence rather than a cognitive function. However, that is not to say that learning about SI is of no benefit. In fact, making people aware of their unconscious and unarticulated processes can assist them in honing their innate skills. It can also give individuals confidence as they realize that they have a competence they were unaware of. At the same time, people often take comfort in realizing that they are part of a larger process, that the systems that they are engaged with affect their beliefs and behaviours as much as their individual intentions. Awareness of one's place in a system and one's ability to interact with that system also unconsciously illuminates the behaviour of others. Thus awareness, or reflectiveness, is the next skill considered.

REFLECTIVE ABILITIES

The ability to understand one's own information capabilities and limits, wants and needs, can be regarded as an essential component of PKM (Davenport and Beck 2001). SI emphasizes a deeper self-awareness – the ability to reflect on one's own behaviour and beliefs. Systems-intelligent individuals recognize that what they believe as fundamental is in fact a reflection of their experiences and particular incidents in their lives (Hämäläinen and Saarinen 2004). People are predisposed to assume that beliefs are at their core and inherent in their identity. Yet the 'core' beliefs people have can be redefined in an instant, for example, through the betrayal of a loved one, which can lead to the restructuring of beliefs and the adoption of new behaviours. The systems intelligent individual 'can manage their own belief systems, the belief systems of others as well as the systems these beliefs systems together constitute, better than those low in System Intelligence' (Hämäläinen and Saarinen 2004, 18). That is, they can recognize that construction of identity, beliefs and other abstract social concepts is emergent and dynamic, thus change and complexity do not lead to excessive anxiety.

Discussion of beliefs and values may appear somewhat abstract and impractical, but beliefs and values affect organizational life daily. To illustrate, employees may have access to the same information within an organization, but the meaningfulness and interpretation of the information will be coloured by the organization's values and each individual's values and beliefs (Stowell 2007). Similarly, being able to ask questions is fundamental to gaining knowledge – uncritically accepting the information and beliefs of an organization is not SI behaviour and is unlikely to lead to improved PKM. Information is now abundant, but ease of access does not necessarily equate to understanding. Stowell notes that to benefit from information available through such technology as the Internet, not only do individuals require the technical and financial wherewithal to access the information, but they need 'the ability to critically evaluate the data and understand the context in which it exists' (2007, 415). In order to critically evaluate information, to self-reflect and to self-criticize, an individual needs to be aware of the system to which the data they retrieve and they themselves belong. Having a deep understanding of how information and knowledge reflect the power of production and distribution (where data comes from, how it is provided and who is providing it) enables individuals to consider their actions and the information they receive in a holistic manner (Stowell 2007).

The concept of PKM by its very terms implies individual self-awareness of one's abilities and limits (Avery et al. 2003), but SI extends this personal awareness to a consideration of the abilities and limits of others and of systems. A systems-intelligent person, for example, enters into dialogue with others in order to explore alternative beliefs, whereas other people typically attempt to justify their own beliefs in interactions. Self-awareness increases the ability to engage with others in an empathetic way. The interconnectedness of individuals and systems that SI is based on is also crucial for PKM. PKM could easily fall into the trap of focusing attention on the individual as a part of a whole system like an organization. It is not enough to study the parts of a system – what is important is to focus on the relationship of the parts to the whole and the dependency of the parts on each other and the whole to them and them to the whole. We should not get so carried away with the 'personal' in PKM that we centre on the individual at the expense of the wider social context. Self-awareness of one's own abilities and expertise is most valuable within a public sphere of action: 'Just as a well-functioning electronic network depends on well-managed individual nodes that are connected to the network, so does community knowledge depend on well-developed individual contributors' (Avery et al. 2003, Personal in PKM, para. 3). Effective PKM, then, is about not only heightened self-awareness but also systemic awareness. SI locates the individual firmly within the system, emphasizing the impact each person's behaviour can have on the system as a whole.

The effects of individuals being aware of their being situated within a system (whether organization, family or society) are primarily seen in behaviour, perceptions and values. Behaviour is influenced, largely unconsciously, by the structure a person operates within, a person's own view of that structure, and what a person perceives others to believe, as informed by the theory of reasoned action (Fishbein and Ajzen 1975). For example, in the workplace we might communicate with our superior based on the culture of our organization, our own view of our place within the organizational hierarchy, and what we believe the expectations of our supervisor are regarding how we will interact with them. However, to be a full participant in a social system like an organization people need to engage and be part of a community that exchanges ideas, asks questions and debates issues (Stowell 2007). PKM aims to develop successful individual contributors, but to do so it must consider a third area important to both PKM and SI – communication.

COMMUNICATION SKILLS

Communication is the active process through which individuals interact with others in the system and the system itself; communication builds the systems people live in and is the process by which change is effected. Traditional models of communication have viewed it as the transfer of information from one person to another, and these mechanistic theories dominate the technological paradigm of KM. Such models are underpinned by the notion that the individual mind is the repository of information and associated cognitive processes, and as such they tend to focus research on the tools and (supposedly) linear steps of communication that facilitate sending and receiving information. If PKM is a conceptual framework 'blending technology, personal skills, processes and methodology' (Jefferson 2006, 36) then a richer understanding of communication is required to explain how workers go about learning, developing and acquiring skills that enable them to flourish in a dynamic environment.

Such an understanding can be found in complex responsive process theory (CRP), an action-based account of communication that stresses the dynamic and complex processes of interacting and which has considerable overlap with SI. CRP posits an alternative view of communication as an action-based process that involves feelings and physical bodies as much as words and thoughts. Like SI, it accommodates the role of intuition and offers a holistic approach to people's interactions. Communicating, then, is about responding to one another and ourselves, with regard to our internal dialogue, in a meaningful way. We evoke and provoke responses in each other rather than share mental content, creating knowledge in the process of interaction (Stacey 2001). Communicative acts are a series of gestures and responses that continually emerge and self-organize in the process of relating (Stacey 2001, 2003). The gestures and responses can be seen to be constrained and enabled by expectations of self and others within the context of a system. Just as the system both enables and constrains communication, so communication has the capacity to perpetuate or alter the system. Adopting a holistic view of communication as a continual process of relating to one's environment gives it a central role in PKM.

The conversational life of organizations, then, should be of primary importance to PKM. When people become involved in an interaction, according to CRP, they bring to it expectations of their own and others' performances. They also arrive with a set of habits, routines, beliefs and so on that are not things 'stored' in minds, but predictable couplings of gesture and response that are typically reproduced as interaction occurs (Stacey 2001). Central to CRP is the idea that new knowledge is generated when established patterns of communicating are disrupted, affecting the unfolding of the interaction. Transformation of patterns of communicating is most likely to occur when participants are aware of each other's expectations, ideas and feelings and how those might constrain their responses. Systems-intelligent individuals are able to consciously or unconsciously identify communication patterns and also understand their contingent nature. They are open to behaving unpredictably and differently to change the tone, direction or outcomes of an interaction.

PKM can be seen as a skill of the systems-intelligent individual and can be developed through the use of techniques that promote systems intelligence. For example, SI advocates using the inquiry mode of systems thinking (Senge 1992) where an individual takes an open-minded and constructive approach to engaging with others. A willingness to learn and to admit one's own limits is important to inquiry. Active listening is also a key skill as systems-intelligent individuals are willing to see the world through others' eyes. They understand that if they are to learn, they need to explore new ways of doing things and new ways of engaging with others. They know what their own communicative patterns are, understand that they are not intrinsic, and are open to altering them. In other words, they have the ability to unlearn old habits and reject past practices in order to move forward (Parent et al. 2007; Truch 2001). The ability to engage in meaningful dialogue, with oneself and with others, is also important. Systems-intelligent people are receptive to the resonances of people's emotions, facial expressions and gestures. All these proficiencies contribute to heightened awareness of the dynamic interaction between the self, others and the system and all correspondingly serve to enhance PKM.

Systems-intelligent individuals are also aware of how the tools they use constrain their processes of relating. The adoption of new communication technologies, such as the use of wikis, may be greeted with suspicion because it threatens comfortable communication patterns. Those high in systems intelligence see the introduction of new technologies as providing opportunities to interact in new ways. It is important to remember that technology is a tool, not a repository of meaning or knowledge in itself. Simply having information available does not develop knowledge. While being able to manage that information is important, it is only when we engage with it that meaning and knowing can develop. Technology that supports PKM needs to emphasize the reciprocal and active nature of communicating in conjunction with the ability to save, store and secure information.

Any change or learning that occurs within the individual or the system, such as an organization, arises out of communicative interaction. To foster positive change and learning, that is, to be systems intelligent, parties must understand the dynamics of conversations in the context of the systems in which they occur. Unfortunately, conversations that result in systemic changes emerging are paradoxically both cooperative and conflicting, and therefore are not easy to manage (Stacey 2001). First, misunderstanding is common. This may lead to frustration and stress, resulting in participants wanting to withdraw from the interaction. Secondly, when a conversation has the potential to disrupt the everyday patterns of being, it also has the potential to threaten continuity of identity, giving rise to anxiety in the participants. Finally, conversations that offer the possibility of transformation often threaten the established power relations. Those in power may seek to close such conversations down as the threat of a shift in power becomes manifest (Stacey 2001). These communicative tensions can be addressed in PKM, however, by encouraging individuals to reflect on the contingency of their core beliefs and identity, and on the systemic context of the communicative event, that is, by enhancing their systems intelligence. Understanding communication as complex, dynamic processes means organizations will be able to provide more effective support for PKM (Avery et al. 2003).

The Benefits of PKM through SI

As discussed above, one of the benefits of using SI as a theoretical basis for the study of PKM is that it is a theory that encourages a holistic approach to individuals. PKM can then comfortably encompass a broad range of skills and attributes that scholars are currently trying to incorporate into definitions of PKM – the combination of applied skills (managing information, using tools to increase productivity and so on) and personal attributes (learning effectively, making judgements, self-awareness). Approaching PKM through an SI lens further addresses a key area of concern for PKM scholars – the potential conflict between individual and organizational goals. Recognizing the interconnectedness of individuals with the systems in which they operate avoids conceptualizing the worker and the organization as a duality. SI thus highlights the context-dependent nature of PKM. It avoids perceiving human behaviour as linear cause and effect reactions and avoids viewing individuals as separate units rather than parts of the same whole. Instead, it invites individuals to view organizations and their place in them as part of a series of interconnections and interrelations. Two key aspects of SI inform the ability to align personal and organizational aspirations: awareness of the pervasiveness of systems and awareness of the influence of the individual.

AWARENESS OF SYSTEMS

SI invites us to consider the goals of PKM in the context of systems. Individuals do not exist in isolation so skills and abilities like learning, organizing, engaging with technology and collaborating should not be examined in relation to the individual alone. A holistic viewpoint needs to be adopted – a recognition that an individual is part of the system, both affected by and able to affect the wider structure, and interconnected with others in the structure.

People with a high degree of systems intelligence understand their place in and effect on the system, even if they are unable to articulate it. SI proposes that making the systemic nature of people's context visible allows individuals to focus more clearly on the way systems enable and constrain not only their own daily existence but the actions of others, thus improving their ability to act with systems intelligence. To illustrate, communication technologies available in the workplace establish habitual communication patterns. The way people use email in the workplace, for example, is shaped by the set formats of the available software but also the conventions of formality, culture and so on within the organization. Being systems intelligent means being aware of the various constraints and enablers involved, being able to choose when to conform and when to be innovative, and being attentive to the impact of those choices. However, just as the organizational boundaries shape people's communicative interactions, personal patterns affect how events unfold (Stacey 2001). PKM needs to address people's ability to balance the influence of systems with their personal habits. If we concentrate on assisting organizational members to develop PKM micro-skills, such as information retrieval, organization, filtering and storage, we need to do so while raising their awareness of the systems they operate within and how those enable and constrain behaviours. PKM has to be contextual and SI highlights the connections between personal and organizational life.

SI recognizes, though, that an appreciation of the pervasive influence of systems can be overwhelming. Systems seem oppressive. Hasgall and Shoham (2008) found that it is difficult for employees to be innovative and apply personal knowledge in new situations because of the systemic requirements of the organization. In addition, employees want recognition of their personal knowledge contributions and the ability to influence organizational processes, and these needs affect their willingness to share (Hasgall and Shoham 2008). Even when the majority of people dislike a prevailing system, they tend to simply adjust and adopt its characteristics because they believe it cannot be changed. People see themselves as mere cogs in the wheel – rather than think of themselves as 'contributing agents of an interactive system' they feel they lack influence, and are limited by others and the overriding system (Hämäläinen and Saarinen 2004, 27). Such feelings and beliefs are enacted through behaviour. For example, if individuals feel their effort is unrecognized at work they may be less inclined to praise the efforts of others (I got no recognition, why should they?) and they may also punish the system (I am not going to work as hard now as I receive no reward). People also tend to make incorrect assumptions about one another without considering the systemic context. If someone is loud and rude in the workplace, there is a tendency to assume they are loud and rude everywhere. In fact, that may just be their pattern of behaviour within that particular system. Similarly, if individuals within a system have an incorrect perception of what others believe, the chances of cooperation towards change are limited. However, it is crucial to remember that while the systems people operate within affect and effect an individual's behaviour, they are also affected and effected by the individual.

AWARENESS OF THE INFLUENCE OF THE INDIVIDUAL

Recognizing the influence of the individual within the system is empowering. Successful, thriving systems can be perpetuated and upheld through individuals behaving and communicating in patterned ways. Likewise, unsuccessful systems can be perpetuated through habitual, patterned behaviour. For example, employees who keep their knowledge local and are either unmotivated to share what they know or refuse to take responsibility for their role in the system serve to maintain a flawed system (Hasgall and Shoham 2008). However, unsuccessful systems can be improved upon if individuals act with systemic intelligence. A systems intelligent person recognizes the processes and patterns that create the system and their ability to influence them. High SI will facilitate the optimizing of PKM skills.

Recent research in PKM demonstrates the importance of individual responses. There is recognition that an organization cannot control how their individual members will behave, that is, even within tightly regulated systems humans have choices. As Hasgall and Shoham comment:

> *the ability to choose between an innovative solution and performance of a routine process as a way to cope with environmental changes is no longer contingent on the managers' decisions, but is based on the ability of each employee to analyze the change in his or her environment and decide on the type of solution.*
>
> *(2008, 52)*

Their study found that organizational routines potentially stifle innovation as they force workers to interact in a particular style using particular tools with a largely predictable outcome. It is when an individual deviates from these prescribed systemic routines that new and innovative ways of being and doing things are developed. For organizations, an awareness that individuals learn through the disruption of set routines raises several issues. First, technology and systems that are designed to support PKM need to be adaptable to individual learning styles (Higgison 2004, Jefferson 2006). What resonates with one individual will not necessarily resonate with another. Therefore, there also needs to be flexibility and leeway for workers to engage with seemingly irrelevant and unrelated information. Organizations with loosely controlled communication channels and processes are more likely to foster individuals becoming effective personal knowledge managers. This means that individuals are able to focus on practical everyday knowledge problems that matter to them rather than a strategic organization-wide vision of what needs to be learned (Sinclair 2007).

SI provides a theory to underpin this observation and justifies PKM's focus on the individual over the organizational focus of traditional KM, while maintaining a systemic context. A fairly small alteration can have a tremendous leverage on a system and a systems-intelligent person is either consciously or subconsciously aware that minor deviations in patterns of behaviour and communication can have transformational properties. With this awareness comes personal responsibility. One study found that choices may be motivated by personal interest as a dynamic and uncertain environment provides space for opportunistic action (Edwards 2007). Another showed that effective KM depends to an extent on employees' willingness to take responsibility, learn and develop (Hasgall and Shoham 2008). SI has an interesting ethical component that proposes that systems-intelligent individuals are able to act in ways that are not motivated just by self interest but also in ways that seek to enhance and improve the system and its impact on others. In this context, PKM is about putting one's personal knowledge to use in a way that not only benefits the individual but also the system and the relationships within it.

> *The ultimate goal of Personal Knowledge Management is not merely to possess knowledge and certain thinking abilities, but to value the use of that knowledge in the service of others and in the enhancement of societal knowledge. The public use of knowledge reaffirms the individual identity of the person who contributes, who has knowledge, who can organize information and who can be a part of a team or a community beyond the self.*
>
> *Avery et al. 2003 (Personal in PKM, para. 6)*

Systems intelligence describes and promotes people's sensitivity to the nuances of a systemic environment. It points out that everybody simultaneously is constructed by and constructs a number of overlapping systems, and fosters the idea that intelligent action within those contexts can serve more than just personal interest.

Conclusions

A weakness of much of the literature on knowledge management is the inability to reconcile the notions of individual knowledge and organizational knowledge, and the struggle to elevate one over the other (Stacey 2001, 2003). There is a risk that a narrow vision of PKM will perpetuate this notion by shifting the focus from the organization to the individual. An SI-informed perspective of PKM helps to avoid establishing a dualism between the individual and the organization. If we consider PKM through SI it is clear that a system is built as much by the interconnectedness of its individual elements as the individual elements themselves. Individuals in organizations are part of a social system and PKM needs to take into account both the personal and systemic aspects of PKM.

SI provides a theoretical framework for the integration of individuals and their environment which also has a practical application as it aims to awaken a competence that people already have and use. It is not a body of knowledge that can be imparted to individuals to make them better people; it needs to be put into practice. Yet it is a challenge for personal learning in that it encourages individuals to embrace change, not for its own sake, but with the goal of improvement in quality of life (Hämäläinen and Saarinen 2004).

SI presupposes that people are able to think beyond the boundaries of their own egos and are willing to act to improve the system, not just for their own benefit but for the benefit of all parts of the system and the good of the system itself (Hämäläinen and Saarinen 2004). PKM is also about individual workers being willing to utilize their skills in a way that benefits both themselves and their organizations, in service of others and for improving group knowledge (Avery et al. 2003).

From an organizational perspective, while organizations cannot control individual members' initiative or desire, they can provide an environment that fosters learning and personal development. Supplying tools and systems that incorporate individual styles and preferences will help individuals to become more effective, which in turn will enhance company effectiveness (Jefferson 2006). There needs to be a willingness on the part of organizations to let individual members control their PKM processes. Organizations need to be unafraid to 'unshackle the giant within', that is, to encourage autonomy within the context of the organization as a system, creating the conditions that support workers taking more responsibility for their PKM (Higgison 2004, para. 10). Recognizing that organizations are patterns of interaction of a group of individuals, simultaneously forming and being formed by their members, rather than a place people go to work helps defuse concerns that can arise when the organization is seen as exploiting workers' knowledge. When employees perceive themselves as having expertise and as able to immediately influence the efficiency and effectiveness of processes in the organization, that is, when they are systems intelligent, work processes are managed well (Hasgall and Shoham 2008). SI helps to align personal and organizational goals by highlighting the interdependence of the individual and the organization and works towards the flourishing of both.

References

Avery, S. et al. (2003), 'Personal Knowledge Management: Framework for Integration and Partnerships', http://www.millikin.edu/pkm/pkm_ascue. html, accessed 18 February 2008.

Davenport, T. and Beck, J. (2001), *The Attention Economy: Understanding the New Currency of Business* (Boston: Harvard Business School Press).

Edwards, T. (2007), 'Organizational Politics and the "Process of Knowing": Understanding Crisis Events During Project-based Innovation Projects', *European Journal of Innovation Management* 10:3, 391–406.

Firestone, J. (2008), 'On Doing Knowledge Management', *Knowledge Management Research and Practice* 6:1, 13–32.

Fishbein, M. and Ajzen, I. (1975), *Belief, Attitude, Intention and Behaviour: An Introduction to Theory and Research* (Reading: Addison-Wesley).

Gao, F. et al. (2002), 'Systems Thinking on Knowledge and its Management: Systems Methodology for Knowledge Management', *Journal of Knowledge Management* 6:1, 7–17.

—— (2003), 'Critical Systems Thinking as a Way to Manage Knowledge', *Systems Research and Behavioral Science* 20:1, 3–19.

Gardner, H. (1993), *Frames of Mind: The Theory of Multiple Intelligences*, 10th edn (New York: Basic Books).

Goleman, D. (1995), *Emotional Intelligence* (New York: Bantam Books).

—— (2006), *Social Intelligence* (New York: Bantam Books).

Gueldenberg, S. and Helting, H. (2007), 'Bridging "The Great Divide": Nonaka's Synthesis of "Western" and "Eastern" Knowledge Concepts Reassessed', *Organization* 14:1, 101–22.

Hämäläinen, R. and Saarinen, E. (eds) (2004), *Systems Intelligence – Discovering a Hidden Competence in Human Action and Organizational Life* (Helsinki University of Technology, Systems Analysis Laboratory, Research Reports A88).

—— (2006), 'Systems Intelligence: A Key Competence in Human Action and Organizational Life', *Reflections: The SoL Journal* 7:4, 17–28.

—— (eds) (2007), *Systems Intelligence in Leadership and Everyday Life* (Espoo: Systems Analysis Laboratory, Helsinki University of Technology).

Hasgall, A. and Shoham, S. (2008), 'Knowledge Processes: From Managing People to Managing Processes', *Journal of Knowledge Management* 12:1, 51–62.

Hazlett, S. et al. (2005), 'Theory Building in Knowledge Management: In Search of Paradigms', *Journal of Management Inquiry* 14:1, 31–42.

Henczel, S. (2001), 'The Information Audit as a First Step Towards Effective Knowledge Management', *Information Outlook* 5:6, 18–23.

Higgison, S. (2004), 'Your Say: Personal Knowledge Management', *Inside Knowledge* 7:7, http://www.kmmagazine.com/xq/asp/sid.7551F69D-2683-471C-A18C-C3365B30C312/articleid.DDDD6EE3-47C6-49CD-9070-F1B1547FD29F/qx/display.htm, accessed 16 June 2008.

Houchin, K. and MacLean, D. (2005), 'Complexity Theory and Strategic Change: an Empirically Informed Critique', *British Journal of Management* 16:2, 149–66.

Jackson, M. (2005), 'Reflections on Knowledge Management From a Critical Systems Perspective', *Knowledge Management Research and Practice* 3:4, 187–96.

Jefferson, T. (2006), 'Taking it Personally: Personal Knowledge Management', *VINE: The Journal of Information and Knowledge Management Systems* 36:1, 35–7.

Jones, R. (2008), 'Breaking Down the Boundaries: Interdisciplinarity and the Future of KM', *Proceedings of the 14th Americas Conference on Information Systems*, Toronto, 14–17 August (CD-ROM).

Jones, R. and Corner, J. (2007), 'Systems Intelligence and its Relationship to Communication Theories', in R. Hämäläinen and E. Saarinen (eds), *Systems Intelligence in Leadership and Everyday Life* (Espoo: Systems Analysis Laboratory, Helsinki University of Technology).

Leppänen, I. et al. (2007), *Intentions and Systems Intelligence: Prospects for Complexity Research, Working Paper 28, September 2007* (Systems Analysis Laboratory, Helsinki University of Technology).

Lloria, M. (2008), 'A Review of the Main Approaches to Knowledge Management', *Knowledge Management Research and Practice* 6:1, 77–89.

Miller, R. (2005), 'The Evolution of Knowledge Management: This Time it's Personal', *EContent* 28:11, 38–42.

Nonaka, I. and Takeuchi, H. (1995), *The Knowledge-creating Company: How Japanese Companies Create the Dynamics of Innovation* (New York: Oxford University Press).

Parent, R. et al. (2007), 'A Systems-based Dynamic Knowledge Transfer Capacity Model', *Journal of Knowledge Management* 1:6, 81–93.

Senge, P. (1992), *The Fifth Discipline: The Art and Practice of the Learning Organization* (Sydney: Random House).

Sinclair, N. (2007), 'The KM Phoenix', *VINE: The Journal of Information and Knowledge Management Systems* 37:3, 255–61.

Stacey, R. (2001), *Complex Responsive Processes in Organizations* (London: Routledge).

—— (2003), 'Learning as an Activity of Interdependent People', *The Learning Organization* 10:6, 325–31.

Stankosky, M. (2005), 'Advances in Knowledge Management: University Research Toward an Academic Discipline', in M. Stankosky (ed.), *Creating the Discipline of Knowledge Management: The Latest in University Research* (Burlington: Elsevier Butterworth Heinemann).

Stowell, F. (2007), 'The Knowledge Age or the Age of Ignorance and the Decline of Freedom?', *Systemic Practice Action Research* 20:5, 413–27.

Truch, E. (2001), 'Managing Personal Knowledge: The Key to Tomorrow's Employability', *Journal of Change Management* 2:2, 102–5.

Wang, H. and Wang, S. (2008), 'A Knowledge Management Approach to Data Mining Process for Business Intelligence', *Industrial Management + Data Systems* 108:5, 622–34.

Wierzbicki, A. (2007), 'Modelling as a Way of Organising Knowledge', *European Journal of Operational Research* 176:1, 610–35.

Wright, K. (2005), 'Personal Knowledge Management: Supporting Individual Knowledge Worker Performance', *Knowledge Management Research and Practice* 3:3, 156–65.

6

Managing your own Knowledge: A Personal Perspective

Larry Prusak and Jocelyn Cranefield

Introduction

Organizational knowledge management, as a discipline and a practice, has now been with us for about twenty years and shows no sign of disappearing. While it may change its name, customs and/or practices, it continues to thrive, especially as organizations live with increasing uncertainty in their environments. But what about us as individuals? Don't we, too, live in very uncertain times, particularly with the recent tectonic shifts in the global economy and in the relations between employers and employees? Isn't it just as important for us to actively manage our own knowledge? The answer everyone gives to this question is, 'Of course I manage my own knowledge – I wouldn't get anywhere without doing it!' Yet when they are asked how they do it – what specific activities do they undertake – they usually give a blank stare and a response that goes somewhat like, 'Well, I try to read some articles on the plane', or, 'Every year I go to a conference', – or 'I go to a conference when I have the budget'. Certainly this is slim pickings for what is perceived to be such a highly important activity.

Peter Drucker has emphasized the importance of *managing oneself* in the knowledge economy – knowing one's strengths, values, and how one best performs (1999). But it seems we think little about the need to manage our own *knowledge* – the foundation upon which we base our way of thinking, what we see as relevant, our problem solving and prioritizing, our interpretation of events and issues and our decision-making. Our knowledge is a large part of what makes us unique. If we manage our knowledge well, keeping it current and relevant, it can give us that sought after edge in performance. If we do not, we could quickly become as stale as last week's loaf of bread.

Four Personal Knowledge Management Practices

What exactly can we do to manage our knowledge? What can an individual learn from what organizations have been doing for the past few decades? And perhaps just as importantly, why aren't many people doing this? Here we propose and discuss four fundamental personal knowledge management practices. They are drawn from the first author's experience of *what works* and his observations of the hundreds of companies for which he has consulted. We support each practice with reference to relevant literature and research, and illustrate it with a real-life example, drawn from a range of industries.

PRACTICE 1: SCAN AND REINVENT

Joseph Stiglitz, a recent Nobel Laureate in Economics, once observed that one of the most important things for a developing nation to do is *'scan globally and reinvent locally'* (1999). He argued that the complexity and diversity of human society invalidates the simplistic concept of passing on global 'best practice'. It is instead necessary to look on a case-by-case basis at what has, and has not, worked in other settings, critically analyse the reasons for these successes and failures, and build on these global lessons in a way that is best suited to one's local needs. Astute local reinvention has led to successes for developing nations and for organizations in diverse business settings.

Reinventing knowledge locally is not merely about tweaking the ideas of others. It requires the skillful selection, analysis and assimilation of the *right* external knowledge and matching it to the *right* local needs at the *right* time. Successful re-inventers know local conditions inside out. They spot the opportunities and they think laterally. When the first author of this chapter visited Taiwan in 2008, he was taken to a very nondescript building where people came and went rather rapidly. What went on there was a commercial operation where engineers could take apart any cellphone under the sun, and would give you a complete schematic drawing of that phone soon afterwards. They kept all records of the drawings and so could fill most requests very quickly. The company's owner said that the only way Taiwanese manufacturers could compete in global markets, especially in consumer electronics, was to understand – at the micro level – every possible product that competed with their own chips and chip-based products.

Lateral reinvention also underpins the work of successful entrepreneurs: The extreme sport of bungy jumping began as a rite of passage in Vanuatu, where young men performed leaps off high platforms with vines tied to their ankles. In 1979, members of the Oxford University Dangerous Sports Club adapted the sport, embarking on a series of spectacular jumping stunts. However, it was A. J. Hackett and Henry van Asch who realized the potential to standardize and commercialize bungy jumping, capitalizing on a growing outdoor tourism market in New Zealand in the 1980s. Today, bungy jumping is a popular adventure tourism offering in many countries and it has been immortalized in a James Bond movie.

These sorts of lessons are familiar to entrepreneurs and businesses, but when it comes to managing your own personal knowledge, what should you make of the maxim scan globally and reinvent locally? We believe that this principle is pertinent to all of us, at the individual level. In order to move ahead – and even to simply keep up – we need to continuously search for new ideas and products, perhaps also for new dreams and visions, within the growing and vibrant global marketplace of ideas. This is a market that has been made far more competitive, and more efficient, by the Internet. If you do not scan and reinvent, you can be sure that a potential competitor will, and that you will lose a step in keeping your own knowledge up to date.

To become an effective re-inventor of your personal knowledge, you need to continually appraise the ideas around you in relationship to your own interests, needs and understandings. You should also consider how well they fit with the zeitgeist – the economic, social and political environment in which they unfold (Davenport et al. 2003). But how should an individual, with far fewer resources than a company, approach doing this?

Some employers support individualized personal development through structured learning programmes. So-called *horizontal learning methods* position people as active learners, allowing them to get up close to the working knowledge of others and acquire knowledge that is tacit and contextual. These methods include cross training, twinning, secondments, internships and study tours (Ellerman 1999; Chang 2002). For example, some healthcare organizations offer secondment opportunities to foster new knowledge (Hamilton and Wilkie 2001), while within tertiary education, faculty exchanges have been found to help revitalize mid-career academics (Kelly 1990). Other employers take an unstructured approach, offering paid leave for personal growth undertakings. Google reportedly encourages its engineers to spend one-fifth of their time working on personal projects (Dickerson 2004). What these initiatives have in common is the recognition that optimum opportunities for building an individual's knowledge often lie beyond one's usual workplace and day-to-day duties.

Such opportunities are, however, far from the norm. We should not rely on our employers to extend our knowledge when the ultimate responsibility rests with us. We must actively look for external opportunities and/or create our own, such as an overseas trip, or a vocation vacation (an emerging form of tourism that provides hands-on work in a range of careers). A few visionary businesses in Japan are offering novel opportunities to their most valued customers. The first author of this chapter met with a group of 22 Japanese executives who were going around the globe as the guests of Fuji Xerox, to visit organizations that have state of the art knowledge systems and processes. Fuji offers this to a select group of their customers and they never have difficulty finding senior executives who want to go. It's no industrial tourism, as they often visit two sites a day in the US, Europe and sometimes in other parts of Asia or Australia. What is interesting is that all of the assembled group take their own notes, ask very smart and interesting questions, and spend up to a week or ten days studying this subject in order to return to their own firms and bring back the knowledge they have obtained. This sort of thing is rarely done in the US, where it would be seen as not worth a senior executive's time and attention. Especially focusing on such an intangible as knowledge. Not so in Japan, a country that avoided being colonized in the nineteenth century by its adroit importation of Western knowledge. In 2009, they had the second richest global economy, with scarcely any resources other than their own knowledge and culture. They are, to a person, aware as to what has allowed them to become this developed.

There are other, less immediate but more ubiquitous ways to perform global scanning. The most common means – available to us all – is via the World Wide Web. This brings us to a key issue to do with managing our personal knowledge: with the unprecedented deluge of global information and opinion coming at us daily via the Internet, what actually counts as knowledge? Who and what should we trust? We explore this issue, and suggest some ways to help address it, below.

PRACTICE 2: VET AND FILTER

If you spend even some of your limited time scanning and searching for new ideas, you need to learn how to evaluate and adjudicate, vet and filter what you are taking in. This is a skill that is not generally not taught in academia, yet it is vital to one's personal knowledge strategy. In a world of rapidly democratizing knowledge, who should we trust? With so many so-called thought leaders, actors, firms, journalists and consultants pushing products and services, we cannot possibly know the reputations of everyone we read or learn from.

Paul Sparrow (1999) has noted that the increasing amount of information in organizations has created a situation of serious information overload for managers. This arises from both the increased volume of information and quality-related issues that increase the mental workload: the low quality, low value, high ambiguity and decreasing 'half-life' (or currency) of much of today's information create increased processing demands. This situation of overload is made worse by growing information complexity – the number of informational elements to be dealt with, the diversity or range of information sources, and the growing interdependence between these (Huber and Daft 1987). All these things can create a degree of stress that results in cognitive inertia, or worse. Sparrow describes how, in coping with the volume of information alone, managers

> begin to neglect large portions of it and try to 'punctuate' its flow …
> [This] begins with omission, then greater tolerance of error, mis-cueing
> or mis-attributing the source of information, filtering its message,
> abstracting its meaning … and finally through seeking escape!
>
> (1999, 144)

Even those of us who are not managers are faced with the task of vetting and filtering a mass of information of highly variable quality. How can we judge the truth, or real value, of what we are reading? How do we know what ideas we can take to the bank? We need to have the right tools at hand – the discernment and judgement – to avoid either information paralysis or information faddishness, and to be able to discern the real wealth in the fire hose of stuff coming at us from the Web.

It is possible to learn how to vet information effectively – evaluating its *cognitive authority* (Wilson 1983), but this takes time and effort. Cognitive authority is about the credibility of an information source, and also the *degree* of its credibility – some sources of information have greater authority than others. You also need to consider the *context* of this authority – a person who is an authority on one subject may unintentionally lead you up the garden path on another. As Fritch and Cromwell (2001) have noted, traditional measures of cognitive authority, such as those we find in books – the author's affiliation, publisher's name and date of publication – are all too often missing on the Internet. Without a structured method for gauging authority we may end up using dubious information recklessly while discarding information that is of high quality. To help address this risk, Fritch and Cromwell (2001) propose a model for vetting Internet-based information that consists of four filters: (1) filtering for *document* (authority and credibility), (2) filtering for *author* (identity, reputation and credentials), (3) filtering by *institution* (identity, reputation and qualifications) and (4) filtering by *affiliation* (of organizations, institutions and individuals).

One way of reducing the amount of Web-based material you need to vet is to use an agent or *recommender system*. These systems filter Web-based material according to diverse criteria such as its content, a user's needs, interests and history of use and the uptake and use of content by others. This is a complex and rapidly evolving area, with assorted kinds of recommendation systems in use. These include collaborative or *social-based*, *content-based* and *economic factor-based* systems (Popescul et al. 2001) and various hybrids (Peis et al. 2008). The algorithms behind such systems may be based on active or passive user input, explicit or implicit user interests, and user-centred or product-centred information. Semantic recommender systems also employ a knowledge base, such as a taxonomy, thesaurus or ontology, to structure Web content according to its meaning.[1] Peis et al. (2008) contend that the most promising recommender systems lie in the future development of mixed systems that combine Semantic Web technology with filters based around trust networks and contextual information. This is a complex, fast-evolving area we should keep our eyes on, but even those of us who rely on such systems will need to vet what is delivered to us from cyberspace.

Our advice is that as a minimum, you should put in enough effort to at least find out *where* the knowledge you are interested in was developed, *who* actually did the research and also, if possible, *who* made the site visits and *who* produced the Web analytics behind what you are reading. To do this you may have to develop a nodding relationship to statistics, or at least an understanding of sampling techniques. This is not always a palatable task, but it is essential if you are to truly gauge the authority of any online material you are building your own knowledge base upon.

---

1   The Semantic Web project aims to provide a common structure for the knowledge that underlies all web content, ultimately leading to interoperability between different agents and between agents and users (Peis et al. 2008).

Knowledge proxies and brokers

To help us reduce the complexity involved in vetting knowledge, we often use knowledge proxies, brokers or referrals, as our guides. Much of the revenue of traditional law and consulting firms is based on this concept: your lawyer or consultant knows what's up; they know from experience who to trust and follow and you can act on their advice with certainty and with good faith that it is true. The Internet, with its open access, has democratized communication opportunities while helping to erode these traditional sources of cognitive (and social) authority.

It is best to do your own vetting and filtering of information, but what if you genuinely do not have time? How about getting trusted others to assist you? In a study of online communities, Cranefield and Yoong (2009) discovered a group of valued contemporary knowledge proxies. Individual educators relied on respected individuals in a blog-centric community of facilitators and advisors. These people, described as *connector-leaders*, interacted with and supported one another as they filtered, vetted, critiqued and adapted ideas from a global network of educational bloggers. They performed daily scanning and filtering activities – which one person compared to a process of triage – before selecting suitable material to cite and comment on in their blogs. In addition, they sent selected material to their followers via email and instant messaging, matching it up with their needs and interests. For the recipients, this was an invaluable service:

> *It's like going to the library, and rather than searching for your own good books, some nice librarian ... says, 'Here are 15 books you might well be interested in' ... these guys have filtered out a whole lot of good stuff, and so I can focus on reading and thinking about it. (Teacher)*
> *Cranefield and Yoong (2009)*

Teachers determined who to follow (cognitive authority) based on a blogger's *street cred* – the extent to which they were a known entity with a track record of having successfully applied their ideas in a classroom setting. The trusted bloggers added further value by recombining the filtered ideas in ways that were of local relevance. They even provided a knowledge matchmaking service:

> *I would actually connect people together. 'Have a talk to this person; they were doing something that might be quite a good solution for your issue'. (Connector-Leader)*
> *Cranefield and Yoong (2009)*

Recombining knowledge is a valuable skill in its own right. Davenport and colleagues (2003) have noted that despite popular belief, most so-called *new* ideas 'owe a considerable debt to related ideas that came before' (59). They have identified a valued subset of people in organizations who know how to 'disaggregate (an idea) into its components, and to adopt the pieces, new or old – that make sense' (60). They call these people *idea practitioners*. Perhaps, at an individual level, we should seek out idea practitioners to associate with, or aim to be idea practitioners ourselves.

As the above example demonstrates, an experienced or well-trained person can be of inestimable value in finding and offering up useful things to study. Some progressive firms offer knowledge referral services, as McKinsey does, to its employees, but most of us do not have this kind of help.

Even with the help of a knowledge broker, you will need to critically read, interpret and socialize the incoming material. This is a very real and fundamental cost of keeping your knowledge fresh and useful, and there is no shortcut to escape it. If you do not put in the time, someone else undoubtedly will – and you will never be quite sure why you lost a job or a bid. You could view this effort as being like exercising, or eating right! If you do not invest in your own knowledge you will surely fall behind someone else who does. The world no longer rewards seniority or hanging around. Today, one's value is surely tied to what one knows and what one can do. There is no escaping this rule.

The thought leader industry, now generating billions of dollars in revenues, is a commercial activity little related to the social and economic reality we live with, and is perhaps most closely related to entertainment. The underlying question therefore remains, *'Who shall I trust?'* Our advice is to fall back on 'trust yourself and your own instincts and emotions' – if the knowledge on offer smells bad, it almost always *is* bad and should be shunned. You may miss some opportunities along the way but in the end, it's the best advice we can offer.

PRACTICE 3: INVEST IN YOUR NETWORKS

We get most of our new ideas from colleagues, friends, co-workers and others in the varied networks we all belong to, and this is fine. Face-to-face (and terminal-to-terminal) connections among those we know and trust have always been a potent force for idea communication and always will be. However, here too it is important to think through how you are going about this. Are you considered trustworthy by your colleagues? Do you reciprocate when asked for help by someone in your network? Do you make real contributions to your network or just take things as needed? One of the least mentioned subjects in the many books on networking is the need to really invest in your network, putting in your own time and resources to strengthen the network's density, content and reach. Once again there is a price to pay for this, in the form of time and effort expended.

The Value of Weak Ties and Human Diversity

There is a text, very well known in sociology, called *Getting a Job* by Mark Granovetter (1974) that examines the advantage of using weak ties, rather than depending on close friends and family, to find a job. Based on an empirical study of how 282 men in the United States found employment, the author examines the value of weak ties, based in overlapping networks, in learning anything new. This value arises because people already share so much with those people they are closest to in their networks. This same principle holds true for your own knowledge networks. If you spend all of your time with like-minded souls, how will you ever challenge what you know, or know anything that is really new? We have seen consultants at several well-known consulting firms write reports for clients that were done by people with the same degrees from more or less the same schools that reached conclusions that were, not surprisingly, interchangeable. How could they not be?

There may well be value in establishing a sustained professional dialogue with someone who has skills that complement our own. One of the authors of this chapter (Cranefield 2009) investigated the process of knowledge transfer amongst online communities of teachers. A few individuals who described themselves as being strongly *intuitive* spoke of the value of building a critical relationship with a more *analytical* partner, and vice versa. These were sustained partnerships that capitalized on each person's complementary strengths, leading to improved individual understanding and confidence. While these people shared some core values and philosophies, they did not end up thinking 'the same way'. The relationships helped them to sharpen and articulate their points of uniqueness.

As Scott Page points out in his important book, *The Difference* (2007), a group or team with cognitive diversity will always produce a better answer than a group of like-minded experts. This finding will eventually revolutionize how we think about both organizational knowledge and our own knowledge sourcing. Just like organizations, people have to learn to be more open to diverse knowledge sources, though it goes against intuitive wisdom and natural inclinations for all of us to flock together. But birds of a feather only get to know other similar birds and never evolve beyond the limits of the group. They are limited by their rule-based behaviours. We can do better.

PRACTICE 4: GET OUT OF YOUR OFFICE

Armed with your laptop, and connected to the WWW, you may feel you have all the access you will need to the world's information, but this will never be the same as real knowledge. Just think of the difference between reading about a country and spending time there, or between using conference call technology to listen in on a meeting and actually being there. We all know that new ideas are more than just words – they contain passion and other emotions – and these things can only be communicated by truly being there. Politicians proclaim loudly how they 'know' what is really going on in their country, and executives say, with great emphasis, 'I know what is going on my firm', when all they really know, or could ever know, is what is going on in their office. The same is true of business school academics who go on and on about organizational life when they have hardly ever visited a firm, to say nothing of having worked in one. This might sound a little obvious, even banal, but it is nonetheless important to say: get out of your office! You need to do this because what you know depends on where you are and where you have been – if you simply stay in your office, all you will really 'know' will be the walls and windows surrounding you!

Lave and Wenger (1991), Nonaka (1998), Cohen and Prusak (2001) and Orlikowski (2002), among others, have demonstrated how *socialization* – interpersonal interactions and the sharing of experiences – is needed for people to acquire the intangible, tacit, dimension of knowledge. Without these fundamental social processes, it is extremely difficult for people to access the subtleties of each other's thinking. Yet, even if we know this, it is all too easy for us to slip into acting as if the only 'real work' happens in our office or usual workplace.

In their book *In Good Company*, Cohen and Prusak (2001) discuss how the single-minded pursuit of efficiency may lead managers to eliminate gathering places because they are seen as 'superfluous or even detrimental' (93). On the other hand, companies which take a strategic approach to fostering knowledge will set out to create informal meeting spots such as cafés, atriums and conversation nooks. This is not just about increasing the opportunities for socialization. It also promotes the building of *social capital* – the fostering of a level of mutual trust that engenders sustained cooperation, knowledge sharing, loyalty and commitment.

There is another reason why getting out of your office can help you to manage your own knowledge, and it has nothing to do with other people. The problem is that if we stay in the same environment for long periods, we can get locked into rigid ways of thinking. According to Nel Mostert, who has run over 125 creative problem-solving workshops at Unilever, people often run into the most useful ideas 'by coincidence' when they are not at work.

> *If you have a seemingly unsolvable problem, you can find the answers everywhere ... with people you meet, places you visit, books you read ... a picture you look at, a dog you see running, a child you see playing. (The) creativity takes place in your own mind.*
>
> *Mostert (2007, 99)*

Creative thinking, or *not* thinking – letting go of a problem and changing our environment – can transport us, within seconds, from having a problem to working out how to solve it. Eight decades ago, researcher Graham Wallas developed a now classic four-stage model to explain the process that occurs when we tackle issues with the aim of finding a creative solution (1926, cited in Shear and Varela 1999). In the *preparation* stage, we define a problem or need, consider it, and gather up information that we think may be useful. We then enter an *incubation* stage, stepping back from the problem while our mind does little conscious work on it. Following this, if we are lucky, we arrive at the *insight* stage – the 'aha' moment. The final stage, *verification*, involves testing out this solution. In novel settings, it seems that your mind can more readily make the creative 'click' or 'aha' between the problem and solution. According to Mostert (2007, 99), you should

> *Get out of your comfort zone, breaking out of the limits of your paradigms. Organizing a creativity session with other people is just one way to try to find the 'coincidence'. Taking a walk, having a coffee, some minutes of 'window shopping' can do the same trick. As long as you allow your own brain the opportunity, time and space to think.*

Many people report being more creative in the mornings, or evenings, than in working hours. There are even online discussion boards devoted to the vexing question of why so many computer programmers have their best ideas in the shower (one participant reports having installed a whiteboard and pens in his shower cabinet!). Perhaps breaking out of the office frame of mind is part of the answer.

Yet another explanation for why getting out of the office may be helpful comes from the work of a group of cognitive scientists. Engeström et al. (1995), Goodwin (1990, cited by Engeström et al.) and Reder (1993) found that expert professionals regularly moved between multiple parallel work contexts – a situation called *polycontextuality*. In order to solve problems, the experts integrated knowledge from, and across, these different contexts. Their innovation and learning was made possible by their ongoing movement between the different contexts.

As you can see, there are plenty of reasons why getting out of your office is a good idea. In terms of the opportunity for truly encountering new knowledge, there is no substitute for this. You simply have to get out and go to some places to really 'get it' when it comes to understanding new ideas with any sort of depth, and to help trigger those great ideas you do not know are coming. Travel and getting around is, of course, no guarantee of anything, but never leaving your office, or library, is a guarantee of your own knowledge becoming stale.

Conclusion

We have proposed four foundational practices for personal knowledge management: scan and reinvent, vet and filter, invest in your networks and get out of your office. The key concept underlying all of these themes is the need to *invest* in managing your own personal knowledge. True knowledge is, and always has been, an expensive thing to obtain. Just think of how much time you have spent in developing whatever skills and talents you already have. If you are going to manage and refresh and keep up your own knowledge assets you will have to spend some of your scarce resources – mostly time and often some money. There is simply no shortcut or technical fix to do this. Whether you are following a technology, a market, a country or firm, a set of propositions, or a concept; all these things require investments in attention, travel and care.

The allure of the Web is often substituted for acquiring real knowledge. The Web is cheap, the material on it can often be read quite quickly, and one can do it anywhere, any time. However, if access to the Web equated with acquiring knowledge there would be a fantastic convergence of knowledge around the world. Many of us would 'know' the same things as each other, and we would become much more interchangeable then we actually are. Since this is obviously not the case, it is clear that at least some people are managing their knowledge – especially those who already have a substantial investment in knowledge that they want to protect by keeping it current.

As individuals, if we are to effectively manage our personal knowledge, we need to continually seek out and capitalize on opportunities – inside and outside our workplace, day by day and minute by minute. As employers, we must consider how to support our employees in developing their personal knowledge in ways that foster commitment and loyalty. The combined, differentiated personal knowledge of many employees can be of inestimable value.

In short, knowledge is a very different thing from information – it is more expensive to develop, retain, transfer and keep current. Knowledge gives each one of us our own advantages in differing markets and contexts, but it takes time, money and effort to manage our knowledge well. The choice is yours!

References

Chang, H.-J. (2002), 'The Stiglitz Contribution', *International Issues* 45:2, 77–96.

Cohen, D. and Prusak, L. (2001), *In Good Company: How Social Capital Makes Organizations Work* (Boston: Harvard Business School Press).

Cranefield, J. (2009), 'Online Communities of Practice and Professional Change: a Three-tier View of the Knowledge-embedding Process'. Ph.D. thesis, Victoria University, Wellington, http://researcharchive.vuw.ac.nz/handle/10063/1147

Cranefield, J., and Yoong, P. (2009), 'Embedding Professional Knowledge: The "Middle Layer" in an Online Community Ecosystem,' in M. Purvis and B. Savarimuthu (eds), *Computer-Mediated Social Networking, Lecture Notes in Computer Science* (Heidelberg: Springer).

Davenport, T. et al. (2003), *What's the Big Idea? Creating and Capitalizing on the Best Management Thinking* (Boston: Harvard Business School Press).

Dickerson, C. (2004), 'The Google Way', *InfoWorld* 20 February, http://www.infoworld.com/t/business/google-way-790, accessed 20 November 2008.

Drucker, P. (1999), 'Managing Oneself,' *Harvard Business Review* 77:2, 65–74.

Ellerman, D. (1999), 'Global Institutions: Transforming International Development Agencies into Learning Organizations', *Academy of Management Executive* 13:1, 25–35.

Engeström, Y. et al. (1995), 'Polycontextuality and Boundary Crossing in Expert Cognition: Learning and Problem Solving in Complex Work Activities', *Learning and Instruction* 5:4, 319–36.

Fritch, J. and Cromwell, R. (2001), 'Evaluating Internet Resources: Identity, Affiliation, and Cognitive Authority in a Networked World', *Journal of the American Society for Information Science and Technology* 52:6, 499–507.

Goodwin, C. (1990), 'Perception, Technology and Interaction on a Scientific Research Vessel', paper presented at the 89th Annual Meeting of the American Anthropological Association, New Orleans, 28 November–2 December.

Granovetter, M. (1974), *Getting A Job: A Study of Contacts and Careers* (Chicago: The University of Chicago Press).

Hamilton, J. and Wilkie, C. (2001), 'An Appraisal of the Use of Secondment within a Large Teaching Hospital', *Journal of Nursing Management* 9:6, 315–20.

Huber, G. and Daft, R. (1987), 'The Information Environments of Organizations', in F. Javlin et al. (eds), *Handbook of Organizational Communication* (Newbury Park: Sage).

Kelly, D. (1990), *Reviving the 'Deadwood': How to Create an Institutional Climate to Encourage the Professional Growth and Revitalization of Mid-Career Faculty in the Community College.* Graduate Seminar Report, Claremont College.

Lave, J. and Wenger, E. (1991), *Situated Learning: Legitimate Peripheral Participation* (Cambridge: Cambridge University Press).

Mostert, N. (2007), 'Diversity of the Mind as the Key to Successful Creativity at Unilever', *Creativity and Innovation Management* 16:1, 93–100.

Nonaka, I. (1998), 'The Knowledge-Creating Company', in *Harvard Business Review on Knowledge Management* (Boston: Harvard Business School Publishing).

Orlikowski, W. (2002), 'Knowing in Practice: Enacting a Collective Capability in Distributed Organizing', *Organization Science* 13:3, 249–74.

Page, S. (2007), *The Difference: How the Power of Diversity Creates Better Groups, Firms, Schools, and Societies* (Princeton: Princeton University Press).

Peis, E. et al. (2008), 'Semantic Recommender Systems. Analysis of the State of the Topic', Hipertext.net 6, http://www.hipertext.net/english/pag1031.htm, accessed 20 November 2008.

Popescul, A. et al. (2001), 'Probabilistic Models for Unified Collaborative and Content-based Recommendation in Sparse-data Environments', in *Proceedings of the Seventeenth Conference on Uncertainty in Artificial Intelligence, 2–5 August, Seattle* (San Francisco: Morgan Kaufmann).

Reder, S. (1993), 'Watching Flowers Grow: Polycontextuality and Heterochronicity at Work', *The Quarterly Newsletter of Comparative Human Cognition* 15:4, 116–25.

Shear, J., and Varela, F. (1999), *The View from Within: First-Person Approaches to the Study of Consciousness* (Exeter: Imprint Academic).

Sparrow, P. (1999), 'Strategy and Cognition: Understanding the Role of Management Knowledge Structures, Organizational Memory and Information Overload', *Creativity and Innovation Management* 8:2, 140–48.

Stiglitz, J. (1999), 'Scan Globally, Reinvent Locally: Knowledge Infrastructure and the Localization of Knowledge', Keynote Address, First Global Development Network Conference, Bonn, 5–8 December, http://www.inwent.org/E+Z/zeitschr/de400-3.htm, accessed 16 June 2009.

Wallas, G. (1926), *The Art of Thought* (New York: Franklin Watts).

Wilson, P. (1983), *Second-hand Knowledge: An Inquiry into Cognitive Authority* (Westport: Greenwood Press).

7

Knowledge Management and the Individual: It's Nothing Personal[1]

Dave Snowden, David J. Pauleen and
Sally Jansen van Vuuren

Introduction

Over the years there has been a great deal of criticism levelled at the concept of knowledge management (KM). According to Snowden (2002a), KM is a term that was hijacked by IT departments and as a result has lost most of its relevance. Snowden has always seen the proper focus of KM as supporting decision-making and creating the pre-conditions for innovation (2000). However, that agenda has now moved on from KM to sense-making, defined as how one makes sense of the world so that one can effectively act in it (Kurtz and Snowden 2003). Inherent in this understanding is the notion that individuals in and of themselves are unable to make sense of the world on their own, but are, as part of the human community, able to engage in sense-making with others (Kurtz and Snowden 2003).

Key contributors to the sense-making literature include Weick (1985) and Dervin (1998), the latter of whom resonates most closely with Snowden.

---

1 This chapter is based in large part on an interview with Dave Snowden conducted by the second author in Wellington, New Zealand in July 2008. The interviewer's objective was to get Dave to discuss his view of PKM. Dave was adamant that he did not believe there was such a thing as PKM, seeing that as an atomistic and aggregative approach which ignores the primacy of social systems. Individuals act within such systems but not as free agents. Community-based collaborative knowledge sharing that skilled individuals can participate in can and should actively direct, to meet their own knowledge requirements: what we refer to in this chapter as *social knowledge networking*. This chapter takes its lead from Dave's comments and the cases he used to illustrate his ideas as well as literature gathered by the second and third authors to provide an academic context.

Snowden's view of sense-making draws on complexity theory as well as aspects of cognitive science, evolutionary psychology and anthropology. Snowden conceptualizes these theories in the Cynefin sense-making framework. The framework was initially used in Snowden's early work in knowledge management, but now extends to aspects of leadership, strategy, cultural change, customer relationship management and more (Kurtz and Snowden 2003; Snowden and Boone 2007). The framework is particularly effective in helping decision-makers to make sense of complex problems, providing new ways of approaching intractable problems and allowing the emergence of shared understandings from collective groups.

Complexity theory has emerged as a new way to understand organizations over the last two decades. Recent thinking in this field has identified the inherent differences between human complex systems and those found in nature (Kurtz and Snowden 2003; Snowden 2000). Most notably, these differences include the human capacity to orientate between multiple identities; an evolved ability to make decisions based on experiential and narrative patterns, rather than a logical examination of the current facts (Kurtz and Snowden 2003); and the ability to purposefully change systems in which they interact (Snowden and Boone 2007). It is this thinking that differentiates Snowden from other sense-making theorists and has led to what he terms 'naturalistic sense-making'.

The premise of this chapter is that if you enable the right sort of ecology then knowledge sharing will tend to happen naturally. The notion of complexity theory provides a basic theoretical model with which to understand the way in which social computing has been effective. Based on current Web-based social activity and individual and collective sense-making the virtual world seems to be the right sort of environment for knowledge sharing and the rise of what we term Social Knowledge Networks (SKN). SKN allow access to the complexity of the world of knowledge that resides on the Internet – the knowledge contained in the experiences and minds of the people who inhabit the Web.

This chapter begins with a discussion on social computing as the right kind of environment to encourage knowledge sharing. It continues with a discussion of complexity and the use of multiple identity management to navigate complexity, and the skills (including sense-making skills) needed to develop and maintain social knowledge networks. Finally, there is a critical discussion on individual vs organizational perspectives on SKN. Included throughout the chapter are concept illustrations called 'Snowden's Cases in Point'.

The Right Kind of Environment

Snowden encapsulates his thinking about the blogosphere in an article on his Cognitive Edge website (2007b). Looking at the blogosphere you can immediately understand that this is the right kind of environment for knowledge sharing. Knowledge sharing is 'just' happening. There are two or three reasons for this. Blogs work at a lower level of fine granularity: that is, they are highly fragmented, ad hoc and unstructured and this matches the way the human brain has evolved to handle data (Snowden 2008a). The human brain does not want to sit down and read a book; it wants to receive multiple fragmented stimuli and that is one of the reasons why people will spend hours surfing the Web or taking part in social groups. The second reason is that meaning in the blogosphere comes through social interaction over time: it is not predetermined. The way it works is if you blog about something, people will link to your blog, you find them via search engines and you link to their blog. If you decide they are saying something of interest, you put it in your RSS feed and gradually a network builds out of that, and if they do not say things you are interested in then you eliminate them from your RSS feed.

SNOWDEN'S CASE IN POINT 1: USING THE BLOGOSPHERE TO MANAGE KNOWLEDGE

As Snowden tries to bring natural sciences into play within organizations, he needs to scan in depth a number of scientific fields including complexity theory, cognitive science, anthropology and a whole body of psychology. So that means he needs to scan a large number of journals, articles and references which exist in these fields. In the old days he would have had two choices. The first was go to the library each month and skim the journals and hope to find useful information. The second option was to employ a summarization service which he never did because he did not trust summarizers to get the essence of the knowledge in these journals.

However none of this is necessary now that that he has tapped into the blogosphere. For example, he connected with a Ph.D. student at University College in London who specializes in neuropsychology. He blogs every day and scans science blogs in Snowden's RSS feed. Basically he is acting as a filtering device and Snowden only needs to read the student's blog to get relevant references. This represents huge savings in time and the reason he is a part of Snowden's network is because Snowden learned to trust him over several months. Other people might not trust him in the same way. He just thinks the way Snowden does, therefore Snowden trusts him to act as a scanning device. He has his own network of other people working in the field, who Snowden has also connected to in part. All in all Snowden has RSS feeds from about 35 science blogs coming in daily or weekly. It takes an hour a day to go through the RSS feeds. So Snowden has effectively got all the things he feels he needs to know about in this one space, all populated by people who have proved themselves as sources. Every six to nine months Snowden tidies the whole thing up, often when he downloads for free a new RSS package to meet his changing needs or out of boredom.

What Snowden is doing here is handling fragmented material, building stuff naturally and structuring his universe into a hierarchy. Every six to nine months he dissolves the hierarchy and reforms it which gives him an adaptive capacity which does not exist in a traditional KM system. It is a fragmented, unstructured, trust-based network. Moreover because he blogs that gives him access to more blogs. His blog is referenced and he references other people. So he became part of this community of people who are sharing and contributing knowledge to a learning environment which is equivalent to the staff common room at university where it is possible to interact with people one did not expect to interact with.

The above case illustrates a basic difference between majority practice KM and SKN on the Internet. While KM tries to force people to work with people they do not necessarily want to work with in a structured environment, the kind of social knowledge networking illustrated above is grounded in the way people actually work. While social knowledge networking appears on the surface to be centred on individually directed interaction, it is more about mutually directed relationships with meaning developing out of interactions with others. It is a much more communitarian (Snowden 2005b) than atomistic. Significantly, you do not necessarily know people as individuals; you know them as identities. They are people who cluster together around areas of interest, such as neuropsychology. In the case above Snowden is tangentially a member of this community.

There are mechanisms within these communities that tend to strengthen the mutual connections among members. In the case above, the student blogger posted that he had just had his second child. This resulted in congratulatory messages that helped strengthen the trust relationship. As in the staff common room, a person can never have a conversation with somebody just about one's discipline; we also need that personal exchange. In the case of the blogger mentioned above, the arrival of a new baby meant he was unable to carry out his part-time work for a period. He posted that his financial situation was difficult at that time and that he would be very grateful for donations or book purchases. His network of readers responded by helping him over a rocky patch. Nobody felt guilty or patronizing about it because he was providing such a valuable service. Snowden bought him a textbook he wanted, and considered it a bargain as he benefited from a trusted summary of a book he could not have found the time (or competence) to read for himself.

What we are seeing here is a emergent form of web-based mutual responsibility different from market-based reciprocation or the balance of favours Davenport and Prusak (1998) have proposed as a knowledge-sharing mechanism and more like the concept of social obligation and gifting often found in traditional cultures such as those of China and Japan (Oyserman et al. 1998).

Using Multiple Identities to Navigate Complexity

The world is a complex system and as human beings we navigate complexity every day. A problem with organizational KM is that it takes place in an ordered system. An ordered system constrains the way that all agents behave so they can only behave in accordance with the rules of the system (Kurtz and Snowden 2003). In this view, organizations are trying to manage knowledge from an engineering perspective. The same can be said for organizationally determined best practice, for example, communities of practice as they are attempts to constrain agents. On the other hand, the blogosphere on the whole verges on being a chaotic system made up of unconstrained agents (Snowden 2007a). Everything is independent of everything else, with different people using different ways and means to do the same things. People do not find the things they expect to find. However, it is possible, as shown above, to build or join trust-based networks where you can find things quickly. As the connections increase, light constraints come into play and the system becomes complex which allows meaning to emerge.

So, for the most part the blogosphere ends up as a series of clusters of people who think in similar ways. Occasionally they interact with another group and there is some transference or linkage but it is not a universally connected system. It resembles a series of isolated villages. These clusters are complex systems and an individual, operating from their personal space, as a part of the cluster can exercise light constraints on the system. Anyone who behaves in a way which is unacceptable to other people in the cluster will be thrown out. If someone does not contribute in a useful way, they will find it difficult to get things from the others. If someone is cooperative, others cooperate with them.

What differentiates the online environment from face-to-face interactions is that an individual can possess multiple identities (Alexander and Wiley 1981; Stryker 1987; Tajfel and Turner 1986). A person can blog under their own name but assume another identity in a group (Kurtz and Snowden 2006). Indeed, in some spaces, such as Wikipedia, as an editor one can be part of a group identity and effectively manage transactions as part of that group identity (Kurtz and Snowden 2006) (see Case in Point 2).

SNOWDEN'S CASE IN POINT 2: WIKIPEDIA PART 1

In Wikipedia Snowden is part of a group who fight off the extreme unionist and nationalist editors on England, Wales, Ireland, Scotland, the United Kingdom, Great Britain and Northern Ireland. Every month or so a war breaks out about whether Wales or Scotland are countries or just part of the United Kingdom. Some people set up 'sock puppets' (false IDs to misrepresent the balance of opinion). Now there is a virtual group of people, whom Snowden can name individually, who manage these situations. When such a war breaks out, they each take on different roles to make sure they look after each other. So in terms of an actor and an agent, they are a cohesive group. This is the way human beings work. Sometimes for ourselves, but most of the time we are in relationships with other people and sometimes we are sort of an ideological identity or we are a physical or organizational identity. And we fluidly move between these identities without thinking about it.

It is incorrect to assume that communities are aggregations of individual self-interest where individuals manage their knowledge and reciprocate with others. The reality is human beings have multiple fluid identities which they shift between, and different identities have different cognitive capacities and work in different ways. The key is to be able to navigate these interactions.

In a complex system, if people try to consciously manage these interactions things inevitably go wrong, just as they do in organizational KM. The secret is to go with the flow as much as possible. However, the reality is that most of us are only capable of managing the immediacy of our interactions against relatively short-term goals. The secret (to navigating complexity) is to increase the level of the interactions one has and to know when to increase the interactions and when to decrease them. Essentially, it is an exploration–exploitation balance (Kurtz and Snowden 2003). If we spend all our time exploring, we never do anything; if we spend all our time doing things, we never explore. The best strategy is to balance the networks and balance those interactions.

The Skills Needed to Build Social Knowledge Networks

Most human beings are born with the basic skills needed to create social knowledge networks. These are certainly innate properties; 98 per cent of our genetic history is as hunter/gatherers (Snowden 1999). Most of our social interactions and the way we retain social relationships derive from this. The habituated pattern of trust interaction is learnt when the brain is very plastic, hence the number of people an individual is likely to trust and to interact with is to some extent correlated with the number of people they interacted with in an extended family up to and just after puberty. People who grow up in isolated environments will tend to have more limited venues of trust. This can be understood as a tribal–non tribal distinction (Kurtz and Snowden 2006).

Most people know how to build social networks because they will not survive much beyond childhood if they cannot build those sorts of relationships. In order to build social knowledge networks one should go with the things which seem natural – the way that you have grown up – because they are patterns in your brain. Trying to force yourself into an unnatural environment will probably not work. There are times when that is possible, but they are rare.

Basic technology skills as prosaic as typing are critical in the web-based environment. Touch typing allows for fast and multilateral online exchanges. Being able to write basic HTML is another necessary skill in the virtual environment. Many of these basic competencies can be developed in a natural evolutionary way in online environments such as Wikipedia. According to Snowden (personal communication), 'Wikipedia is not so much an encyclopaedia; it's a place to experiment with social interaction' (see Case in Point 3).

SNOWDEN'S CASE IN POINT 3: WIKIPEDIA PART 2

Editing Wikipedia pages on a topic of interest can result in learning a considerable amount. First of all one learns how to maintain trust and relationships with people who are using false IDs. Then there is 'Wiki love', which means that you must not oppose people; that you must build consensus with the others; you must cite everything which is challenged and if you get this wrong you will be punished by people very quickly. You also interestingly start to realize that right will win out. Snowden has never yet been in a Wiki battle where at the end of it something did not come out which could be held to be correct. He did not always agree with it, but he never ended up with something he violently disagreed with. So the sock puppets and the point of view pushers actually do not win.

The other thing that becomes apparent is that Wikipedia has developed natural immune systems. Sock puppets exhibit pattern behaviour. For example, every time there is a consensus on whether Scotland and Wales are countries somebody new suddenly leaps in and starts doing the reverse edits and getting very disputatious. This is now seen as a familiar pattern. So as soon as one of these comes along the group makes a case to a 'check user', who then checks the IP addresses involved and delivers a verdict. If it is guilty then we have a sock puppet and an administrator bans the ID. Thus all these natural immune systems are built up in the system. So anyone who wants to understand complexity and how to work in this new world should go and spend six months in Wikipedia. They will be forced to learn some HTML. They will be forced to learn social interaction. They will learn to live in a virtual environment and maintain multiple relationships.

Because social knowledge networks rely on knowledge reciprocity, another critical skill set – actually more of a knowledge set – is fluency in a range of transdisciplinary subjects. People have to read books which stretch them in subjects that they are not familiar with. The world increasingly requires generalists rather than specialists (Snowden et al. 2005a). Reading widely should be a great advantage over the next decade or so.

Developing Sense-making Skills

Besides online interaction, old-fashioned face-to-face interaction in different social contexts also builds up social and identity switching abilities (Snowden 2005a). These are diversity skills acquired through practice. If you did not develop these social networking skills in childhood, they can be acquired by learning through doing (Snowden 2005a).

People cannot survive through individual sense-making. Sense-making is a social activity reliant on family, friends and society as a whole (Kurtz and Snowden 2006). One way to develop sense-making capabilities online is through social knowledge networks. Individuals in the network, and the network itself, collectively sort through information, events, stimuli and a host of other inputs and present them in coherent forms. In order to manage uncertainty, that is, to make sense of it, multiple filters are necessary as contradictory signals will come in (Snowden 2002b), but even then it is possible to make a lousy subconscious decision. So the more experiences you build in your brain the more likely you are to make a decision which is reasonably stable.

One way to make sense of uncertain and complex environments is to manage the level of constraint (Snowden 2005a). An increase in constraint increases predictability, but also reduces resilience and adaptability. It may also increase stress in the system to the point where any break would be catastrophic (Kurtz and Snowden 2003). If all constraints are removed then there is complete chaos which will result in novelty, but it will not be manageable. If constraint is maintained at flexible levels, by modifying them as necessary, then a *complex adaptive system* where novel and new ways of thinking will naturally *emerge*. A critical sense-making skill is to become aware of constraints and boundaries and know how to apply them in one's interactions.

The reality is we are determined by our interactions. By changing the number and nature of these interactions we can achieve change, cope with uncertainty and extend our capacity. The key is to focus on interactions, not on oneself.

Social Knowledge Networking: Individual vs Organizational Perspectives

There would seem to be conflict between how an individual might set up and maintain a social knowledge network and the objectives of an organizational KM programme. However, the tension within organizations is generally not an individual–organization tension, but rather a group–organization tension: for example informal trusted networks are more effective at knowledge transfer than formal systems, but people learn camouflage behaviour in formal knowledge systems, using the language of trust but not the practices (Snowden 2002a). So sometimes the organization tries to impose constraint on the way that a group of people behave, but the group does not actually want to behave as directed. At that point the systems are clashing. What happens next? Does the constraining system actually change the behaviour of the group? Often, all the organization achieves is verbal conformance or camouflage behaviour (Snowden 2002b). So people will actually do what the system expects in order to receive their salary, but in reality, underneath the system's radar, they will do something different. The irony of this is that it builds inefficiency into the system at the same time those imposing the constraints see the organization as becoming more efficient. The reality underneath is that more and more people are paddling around in a desperate attempt to keep the organization afloat until it finally it breaks catastrophically (Kurtz and Snowden 2003).

From an organizational KM view, the lesson is that organizations should not overly constrain the way employees interact with colleagues, for example by coercing knowledge sharing through prescribed technologies or social interaction. If this is not done, employees may reach the point of not wanting to do any more and, if they can, they will leave.

On the other hand, if organizations can reduce constraints and set boundary conditions (Snowden and Boone 2007), they can create a safe-fail experimental approach to KM. For example, the organization can stop trying to define everything: effectively it allows a thousand flowers to bloom. As the ideas flower the ones that look interesting are nurtured and the ones that look counterproductive are pruned. This style of management allows more freedom within the system, as it is a lightly constrained system rather than a rigidly constrained system. Moreover, it is a safe to fail design (Snowden and Boone 2007). Ironically, this gives management more control, because as it does not overly constrain the system, the groups do not need to go underground. Things remain visible to management.

This is, in fact, organizational social knowledge networking. It is a way of distributing cognition and sense-making across the whole organization (Snowden 2007b). Cognitive Edge's sense-making software products support this by basically allowing leaders in an organization to distribute problems immediately to their employees and receive the results back, without the employees necessarily knowing the nature of the system that they are being consulted about. In fact, looking at the way networks operate both within companies and outside of companies and the fact that the boundaries within organized companies are breaking down all the time, we then begin to see all sorts of things can be done in a modern technology environment. We are actually returning to the tribal and clan structure in nature of social interaction

(Snowden 2007a). Following a period of two or three centuries where we have been trying to create machines, we are now seeing a return to much more organic approaches (see Case in Point 4).

SNOWDEN'S CASE IN POINT 4: SKN AND THE ORGANIZATION

Snowden suggests a way of reducing 10–15 percent of the average IT budget and improving service by stopping organizational attempts to control social computing. He would do something very simple at the corporate level through the creation of one rigid barrier. This barrier would prohibit anyone from attaching attaching anything to email, Skype or Facebook. The first time this happens, there is a verbal warning, the second time is a written warning and the third time results in dismissal. This is an absolutely rigid rule, because there is no excuse these days for not using an html link back into a secure folder address. This is the only way to achieve security. He would punish people if they broke the rule, because security is becoming more an issue.

Second he would have a pop server for his own email, which is company email, and he would satisfy the audit requirement by simply streaming all data off the pop server before it reached the reader. This creates a record of what people have now. He would let people choose their own email system because they can only link to files if they actually have hot links. This makes the data secure. People should not be writing anything in emails which they are not prepared to allow outside the company anyway. If someone wants to write something deeply secure, they should print it in a document and put it somewhere safe and secure, which has the added benefit of reducing email traffic. There are some collaborative environments, so instant messenger and chat programs can exist within the firewall. It is neither possible nor necessary to keep people away from Facebook, but they should be made aware that they are operating outside the firewall. At the moment organizations only allow employees to do things inside the firewall, so people do whatever they want because there is no natural caution. When people know they are outside the firewall, they will be more careful.

Most people will think this is radical. To Snowden it is self-evident. The pressure on people to work in both home and work environments is increasing. So employees are forced to work in a secure environment in the workplace but are also expected to work in the evenings and the weekends. That means they will put stuff onto USB sticks or email to a private email address. The reality is these days we are moving towards a limited number of devices. An IPhone and MacBook comprise a system that constantly interacts with all the same data or access to the same data at all times. And the user moves fluidly between different environments without thinking about it. That is going to increase. So the artificial boundaries of the firm are going to break down at that point.

Conclusion

Social knowledge networking can be summed up as the right tool at the right time for the human condition. Human beings are natural tool users and technology is a powerful tool. People want tools that fit their hands. They are not interested in tools that require them to bio re-engineer their hands. This is what KM has been requiring people to do these last ten years – bio re-engineer their hands, their minds, even their souls. And that is where we are now. Social knowledge networking, on the other hand, can be picked up and used naturally. It is a way that individuals, as part of a network, can stay current, fluid and knowledgeable in a constantly changing, complex world. Individuals need to first acknowledge the importance of collaborative networks in their personal knowledge strategies and then learn the skills that will allow them to make sense of and work effectively in complex online networked knowledge environments.

Snowden summed up what he believes KM is about in a recent blog (2008b), summarized below. These seven principles highlight his understanding of what underpins successful KM. Social knowledge networking is a key and evolving element of KM as it relates to individuals and their networks and its importance can be seen in several of these principles.

1. Knowledge can only be volunteered: it cannot be conscripted.

2. We always know more than we can say, and we will always say more than we can write down. The process of taking things from our heads, to our mouths (speaking it) or to our hands (writing it down) involves loss of content and context.

3. The way we know things is not the way we report we know things.

4.   We only know what we know when we need to know it. Human knowledge is deeply contextual and requires stimulus for recall.

5.   Tolerated failure imprints learning better than success.

6.   In the context of real need few people will withhold their knowledge. A genuine request for help is not often refused unless there is literally no time or a previous history of distrust.

7.   Everything is fragmented. We evolved to handle unstructured fragmented fine granularity information objects, not highly structured documents.

References

Alexander, C. and Wiley, M. (1981), 'Situated Activity and Identity Formation', in M. Rosenberg and R. Turner (eds), *Social Psychology: Sociological Perspectives* (New York: Basic Books).

Davenport, T. and Prusak, L. (1998), *Working Knowledge* (Boston: Harvard Business School Press).

Dervin, B. (1998), 'Sense-Making Theory and Practice: An Overview of User Interests in Knowledge Seeking and Use', *Journal of Knowledge Management* 2:2, 36–46.

Kurtz, C. and Snowden, D. (2003), 'The New Dynamics of Strategy: Sense-making in a Complex and Complicated World', *IBM Systems Journal* 42:3, 462–83.

—— (2006), 'Bramble Bushes in a Thicket', in M. Gibbert and M. Durand (eds), *Strategic Networks: Learning to Compete* (Oxford: Blackwell).

Oyserman, D. et al. (1998), 'Cultural Accommodation: Hybridity and the Framing of Social Obligation', *Journal of Personality and Social Psychology* 74:6, 1606–18.

Snowden, D. (1999), 'The Paradox of Story', *Journal of Strategy & Scenario Planning* 1:5, 16–20.

—— (2000), 'The ASHEN Model: An Enabler of Action', *Knowledge Management* 3:7, 14–17.

—— (2002a), 'Narrative Patterns: Uses of Story in the Third Age of Knowledge Management', *Journal of Information & Knowledge Management* 1:1, 1–6.

—— (2002b), Complex Acts of Knowing: Paradox and Descriptive Self-awareness', *Journal of Knowledge Management* 6:2, 100–11.

—— (2005a), 'Multi-ontology Sense Making: A New Simplicity in Decision Making', *Management Today, Yearbook 2005* Vol. 20 http://www.kwork.org/Stars/Snowden/Snowden.pdf

—— (2005b), 'From Atomism to Networks in Social Systems', *The Learning Organisation* Special Issue 12:6, 552–62.

—— (2007a), 'Social Computing and the Enterprise', *Cognitive Edge* http://www.cognitive-edge.com/blogs/dave/2007/12/social_computing_the_enterpris.php

—— (2007b), 'The Blogosphere as an Artifact of Distributed Cognition', *Cognitive Edge* http://www.cognitive-edge.com/2007/03/_only_if_we_meet_them_half_way.php

—— (2008a), 'Everything is Fragmented – Blog Storming in Six Stages', *KM World* http://www.kmworld.com/Articles/News/News-Analysis/Everything-is-fragmented%e2%80%94-Blog-storming-in-six-stages--50451.aspx

—— (2008b), 'Rendering Knowledge', *Cognitive Edge* http://www.cognitive-edge.com/blogs/dave/2008/10/rendering_knowledge.php

—— and Boone, M. (2007), 'A Leader's Framework for Decision Making', *Harvard Business Review* 85:11, 68–76.

—— et al. (2005), 'Emergence, Complexity and Organisation', *E:CO Annual* 7, vii–x.

Stryker, S. (1987), 'Identity Theory: Developments and Extensions', in K. Yardley and T. Honess (eds) , *Self and Identity: Psychosocial Perspectives* (New York: Wiley).

Tajfel, H. and Turner, J. (1986), 'The Social Identity Theory of Inter-Group Behavior', in S. Worchel and L. Austin (eds), *Psychology of Intergroup Relations* (Chicago: Nelson-Hall).

Weick, K. (1985), 'Cosmos vs. Chaos: Sense and Nonsense in Electronic Contexts', *Organizational Dynamics* 14:2, 50–64.

8

Managing Personal Connectivity: Finding Flow for Regenerative Knowledge Creation

Darl G. Kolb and Paul D. Collins

Introduction

On a recent visit to Kuala Lumpur, we met up with some friends and colleagues who were there working as consultants. These consultants are a married couple, who are truly global nomads. They have a base in Perth, but spend several months of the year in France and New Zealand. Their client work takes them all around the world, to places including the Philippines, Saudi Arabia, New Zealand, Australia and Korea. Their consulting practice is based on knowledge work and it is very personalized, that is, there is no headquarters or back office coordinating their efforts, or supporting their movements. They are intellectually, physically and logistically independent. Of course, they are also intellectually, physically and logistically interdependent with others around the world, including their clients, friends and families. During our intersecting visit in a city that was home to neither of us, we noticed how much time they spent organizing their work and travel. We also noticed that they simultaneously maintained a degree of 'normalcy' within their hectic schedules and transient lifestyle. For example, they try their best to stay in the same hotel each time they stay in a particular city. They also actively get to know the local markets and stores around the hotel, all of which lends a sort of temporary 'local' neighbourhood feel to the area for them.

The converse of the global nomadic life for our friends is time away from airports and hotels – time spent either in a remote farmhouse in France or a beach house in New Zealand, both with very slow dial-up Internet access.

To the extent that it is possible, without putting off their clients, they try to cluster client engagements into periods of intensive activity, which are then punctuated with periods of remote retreat, not just from clients, but also from airports, cities and crowds in general. The stark contrast and healthy interaction between highly connected work and its counterbalancing disconnection is the main theme of this chapter. Whether you are a globally mobile nomad or a cubicle dweller, whether you are a part-time portfolio worker or a ubiquitously networked, phone-in-the-ear workaholic, when it comes to personal knowledge management, we all need at times to both connect and disconnect.

In this chapter, we will introduce knowledge creation and management through a lens of 'connectivity' and explore how 'dualities' between generative and regenerative knowledge processes match the inherent duality of connectivity, that is, connects and disconnects. The connectivity metaphor is further explored for other attributes, which are also applied to personal knowledge management.

Duality of Knowledge Creation

Where knowledge comes from is a question beyond the scope of this chapter. However, what we would like to propose is that knowledge is created and maintained within a duality of connects and disconnects and that this duality provides not just theoretical insights, but also practical implications for those who want and/or need to manage personal knowledge. Underpinning this connective perspective on personal knowledge creation and management are the following three premises:

Premise 1: Personal knowledge is seldom, if ever, 'stand-alone' knowledge.

Premise 2: We need to be connected to create knowledge.

Premise 3: We also need periods of regenerative disconnection.

When these conditions are met, we may experience 'connective flow', which means having enough, but not too much connectivity (Kolb et al. 2008).

Following the view that knowledge, as part of all reality, is socially constructed (Berger and Luckmann 1967; Giddens 1984), our first premise reminds us that we learn in context with others. We 'stand on the shoulders of giants' when we adopt given wisdom, or rote learning. And, importantly, if our own original thoughts are to be useful to ourselves and others, they must fit within existing structures of meaning, that is, they must 'make sense' to our referent group. The second, related premise is that our processing of ideas, whether we are introverted or extroverted, normally involves an interaction – usually through conversation or reading – with others' thoughts and perspectives (Orlikowski 2002). So, the act of creating or crafting knowledge requires us to 'connect' with others, be it in face-to-face conversations, on the phone, via text messages or in virtual, mediated environments. Finally, and somewhat contradictorily, the third premise suggests that our ability to absorb and adopt new information and knowledge is enhanced by reflective learning, which generally requires some form of disconnection from others. In an increasingly interconnected world, most of us still need to disengage somewhat sometimes to 'make sense' of things, or to get perspective. We need to let our brain process the never-ending stream of information that comes our way in an ever-increasing variety of media and modes. As our globe-trotting colleagues described above know, and Peter Murphy suggests (2007), creative professional work requires an 'off' switch if we are to keep our generative juices flowing.

Dualisms and dualities have long existed in educational philosophy. As far back as Plato and Aristotle, there has been a debate about which is more important – practical experience or abstract ideas? Action or reflection? Is it our thinking that makes us human (*Je pense, donc je suis:* 'I think therefore I am'), or is it our actions ('A coward dies a thousand deaths, but a hero [acts and] tastes of death just once')? In modern times, we resolve this by saying that while action is important, reflection on our actions is the necessary ingredient for increased insight and understanding. Experiential learning models (for example Kolb 1976), incorporate action and reflective components, that is, action, reflection, conceptualization (generalization) and active experimentation, which leads back to further action, and so on. The crux of the experiential learning model, however, is the action–reflection nexus, which constitutes a 'duality'. Whereas a 'dualism' portrays phenomena as mutually exclusive, that is, 'individuals' and 'groups', a duality highlights the interaction of the concepts, that is, individuals constitute and thereby determine the nature of the group, while the group simultaneously shapes, constrains and enables individual actions (Jackson 1999).

So, to generate knowledge, we as individuals act, which stimulates our thinking about our actions, which in turn affects our subsequent actions, upon which we reflect and modify our actions, and so on. You might also say that some of us think about something. We then try out our ideas by experimenting (putting ideas into action). We analyse the data from our experiments/trials, modify our next experiments, and so on, learning as we go through systematic (or random) trial and error, with our understanding and wisdom hopefully increasing over time. In a positive 'virtuous circle', action and experience stimulate our thinking and thinking stimulates us to act, thereby gaining more experience, and so on. But, in a negative 'vicious cycle' scenario, we can have a bias toward action that means we go, go, go, but seldom stop to reflect on our actions. Or, conversely, we think about doing something, but never get around to doing it. Both have negative effects on learning and knowledge, not to mention embedded existential dilemmas, mindless busyness vs fruitless procrastination.

From the action/reflection duality of learning, if we accept that knowledge creation and management also take place in relationship with others, then another underlying duality is based on the myriad connects and disconnects that take place between individuals and groups. Here, we can apply a 'connectivity' lens, suggesting that 'connects' and 'disconnects' occur at all levels of social and technical interaction (Kolb 2008), as shown in Table 8.1.

Table 8.1   Dimensions and duality of connectivity

Dimension	Connects	Disconnects
Geophysical	Sail and steam ships, rail, air travel facilitate exchange at reasonable cost.	Enduring effects of spatial distance and local context; global risk deters physical travel.
Technical	Internet, satellite, wireless mobile technologies increasingly affordable and accessible.	Unevenness of Internet use and reliability, technical gaps still persist and plague most users.
Interpersonal	Personal wireless communication devices (for example mobile phones), cyberspace offers endless opportunities to connect with others from anywhere to anywhere on the Internet.	Isolation, alienation, avoidance of 'real life', individualism, language differences; struggle for identity within a vast number of 'others'.
Group	Advances in remote communication devices, ubiquitous Internet, email access, better understanding of virtual teams.	Control, trust issues, leadership in virtual environments, social preferences for face-to-face.

Organizational	Globalizing markets, consolidation, alliances and hard networks, increasing reliance on information as 'means *and* end' of productivity, flexible work arrangements, anytime/anywhere.	Communication challenges, social needs, power, need for context, structure; higher complexity, legacy systems, customer needs and preferences, technical limitations, and so on.
Networks	Compelling business case for collaboration, 'Rise of the Network Society' (Castells 1996, 2000); networks increasingly personal, ubiquitous.	Internet as medium, not network; distribution effects do not ensure efficacy.
Economic	Globalization of trade, market convergence, economies of scale and scope, lower transaction costs, start-up firms 'born global'.	Trade barriers, regulation, customer needs and preferences, limits to growth, local (cluster) advantages.
Cultural	Internet as cross-cultural, 'neutral' space, convergence, alignment, homogeneity of values, norms and worldviews, 'global culture'.	Cross-cultural communication problems, resistance to globalization, resistance to cultural hegemony, resurgence of local identities, loyalty.
Political	Supra-national alliances, allegiances, NGOs, grassroots participation on the Internet.	Global risk, wars, grassroots resistance to globalizing forces, global powers reinforcing territoriality.
Philosophical	New forms of communitarianism; we are already close to those we care about; we are all in this together.	Fear of lost identity; individualism, sectarianism, fundamentalism; we are each alone, existential angst.

Source: Kolb (2008).

At a personal level, the duality of connectivity means that individuals must connect with others to gain existing knowledge (rote learning; normative education), explore and expand the known into new realms (research and development) and/or create integrated combinations of knowledge for holistic outcomes (cross-functional collaboration). At the same time, individuals will experience 'disconnects' in one form or another. For our global nomadic friends, the whole range of connects and disconnects shown in Table 8.1 may arise during their international cross-cultural business consulting practice. They may be stopped at borders, face philosophical indifference to their consulting methods, bureaucratic gaps in and between organizations, and so on. Their ongoing challenge is to transport, translate and integrate their personal knowledge from their heads and hard drives across borders, time zones, organizational and institutional boundaries, economic barriers and philosophical chasms to connect with their clients, who to some, but perhaps a lesser, extent have to bridge similar connective gaps in order to take on board the consultants' knowledge and process expertise.

The bedevilling aspect of the connectivity duality is that it is not a fixed state, that is it does not remain intact forever. As discussed below, connectivity comes and goes. As any knowledge worker knows, one day you are making great connections (physical and intellectual) and the next you feel disconnected and isolated. This is indeed a dynamic duality, not even a continuum where you shift and stay on one end or the other. Indeed, the more you connect on one dimension, the more disconnection you may experience on another. For example, the more effort one puts into travel to meet others face-to-face (geophysical) and/or the more one uses ICTs for communication (technical), the more one's interpersonal, group or organizational connectivity may suffer from disconnects. We all know someone whose personal connections seem to exist primarily through a computer screen and who subsequently struggles to stay connected to others who are physically proximal, that is, sitting right next to them! So the cubicle dweller is often no more closely connected than the remote teleworker, and neither can take their connectivity for granted.

Managing connects and disconnects begins with an understanding of their underlying duality. And seeing the many dimensions on which we connect and disconnect with others can offer a perspective on the challenges and opportunities of making and keeping social and technical links vital for personal and work life. The fact that geophysical and technical connections are outnumbered by social dimensions reflects the reality that connectivity is largely socially constructed (Orlikowski 1992) and therefore is dependent on the number, type and quality of social relationships we have. But connectivity is a more comprehensive metaphor than just social networking (Cross et al. 2002; Granovetter 1973) and a more dynamic one than the network society (Castells 1996, 2000). As will be shown below, the attributes of connectivity make it more challenging than merely having more contacts in your email contacts list. As stated in Premise 3 above, connectivity-as-duality suggests that we must accept and manage the disconnects as effectively as we manage the connects. We return to the issue of personal disconnectivity for reflection, generative and regenerative knowledge management later in this chapter. But first let us look at some other attributes of connectivity as they pertain to personal knowledge management.

Connective Attributes

In addition to the fundamental connective dualities that exist on multiple dimensions, there are other attributes of the connectivity metaphor that also apply to personal knowledge management. These attributes include 'latent potentiality', 'actor agency', 'temporal intermittency' and 'unknowable pervasiveness' (Kolb 2008, p. 129) and can be applied to personal knowledge management, as shown in Table 8.2.

Table 8.2   Implications of connectivity attributes

Attribute of connectivity	Implications for personal knowledge management
Latent potentiality	Networks reside in the background until we bring them into the foreground; the power of connectivity may be actively used or may lie dormant.
Actor agency	Individuals can and do choose when, how and how much to connect with others.
Temporal intermittency	Connective time is never totally seamless or continuous; time zones, asynchronous media and human biological patterns (e.g., sleep) interrupt even the most robust form of technical connection.
Unknowable pervasiveness	Technical connections link us to unknown others; many forms of connective media (forwarded email, web pages, blogs, social networking sites) easily and often extend beyond a known (or desired) recipient audience.

To illustrate the attributes of connectivity, let us leave our global nomads and feature the humble cubicle worker. On the one hand, the knowledge worker in an open plan office faces the lowest barriers and least obstacles (physically at least) to making collaborative contact with those around her/him in order to share and create new knowledge. On the other hand, the attributes of connectivity described in Table 8.2 suggest why this is still a problematic non-trivial exercise in some instances. As a thought experiment, let us consider an open plan office with 20 people working at individual desks in cubicle structures (a common call centre-type arrangement). The physical propinquity of the group is high and let us assume they are working on a fast local area network (LAN) with high-speed Internet access, so technical connectivity is state-of-the-art.

The first attribute of connectivity to consider in our hypothetical office is *latent potentiality*. This suggests that if we assume everyone in the room has something to offer everyone else in the room (*potential*, from the Latin root for 'power' or 'life'), that 'something', be it knowledge, power, influence or social support, is not always activated. It is latent, underlying, but not in use. In short, it is there, but not activated. At the moment when a technical resource (like a fact or figure) or some social support (over a cup of coffee or tea or lunch) is required, the connectivity is mobilized to deliver. A question may be yelled across the room (or just as likely sent by email or instant messaging) for the fact or figure to be extracted from the group. Or a call, 'who wants lunch?' may similarly be yelled or emailed or messaged throughout the Cubicle Clan to find a friendly partner or foraging party for an expedition down the hall or across the street. Of course, the connective range of this group might extend far beyond the cubicle walls, in which case, in a similar fashion it can lie dormant and silent for long periods of time (years, in fact), and yet may be mobilized for its potential at the moment it is deemed necessary or desired.

Actor agency conjures up the 600-year debate about the nature of human 'free will'. To what extent can we 'act alone', and to what extent are we constrained by the conventions and normative pressures of the crowd, the mob and/or the social groups to whom we belong? As one Dilbert cartoon portrayed it, the boss encourages virtual work and the cubicle dweller responds by being 'offline' while making faces at the boss through a glass window with the door locked between them. The boss declares, 'I think we have a problem'. Actor agency is at the heart of distributed knowledge work, in that we must rely on highly independent individuals to choose to work together for some corporate or collective goal. This is the managerial challenge. However, from the workers' point of view, ubiquitous connectivity offers both a blessing and a curse, wherein we can work anywhere we like, but also anytime we like and the time can get out of hand. The good news is that rather than being an uncontrollable intrusion into our personal lives, knowledge workers can accept and achieve this connective balancing act, if we take our ability to disconnect as seriously as we take all the opportunities and pressures to connect (Cousins and Robey 2005).

Temporal intermittency means that connectivity is not perfectly continuous and that connective gaps can exist in any medium and/or any social dimension. Servers go down, mobile (cell) phone coverage is spotty and technical glitches often take time out of the knowledge workers' day (Brown and Duguid 2000). Moreover, returning to our illustrative collocated workplace, the workers in Cubicleland must go home to sleep and the exceptions (like the occasional 'all nighter' or summer interns getting couches to sleep on at certain software houses) do not disprove the rule that we cannot stay connected 24/7, despite the popularity of that concept. Of course, the flip side of temporal intermittency is that work can be shifted to 'follow the sun' in other parts of the world overnight, so that the project or workflow never sleeps. But despite their positive opportunities, time zone differences are probably still the temporal gap that plagues knowledge workers the most. For example, in the author's collaboration from New Zealand with colleagues on the west coast of the US, we sometimes end up with virtual meetings with our host research organizations mid-morning Friday in Seattle, which can be 5 a.m. on a Saturday morning in New Zealand!

The connective attribute of *unknowable pervasiveness* strikes us when a blogger comments on the products we design, the way we manage or the courses we teach. Or, when we go for a job interview and the interviewer brings up our Facebook photos from a big night out – one we wish we could delete in more ways than one. The desirability of a pervasive Internet has set the developed and developing world into a frenzy of wiring the world together. However, the unknowable extent of ubiquitous connections that are being unknowably linked to us gives cause for concern. At a personal level, if knowledge is personal, yet collaborative and shared, when the blurred line between 'personal' and 'shared' (or found, discovered, exhumed, and so on) gets crossed, the basis for cooperation, that is, respect, honour and mutual accountability, quickly dissipates. Managing personal knowledge becomes imperative in a world where we cannot know all the people who can 'know' us through connective media. Living in a connected world makes it easier to become a cyber celebrity, but at the same time, it is also much easier to become a victim of cyber-stalking.

Finding Flow

In seeking to understand how connectivity affects team performance, we have developed a model of 'requisite connectivity', which suggests that both conditions of too little (hypo-) and too much (hyper-) connectivity are associated with lower team performance. As shown in Figure 8.1, 'requisite connectivity' occurs as a *threshold* condition of sufficient connectivity for the purpose at hand and also as an *optimal* condition, which we call 'connective flow', which borrows from the psychological concept of 'flow' (Csikszentmihalyi 1990). 'Connective flow' is a 'sweet spot' of sufficient connectivity for the situation, but not so much as to be a distraction.

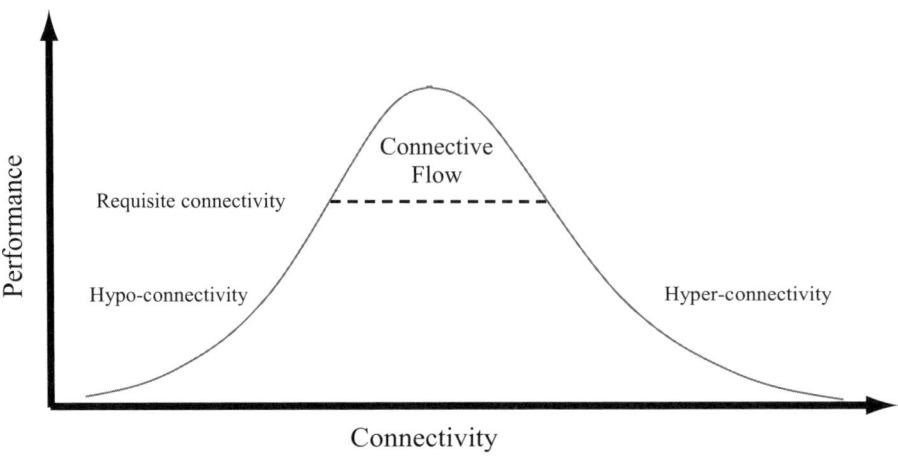

Figure 8.1   Requisite connectivity model
Source: Kolb, Collins and Lind (2008)

Our study of distributed product development and project teams has provided evidence of a strong, positive correlation between connective flow and team performance. Our sample includes concurrent engineering projects, multi-site product development programmes, professional services and other knowledge-intensive work around the globe, including participants in Auckland, Bangalore, Boston, China, Hyderabad, Jakarta, Kuala Lumpur, Seattle, Singapore and Sydney.

There are a few points to make regarding connective flow. First, while 'requisite connectivity' may be achieved and may endure throughout the lifespan of a team (and hopefully it does), the optimal condition of 'connective flow' is more fleeting and ephemeral. Like connectivity in general, it comes and it goes. Even successful collaborative teams can experience too much or too little connectivity at times and cannot take requisite or optimal connectivity for granted. Secondly, while relatively fragile in some teams, connective flow is nonetheless a worthy goal for collaborative learning and distributed knowledge work. This is because when we are not worried about making contact or not hearing from colleagues (hypo-connectivity) and also not overwhelmed with the number of emails, phone calls and text messages we have to respond to before we can 'get down to work' (hyper-connectivity), we are able to be more productive. This allows us to focus on tasks that are built upon, but also go beyond, communication – tasks involving idea generation, creative problem-solving and/or strategic thinking. Thirdly, teams who choose to or are forced to work in zones of hypo- or hyper-connectivity may still get things done, but they are simply not as efficient or effective as teams that are experiencing connective flow. Efficient but ineffective teams may use 'cut and divide' approaches to collaboration, such as often occurs in student learning teams, where the team wants to hold a minimal number of team meetings while still achieving input from each team member to offset social loafing. Meanwhile, many professionals find themselves in teams which are highly inefficient in terms of wasted time, off-topic socializing and/or poor leadership, but the team is effective, largely due to the competence, commitment and professionalism of its individual members. Despite the long hours, they ultimately 'get it done right!'

While ours is a team-level study, we have heard the professional knowledge workers in our study refer to the practical challenges and solutions associated with managing communication within a distributed work environment. Some of these practices will be discussed below, but the gist of what we have learned is that, notwithstanding national, organizational and team culture, each individual interprets and responds to connective demands differently. However, individuals generally experience the connective states portrayed in our model, namely hypo-connectivity, hyper-connectivity and to some extent requisite connective flow. Requisite connectivity is lost when projects break down or go bad. Leaders of distributed teams have the added challenge of initiating and maintaining connectivity within the team, often in addition to their technical contribution as engineer or consultant. While leading online goes beyond the scope of this chapter, it is likely to become an increasingly important issue in distributed work contexts and mediated organizational communication networks (Cummings 2008; Weisband 2008).

Managing Connective Flow

If we take the duality (connects and disconnects) of connectivity and learning seriously, what practices might help us better create and manage personal knowledge? What are some 'simple rules' that can help us maintain connective flow? The following list of recommended practices come from our studies of connectivity in distributed work teams, plus the reflections and suggestions of executives, owner-managers and independent knowledge workers over the years we have been studying this phenomenon.

PRACTICE 1: THINK AND CREATE WHEN YOU'RE AT YOUR BEST

Using a Work Style Analysis or other tool, find out when your brain is at its best for creative, generative work and use that insight to manage your task priority. For example, if you are most creative in the morning, do your creative work then, and do email and more mundane tasks after lunch.

PRACTICE 2: JUST SAY 'NO' TO HYPER-CONNECTIVITY

Exercising personal choice (actor agency) means making choices! You can decide when 'enough is enough'. And, you can (generally) say 'no' to too much connectivity. However, the choice is yours to make. No one else is going to look at your inbox and decide how much is too much.

PRACTICE 3: NO MEANS NO (MOST OF THE TIME)

Making personal choices doesn't need to make you rigid. The one thing we understand about connective flow is that it is contextual and contingent. The 'right' amount depends on the circumstances and situation. Genuine work or personal crises may require 24/7 contact, but the idea is to not be constantly in crisis mode.

PRACTICE 4: RESPECT OTHERS' REFLECTIVE SPACE

If it works for you, why not respect others who also need to reflect and recharge their batteries? In fact, if you are a manager and you can spread the practice of generative knowledge work, you are likely to get a higher performing team.

PRACTICE 5: EXPECT AND MANAGE YOUR CONNECTIVE EMOTIONS

Change often presents a personal challenge and changing your communication practices may bring a fear of missing out, and/or feelings of isolation, anxiety and loneliness. We can become vulnerable to the suspicion that if others can live without my constant input, what is the value of my ideas and expertise? Don't dwell on them, but also don't disengage from your emotions around connective practice; admit and process them with trusted peers and/or seek professional support.

Conclusion

The irony of personal knowledge management is that while there is no such thing as 'stand-alone' knowledge, each of us must, to greater or lesser degrees, stand alone to create knowledge through reflective and regenerative practices. As we reach the point where more and more of the world's population is connected, we must now consider the benefits of being disconnected – at least some of the time. While only a small percentage of the population ever 'drop out' and become hermits, it might also be said that few of us can live the realities of 24/7 ubiquitous networks and social networking. Converting experience and action into knowledge and wisdom has always been a challenge for humankind. Currently, as information is literally overflowing around and over us, we must seek connective states that allow us to gather information and experience and process it into knowledge and meaning. Applying a lens of connectivity to personal knowledge management, we can see multiple dimensions, each with connects and disconnects to be managed. We also see attributes that explain why managing connectivity is no mean feat. To say that connectivity is both a blessing and a curse is an understatement. However, it is a good place to start.

References

Berger, P. and Luckmann, T. (1967), *The Social Construction of Reality* (New York: Anchor Books).

Brown, J. and Duguid, P. (2000), *The Social Life of Information* (Boston: Harvard Business School Press).

Castells, M. (1996), *The Rise of the Network Society* (Oxford: Blackwell).

—— (2000), *The Rise of the Network Society*, 2nd edn, Vol. 1 (Oxford: Blackwell).

Cousins, K. and Robey, D. (2005), 'Human Agency in a Wireless World: Patterns of Technology Use in Nomadic Computing Environments', *Information and Organization* 15:2, 151–80.

Cross, R. et al. (2002), 'Six Myths about Informal Networks – And How to Overcome Them', *MIT Sloan Management Review* 43:3, 67–74.

Csikszentmihalyi, M. (1990), *Flow: The Psychology of Optimal Experience* (New York: Harper and Row).

Cummings, J. (2008), 'Leading Groups from a Distance: How to Mitigate Consequences of Geographic Dispersion', in S. Weisband (ed.), *Leadership at a Distance: Research in Technologically-Supported Work* (New York: Lawrence Erlbaum Associates).

Giddens, A. (1984), *The Constitution of Society: Outline of the Theory of Structuration* (Oxford: Polity Press).

Granovetter, M. (1973), 'The Strength of Weak Ties', *American Journal of Sociology*, 78:6, 1360–80.

Jackson, W. (1999), 'Dualism, Duality and the Complexity of Economic Institutions', *International Journal of Social Economics* 26:4, 545–58.

Kolb, D.G. (2008), 'Exploring the Connectivity Metaphor: Attributes, Dimensions and Duality', *Organization Studies* 29:1, 127–44.

—— Collins, P.D. and Lind, E.A. (2008), 'Requisite Connectivity: Finding Flow in a Not-So-Flat World', *Organizational Dynamics* 37:2, 181–9.

Kolb, D.A. (1976), 'Management and the Learning Process', *California Management Review* 18:3, 21–31.

Murphy, P. (2007), 'You Are Wasting My Time: Why Limits on Connectivity Are Essential for Economies of Creativity', *University of Auckland Business Review* 9:2, 17–26.

Orlikowski, W. (1992), 'The Duality of Technology: Rethinking the Concept of Technology in Organizations', *Organization Science* 3:3, 398–427.

—— (2002), 'Knowing in Practice: Enacting a Collective Capability in Distributed Organizing', *Organization Science* 13:3, 249–74.

Weisband, S. (ed.) (2008), *Leadership at a Distance: Research in Technologically-Supported Work* (New York: Lawrence Erlbaum Associates).

9

No Knowledge but through Information

William Jones

Introduction

What should personal knowledge management (PKM) be about? What should personal information management (PIM) be about? How should the two relate? As areas of study, should one subsume the other? Or should each be regarded as a separate area of inquiry? If so, where do areas overlap?

This chapter is about definitions, but the intent is not to arrive at formally 'correct' or even consensual definitions. Instead, the focus is on useful definitions and the useful distinctions made by these definitions. Definitions for phrases like PKM and PIM are not 'out there' awaiting our discovery. Rather, these definitions are for us to invent to serve our purpose. Good definitions are a lens giving greater focus to our research and greater clarity in the interpretation of results. We seek to understand. But we also expect that better understanding leads eventually to greater utility.

For example, we want to manage better, but management – whether management of information or knowledge or the detritus in a garage – is a means to an end. In companies, better management of information and knowledge should translate to various intermediate measures with enduring impact on the bottom line. Better management means better communication, better cooperation, better sharing of expertise so that, for example, the working time of people in the company is angled more towards useful products and services and less towards the maintenance of bureaucratic routine.

At a personal level, we want to manage so that our resources – our money, energy, attention and, above all, our non-renewable time – are put to better use in accomplishing our life's goals, fulfilling our life's roles (as spouse, parent, friend, employee and so on) and meeting our life's challenges (the challenge of raising a family, the challenge of a life-threatening disease, the challenge of old age).

This chapter argues for the following:

1. *Information is a thing; knowledge is not.* Information as thing (Buckland 1991) can be pointed to and experienced (or ignored). Information can take form in information items such documents or email messages, which can be modified, stored, retrieved, sent, received, deleted and otherwise manipulated (Jones 2007). Knowledge as 'no thing' (Zins 2007) cannot be experienced directly. Knowledge cannot be examined. Knowledge is embedded, distributed. Knowledge is hidden. Knowledge is inferred through its impact on observable behaviours (information). Knowledge cannot be represented directly. All attempts to represent knowledge give us information in one form or another.

2. *There is no management of knowledge except through the management of information.* If knowledge lies hidden, not to be experienced directly but rather to be inferred, then knowledge management must, to a large extent, be about its elicitation as information which can then be managed directly. Knowledge management also encompasses efforts to move in the other direction – from information to knowledge. For example, a company develops a new set of 'best practices'. Knowledge management includes various uses of information aimed at effecting a change in the attitudes and behaviour of people within the company. Best practices are expressed not only in a formal document (which few will ever read) but also in posters displayed on cubicle dividers, in broadcast email announcements and in a film that employees are required to see as a group and discuss afterwards.

3. *PKM is a very useful subset of PIM.* Personal information management is a large area. How does a person – any of us – make use of information to accomplish a life's goals, fulfil a life's roles and meet a life's challenges? How – with better tools, techniques, training,

policies, procedures, strategies, organizational schemes, and so on – might we do this better? Personal knowledge management as a subset of PIM gives additional focus. What do we know? Do we know what we think we know? Are we under-selling or over-selling ourselves? What should we be learning? How should we be learning so that the knowledge we need is integrated into our everyday lives? At the same time, PIM, as a superset of PKM, provides additional grounding. All of our feats of PKM will be accomplished, necessarily, through the use of information.

The remainder of the chapter will explore each statement in turn.

Information is a Thing; Knowledge is Not

What's the difference between information and knowledge? The question endures. Zins (2007) describes the results of a survey of 57 respected experts in information science from 16 separate countries. Each was asked to define the terms 'data', 'information' and 'knowledge'. Some participants asserted directly the ordering we often observe implicitly as in 'Information is the end product of data processing. Knowledge is the end product of information processing' (482). Others asserted that such an ordering is a 'fairy tale' (481).

Whether or not the ordering is correct, information would appear to play a pivotal role in efforts to understand both data and knowledge. In the Zins report, definitions for 'data' and 'information', though distinct, frequently overlap. Likewise, definitions for 'information' and 'knowledge' overlap. For no participant, however, is there any evidence for an overlap between or confusion among the terms 'data' and 'knowledge'.

What is information? This question has been a repeated topic of discussion in its own right (Machlup 1983; Braman 1989; Buckland 1991, 1997; Cornelius 2002; Capurro and Hjørland 2003). Buckland (1991), after an analysis of the many senses in which the word is used, concludes that 'we are unable to say confidently of anything that it could not be information' (256).

Indeed, the efforts people make to understand their world are usefully characterized as acts of information processing (for example, Broadbent 1958). According to this view, our intelligence comes from our ability to process the raw data received through our senses into concepts, patterns and implications. Everything 'out there' that we are able to perceive is potential information.

Whether sensory data actually yields information depends. The seminal work of Shannon (1948) and Shannon and Weaver (1949) introduced the notion that the information content of a message or event can be measured according to its impact on a recipient's uncertainty. The message that 'Bob is coming to the meeting' has no information value, for example, if its intended recipient knows this already or if the message is given to the recipient in a language they do not understand. In neither case does the message do anything to reduce the recipient's 'uncertainty' concerning who will be attending the meeting.

But making information exclusively about the reduction of uncertainty has come to be seen as overly restrictive (see Aftab et al. 2001; Cornelius 2002; Capurro and Hjørland 2003). An exchange of information has a sender as well as a recipient, for example, and the exchange is not always collaborative. The sender may intend to 'clarify the situation' and so reduce the recipient's uncertainty, but of course the sender may have many other intentions. The sender may want to impress or persuade. The sender may want to increase the recipient's uncertainty ('have you considered these other possibilities...'). The sender may even want to confuse or deceive.

Expressions of intention occur often in the definitions of information provided by participants in the study described by Zins. Intention provides us with one way to distinguish information from data. Information is 'the intentional composition of data by a sender with the goal of modifying the knowledge state of an interpreter or receiver' (485). Information is 'data arranged or interpreted ... to provide meaning' (486).

A thing can be information or informative from the standpoint of the sender and gibberish or a non-event from the standpoint of intended recipient. I click the 'OK' button on a website with the intention of making a hotel reservation. As far as I'm concerned the choices I've made as summarized on the web page are information. But there is no information on the recipient's side if the transmission doesn't arrive, arrives garbled or is overlooked. To take another example, depending upon our life philosophy or religious conviction, we may or may not see nature as an intentional agent in the transmission of information. Regardless, we express the intention to treat sensory data as information when we say things like 'What is my body/this tree/the sky/this room trying to tell me?'

Just as the context-dependent notions of intention, uncertainty and meaning can be used to distinguish information from data, information as 'out there' can be distinguished from knowledge as 'in here'. Participants in the Zins report describe knowledge as 'embodied in humans', 'assimilated' (480), 'in the mind of the knower' (481), 'held in human brains' (483), 'the interiorized content of information' (485), 'internalized or understood information' (486).

Information as external is also 'information as thing' (Buckland 1991). With reference to this slant on information, one participant in the Zins study referred to knowledge as 'no thing' (481). Blair (2002) explores the 'thingness' of data, information and knowledge through their substitution for one another in sentences such as 'Put the data on the desk' or 'Get the data and fax it to New York' (1020). 'Information' substitutes readily for 'data'. But 'knowledge' does not.

We acquire information quickly; we acquire knowledge only gradually. We can, for example, quickly acquire a book of German grammar and a German-English dictionary, but we acquire the ability to speak German only over time. We might say 'I had the book of German grammar last week but seem to have lost it'. But we would not, unless as an aftermath of a serious stroke, say something like 'I knew how to speak German last week, but seem to have lost this ability'. Just as knowledge is acquired gradually, we can also speak of its gradual loss. We might say, for example, 'I knew how to speak German in college but seem to have lost this knowledge over the years'.

Knowledge is everywhere, but nowhere in particular. Knowledge is distributed. We have knowledge. But rats too acquire a kind of knowledge as they learn, for example, to complete a maze. As Lashley (1950) made apparent in a famous series of experiments, this knowledge is not a thing that can be excised from the hapless rat through surgery. Performance on the maze degrades only gradually as a function of the amount of brain tissue removed. The knowledge is apparently distributed throughout the cortex of an animal.

Larger assemblies of organisms, organizations of people and whole societies can also be seen to embody various kinds of knowledge. In his careful study of navigational activities on a carrier ship, for example, Hutchins (1994) described an organic process in which different abilities and responsibilities were distributed among the crew in a redundant fashion. This overlap in responsibilities and training procedures gave the ship as a whole an ability to repair and recover from losses in individual personnel.

Knowledge is not a thing to be managed directly. Knowledge is managed only indirectly through information. As one participant writes 'Knowledge is not transferable, but through information we can communicate about it' (Zins 2007, 486). Another participant writes 'represented knowledge is information' (481).

Consider the example of a manager who wishes to instil in their staff the knowledge of a new procedure of cost accounting. The manager's objective is that staff will follow this new procedure. One might wish there were a simple 'neural plug-in' that could be applied to each member of staff to accomplish the desired change. But this is not possible. Instead, the manager must use various forms of information. The new procedure is introduced in a meeting. It is reinforced through email reminders and through diagrams posted around the office. Sticky notes could even be placed on the sides of display screens used by staff.

Speeches in meetings, email messages, paper notes that stick – the manager uses these and other forms of information as part of the intention to communicate new procedures and to effect a change that is eventually internalized in the staff.

These efforts will be judged a success when staff observe changes of procedure as a matter of course. Knowledge is, as O'Dell et al. say, 'information in action' (1998, 5). Similarly, we might say that information is 'data in motion' – data communicated, data sent or received with intention.

Alas, notwithstanding the manager's intentions when sending directives, to some of the staff these may be better described as data – ignored or not understood and certainly having no impact on their behaviour or ways of thinking.

Will a message have a desired impact on its intended recipients? Obviously, the answer depends upon the content of a message. Some changes in office procedure are much easier to communicate and instil than others. But messages of roughly the same content can have very different impact depending upon attributes of their packaging and delivery.

Elsewhere, I have defined two terms that are useful in this chapter's discussion:

> *An **information item** is a packaging of information as a thing.*
> *Examples of information items include: 1. paper documents, 2. electronic*

*documents, digital photographs, digital music, digital film and other files, 3. email messages, 4. web pages or 5. references (for example, shortcuts, aliases) to any of the above. Items encapsulate information in a persistent form that can be created, modified, stored, retrieved, given a name, tags and other properties, moved, copied, distributed, deleted and otherwise manipulated. An information item has an associated **information form** which is determined by the tools and applications that support these operations. Common forms of information include paper documents, e-documents and other files, email messages and web bookmarks.*

(Jones 2007, 37)

The office manager uses at least three forms of information to communicate a change in office procedure: (1) the spoken words of a meeting, (2) an email announcement and (3) sticky notes. The second and third are information items. The first is not (though its digital recording would be).

The ways in which an item is manipulated will vary depending upon its form and the tools available for this form. The tools used for interaction with paper-based information items include, for example, paper clips, staplers, filing cabinets and the flat surfaces of a desktop. In interactions with digital information items, we depend upon the support of various computer-based tools and applications such as email applications, file managers, Web browsers, and so on. The ways we delete a paper document differ from the ways we delete an electronic document (for example, tossing in the trash or shredding vs using 'Cut' or 'Delete') but some notion of deleting applies to each (a similarity the Macintosh reinforces through its metaphorical 'trash can').

The information item establishes a manageable level of abstraction for discussions of information and knowledge management. There are, for example, many essential similarities in the way people interact with information items, regardless of their form. Whether people are looking at a new email message in their inbox, a newly discovered website or the business card they have just been handed at a conference, many of the same basic decisions must be made: 'Is this relevant (to me)? To what does it relate? Do I need to act now or can I wait? If I wait, can I get back to this item later? Where should I put it? Will I remember to look?'

A person's interactions with information will also vary greatly depending upon its form. Interactions with incoming email messages, for example, are often driven by the expectation of a timely response and perhaps also by the awareness that, when an email message scrolls out of view without some processing, it is apt to be quickly forgotten. A paper printout of the same message may be easier to read at an opportune moment (for example, while stuck in traffic or standing in the subway) but the printout is also more difficult to retrieve later if misplaced.

Some forms of information favour the sender, others the receiver (see Grudin 1988). For example, we usually speak more quickly and easily than we write so that as senders of information, we may prefer the spoken to the written word. But as recipients of information, we generally read faster than we listen. Moreover, we can skim and skip through written information – something not easily done with an oral recording. Asymmetries between sender and recipient in the costs and benefits of different forms of information have implications for both information and knowledge management, which are explored further in the next section.

There is no Management of Knowledge Except through a Management of Information

'Management' comes from 'manage', which derives from the Latin *'manus'* – hand.[1] The management practised by many of our forbears, those with no staff to order, was necessarily hands on. My grandfather was a dairy farmer. His management of his livestock and his crops was literally 'hands on'. The same could be said for my grandmother as she managed the household. Or of the grocer who managed his store in town.

In our time, the expression 'hands-on style of management' is not a redundancy nor even meant to be taken literally. Managers who are 'hands-on' are more directly involved with their staff and with day-to-day details. Managers who literally manage their staff with the use of their hands run the serious risk of being sued for harassment.

But we are still quite literally hands-on in many of our efforts to manage information. We compose an email message with finger presses into the keyboard and then we send the email with a click of the mouse button. Likewise, we use our hands on keyboard and mouse to work with electronic documents and with web pages. We make printouts for an even more direct interaction with our information. Paper forms of information endure (Sellen and Harper 2002)

---

1   Sources used for definitions are the online services, Merriam-Webster OnLine (http://www. merriam-webster.com/dictionary/) and Wiktionary (http://en.wiktionary.org/wiki).

in large measure for their hands-on affordances. Paper and the means to write on paper with pencil or pen are nearly always at hand. Paper can be folded, torn and thrown away. Writing, sketching or doodling on paper is easy and satisfying. There is a 'feel' to paper that we may never achieve with digital forms of information.

Knowledge as 'no thing' cannot be managed directly. If we think we have knowledge 'at our fingertips' we are most likely touching information in some form instead. This is not to say that knowledge management is not possible, but we do so through its expression in information. There is no management of knowledge except through the management of information.

What are we doing when we manage information? What must we do to manage knowledge? These questions are each considered in turn.

WHAT ARE WE DOING WHEN WE MANAGE INFORMATION?

Information as data – as bits – is a resource to be managed. The DAMA International Foundation in a pamphlet provided for download from their website states that 'The basic premise of Data Management (DRM) is that information and data is like any other business resource – and should be managed as such.' (DAMA International Foundation 2005, 5). The pamphlet goes on to say that 'the amount must be optimized. In other words, the company should always have enough – but also minimize excess and redundancy' and 'resource should be shared and leveraged in as many ways as possible, in order to maximize its value while diminishing its overall costs'.

These are sensible steps for a company to take with data, information or any other resource. Steps must be taken, for example, to ensure that information is properly maintained. Information should be securely stored. Access to information should be controlled. Its use should be monitored. For information or data, viewed as a resource, considerations apply that are not that different from those that might apply to money or laptops or employee time.

But for information as 'data in motion' additional considerations arise. Information can be copied and communicated. Information is sent and received with a purpose or intention in mind. Is information getting to the right people? Is it having a desired effect? Depending upon context, depending upon the recipient, the same information may save valuable time and money or be a waste of these resources.

One of the neater definitions of management[2] is 'the judicious use of means to accomplish an end'. Mary Parker Follett, writing at the turn of the last century defined management (of people) as 'the art of getting things done through people' (Daft 1988, 5). Substitute 'information' for people and we have a nice definition for information management – the art of getting things done through information.

An ideal in information management is to have 'the right information (in the right place, in the right form, enough, not too much, and so on) to meet our current need' (Jones 2007, 7). We come closer to this ideal to the extent that we are able to create and maintain a mapping between information and need.

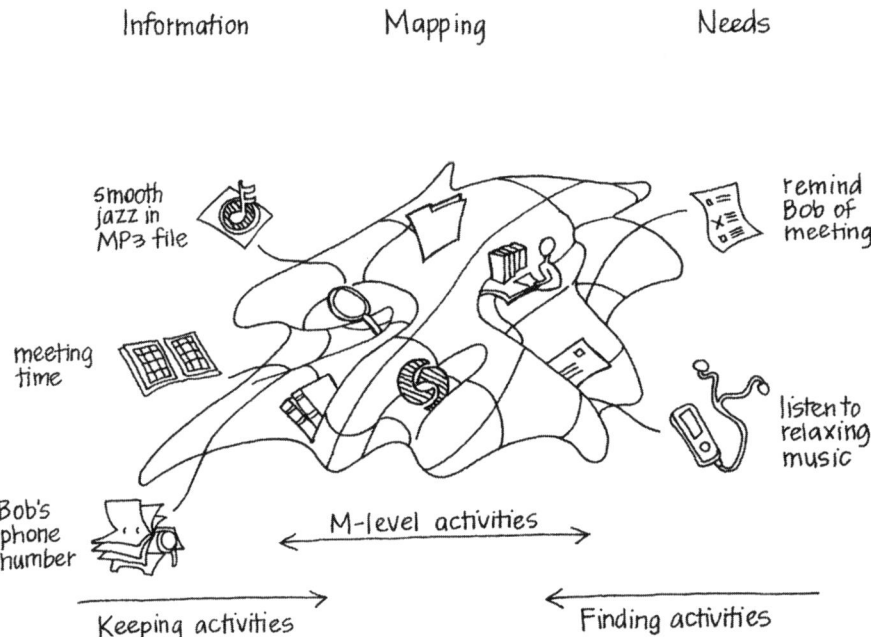

Figure 9.1   Information management activities viewed as an effort to establish, use and maintain a mapping between needs and information. Illustration by Elizabeth Boling. Variation of a figure from Jones (2007)

---

2   Found in both Merriam-Webster OnLine (http://www.merriam-webster.com/dictionary/) and Wiktionary (http://en.wiktionary.org/wiki).

A simple, stylized mapping between information and need is depicted in Figure 9.1. Only small portions of the mapping have an observable external representation. In a company or as individuals, for example, we maintain folder structure or a tagging scheme which is visible in our filing systems, digital and paper-based. However, much of a mapping has only hypothesized existence in the memories of individuals and perhaps also in the policies, procedures and daily workflows of an organization. Large portions of the mapping are potential and not realized in any form, external or internal. A sort function or a search facility, for example, has the potential to guide from a need to desired information.

With respect to the mapping, we have two basic kinds of information management activity corresponding to the two directions in which the mapping can be traversed: keeping activities attempt to take us from information encountered to anticipated need, while finding activities attempt to go in the other direction – from need to information.

Finding: from need to information

In their efforts to meet a need, people seek. People search, sort and browse. People scan through a results list or the listing of a folder's contents in an effort to recognize information items that relate to a need. These activities are all examples of finding activities. Finding is broadly defined to include both acts of new finding where there is no previous memory of having the needed information, and to include acts of re-finding. More broadly still, finding includes efforts to create the needed information as in 'finding the right words' or 'finding the right ideas'.

Keeping: from information to need

Many events of daily life are roughly the converse of finding events. Instead of having a need for which we seek information, we have information in hand and must determine what, if anything, we need to do with this information. In organizations and as individuals we encounter and generate large amounts of information. Decisions and actions are much the same no matter the information or its source. Is the information at all relevant, or potentially useful? Do we have an anticipated need for this information? What are the costs of not having this information? Some information – tax-relevant information for past years, for example – must be kept even though the likelihood that a need for this information will arise is very small since the costs of not having this information, should the need arise, are very high (Jones 2004).

Finding and keeping activities traverse the mapping in complementary directions. Four kinds of information management activity focus on the mapping itself. Elsewhere, I refer to these collectively as *meta-level activities* or, simply, 'm-level' activities (Jones 2007).

Maintaining and organizing

How do we organize information for repeated use; safeguard this information against loss; ensure that information is current and correct; update formats to keep pace with changes in standards and in supporting tools; and ensure that old information is deleted, archived or otherwise moved out the way? What about versions? What about duplicates and near-duplicates? These are all questions of maintenance and organization.

Managing privacy and the flow of information

Information management aims to ensure that the right people have the right information at the right time. But steps must also be taken to ensure that other people – the wrong people – do not also have access to this information. And how to ensure that the right people are not distracted or overwhelmed by the information they receive?

Measuring and evaluating

Choices are made in support of all the activities described so far. Schemes of organization are selected; strategies, policies and procedures are adopted; supporting tools are put in place. We then need to ask, periodically or continuously, 'is it (the resulting mapping between information and need) working? Can it work even better? If so, what should change?' These questions depend both upon the measurements we are able to make and also on the evaluations we must make in cases where measurements (and the underlying objectives these measurements reflect) are in competition with one another.

Making sense of our information

Efforts to make sense are the most 'meta' of meta-level activities. 'Does it make sense?' The question can be applied to choices made in each of the other meta-level activities. The question has broad application and reaches to deeper levels of understanding concerning ultimate goals and tradeoffs. We might hear ourselves saying something like 'I understand what you want to do but it doesn't make sense'. Choices that make sense with one need in mind, may not make sense when other needs are also considered. Does the mapping make sense? Our information is now totally secure against unauthorized access but we cannot easily access the information either. Does this make sense? We make sense of information. We use our senses. We also 'make' and manipulate. Information is a thing to be piled and sorted, arranged and rearranged. Information is a thing to be touched. Information is in the mapping. Information is also how we represent the needs of a mapping (including goals and constraints). Information, perhaps in the form of graphs, is how we represent a hierarchy of need. Information is how we represent the synergies and conflicts between needs. Information is how we represent the mapping itself. It is all information.

WHAT MUST WE DO TO MANAGE KNOWLEDGE?

To make a variation on an old joke, ask any three people involved in 'knowledge management' for a definition of same and you are likely to get three different definitions. Wait a few more minutes and you will get three more.

In his blog post, '43 knowledge management definitions – and counting…', Ray Sims (2008) documents a diversity of definitions for knowledge management. Many of the definitions seem to have little in common with each other save for the repeated use of the word 'knowledge'.

One of the better, more forthright, of the definitions comes from Levinson (2008):

> *Unfortunately, there's no universal definition of knowledge management (KM), just as there's no agreement as to what constitutes knowledge in the first place. For this reason, it's best to think of KM in the broadest context. Succinctly put, KM is the process through which organizations generate value from their intellectual and knowledge-based assets. Most often, generating value from such assets involves codifying what employees, partners and customers know, and sharing that information among employees, departments and even with other companies in an effort to devise best practices.*

The definition notes that 'generating value' (from knowledge-based assets) involves information – the 'codifying' of what people know and 'sharing that information'. We can consider KM to require two essential transformations: from knowledge to information and then, to complete the transfer of knowledge, from information back to knowledge. The first transformation is often referred to as *knowledge elicitation*. We need a name for the second transformation as well. Call it *knowledge instillation*.

Knowledge elicitation[3]

Each of us knows a lot about matters big and small. We know, for example, how to spot and move away from erratic, potentially dangerous people on a street or subway platform. We may know (not I) how to use the buttons on a video game controller. Some of this knowledge is relatively easy to express. We know to stay clear of people who are shouting and screaming. But the more knowledge is integrated into our beliefs, our judgments and our actions, the less easy it is for us to give expression to this knowledge. Polanyi (1967) makes the distinction between *explicit knowledge* – knowledge readily expressed, and *tacit knowledge* – knowledge not easily expressed. Polanyi offers, as an aphorism, that 'we know more than we can tell' (4).

We can never tell all of what we know but methods of knowledge elicitation can help us to tell *more* of what we know. A review of all the various techniques of or with potential application to knowledge elicitation is beyond the scope of this paper. Techniques involve the use of repertory grids (Kelly 1955), concept maps (Novak 1998), affinity diagramming (Bondarenko and Janssen 2005), interviews – free-form or structured and observations (for example, as an expert works through a selection of problems or cases) (Hoffman 1989). The person whose knowledge is being targeted may be asked to think aloud and a transcription of the recording of this think-aloud may later be subjected to a protocol analysis (Newell and Simon 1972).

---

3   The term *knowledge elicitation* is often used interchangeably with but is to be preferred to the terms 'knowledge acquisition' or 'knowledge capture'. These terms were used frequently in the 1980s in connection with efforts to build expert systems. Attempts were made to 'acquire' or 'capture' the knowledge of human experts for use in computer-based expert systems. However, these terms were not apt then and are even less apt now when knowledge management is more about attempts to facilitate the exchange of knowledge among people. Knowledge was never captured. Knowledge could only be said to have been acquired by an expert system after a time-consuming process of iterative tinkering of rules and representations. Whatever eventually found programmatic expression in the expert system bore only a passing resemblance to the forms of information (transcripts, rules inferred, diagrams and so on) initially used to represent the results of interviews with the expert.

A point to make is that these methods are as much, if not more, about information as about knowledge. Each method involves several forms of information. Included, to be sure, are eponymous forms of information such as concept maps, affinity diagrams and repertory grids. Information in other forms is used to set the stage for a session with the expert. And the results of this session are recorded using other forms. In sessions with an expert underwriter in which I participated, for example, the underwriter worked through a paper stack of applications for life insurance, thinking aloud as he did so. His utterances were recorded and later transcribed. Paper-based applications, cassette recordings (this was in the 1980s) and electronic transcription were each used in knowledge elicitation.

Knowledge instillation 'Instillation' comes from 'instil' as in 'to cause to become part of someone's nature'. Instillation neatly contrasts with 'installation'. Much as we might like to, we cannot simply 'install' a new body of knowledge in our brains or in an organization as we might install a new software program on our computers. Knowledge elicitation is only step one. Knowledge instillation is often the more difficult step in the transfer of knowledge. Popular books on knowledge management write of the barriers to transfer and change (for example, Argyris 1994). We read of the importance of creating a culture to promote knowledge transfer (for example, O'Dell et al. 1998) and of creating communities for the sharing of knowledge (for example, Snyder and McDermott 2002).

Challenges remain even when recipients are willing. Of potential relevance is the wealth of education research on methods of teaching and learning (see, for example, Bransford et al. 2000). Of direct relevance, for example, is an ongoing debate concerning the extent to which – putting it plainly – people can be taught or need to learn for themselves (see, for example, Duffy et al. 1993; Schwartz and Bransford 1998).

Person-to-person contact remains one of the most effective ways to transfer knowledge. In educational contexts, for example, students working with individual human tutors test at levels of performance as much as two standard deviations higher than students in a conventional classroom (Bloom 1984). Identifying expertise and locating experts is an area of research in its own right (for example, McDonald and Ackerman 2000). Now the Web provides a basis for a transfer of knowledge on a variety of topics ranging from home repair to cancer treatment.[4]

---

4   See, for example, http://www.cancercompass.com/message-board.htm.

We can also recognize that instances of KE and KI are commonplace and by no means limited to companies and classrooms. If someone asks you for directions or if you try to teach someone a skill that you have and they do not (for example, driving a car or driving a golf ball), you are doing KE. You may imagine the route or the way you drive in your 'mind's eye'. Or you may actually do the thing you mean to tell or teach. You may go to the destination or you may take the golf swing – observing your actions as you do so. In these examples, your objective is to render your skill, your knowledge, into forms of information (spoken instructions, hand gestures, re-enactments) that can be communicated to someone else. But acts of KE are only step one. Step two is for the other person to really understand, to 'get it', and not just to nod as if they do. The ultimate proof is in the action but by then the costs of failure may be too high. Managers and parents alike often apply techniques to test for transfer, such as having the intended recipient repeat the instructions or testing for choice points ('what will you do if…').

PKM is a Useful Subset of PIM

We are almost ready to address the questions posed at the outset of this chapter: what should PIM and PKM each be about and how should the two fields of study relate? But first, one more basic question. The previous section explored essential activities of information management and knowledge management. What does it mean to add 'personal' to these terms? The question is considered first for PIM and then for PKM.

SIX SENSES OF PERSONAL INFORMATION

How is information personal? Think of the possible connections between 'information' and 'me'. As summarized in Table 9.1, information can be owned by me; about me; directed towards me; sent or published by me; experienced by me or, 'relevant to' me. Each kind of personal information is briefly described in Table 9.1.

Table 9.1   The senses in which information can be personal

	Relation to 'me'	Examples	Issues
1	Controlled by, owned by me	Email messages in our email accounts; files on our computer's hard drive.	Security against break-ins or theft, back-ups, virus protection, and so on.
2	About me	Credit history, medical, Web browsing, library books checked out.	Who sees what when (under which circumstances)? How is information corrected or updated? Does it ever go away?
3	Directed towards me	Phone calls, drop-ins, TV ads, Web ads, pop-ups.	Protection of me and my money, energy, attention and time.
4	Sent (posted, provided) by me	Email, personal websites, published reports and articles.	Who sees what when? Did the message get through?
5	(Already) experienced by me	Web pages that remain on the Web; books that remain in a library; TV and radio programmes that remain somewhere in 'broadcast ether'.	How to get back to information again later?
6	Relevant (useful) to me	Somewhere 'out there' is the perfect vacation, house, job, lifelong mate, if only I could find the right information!	If only I knew (had some idea of) what I don't know; how to filter out or otherwise avoid information we do not wish to see? (How to do likewise for our children?)

Adapted from Jones (2007).

1. *Controlled by (owned by) me.* The information a person keeps, directly or indirectly (for example, via software applications), for personal use is personal information. Included are email messages in an email account, files on the hard drive of a personal computer and also the papers kept on surfaces and inside conventional filing cabinets.[5]

2. *About me.* Information about a person but available to and possibly under the control of others is a second sense of personal information. Personal information in this category includes the information about a person kept by doctors and health organizations, for example, or the information kept by tax agencies and credit bureaus.

---

5   Note that even though information is, at least nominally, under the person's control, the rights of ownership for portions of this information are sometimes in dispute. In the context of a person's work inside a company or in collaboration with others, for example, it is often unclear who owns what information.

3.   *Directed towards me.* Included in this category is the email that arrives in the inbox and also the pop-up notifications that this new email has arrived. Alerts raised by a person's computer, the 'push' of advertisements on a visited web page or the television or the radio, and the ringing telephone are all examples of information directed towards a person. The information itself may or may not be personally relevant. But the sender's intention is personal and so too is the potential impact of the information on the person. Information directed to a person can distract the person from a current task, consume a person's attention and convince the person to spend time, spend money, change an opinion or take an action. We may be inclined to think of this incoming information as a nuisance, but sometimes this information serves the recipient well – a fire alarm in the case of a burning building, for example, can be a lifesaver.

4.   *Sent (posted, provided) by me.* Information sent by the person (or posted, published) is a fourth kind of personal information. This information may or may not contain information about the person. But the person as sender is personally invested in seeing that the information gets to its intended recipients. And perhaps the person is also invested in efforts to keep the information away from other people. For example, we may try to control, albeit imperfectly, who first sees the information in an email message we send. We may try to do this through choice of distribution lists and by including notices on the email messages such as 'Confidential, please do not distribute'.

5.   *Experienced by me.* Information experienced by a person is also personal information. Some of this information is under the person's control and so also personal in the first sense of personal. Other information is not under the person's control: the book a person browses (but puts back) in a traditional library, for example, or the pages a person views on the Web. This fifth sense of personal information has special relevance to the first of two PKM questions: what do I know (already)?

6.   *Relevant (useful) to me.* A final sense in which information can be personal is determined by whether this information is relevant or useful to the person. Out there, somewhere, is an article that is

perfect for a report we are writing or an advertisement for a vacation package that perfectly fits our needs With respect to this expanded 'sixth sense' of personal, we depend upon filters both to filter in the information we would like to see and to filter out the information we do not want to see.

These broad categories have value not for what they exclude – in their union, they exclude very little. Rather, the categories each in their turn provide an important focal point for a discussion of PIM.

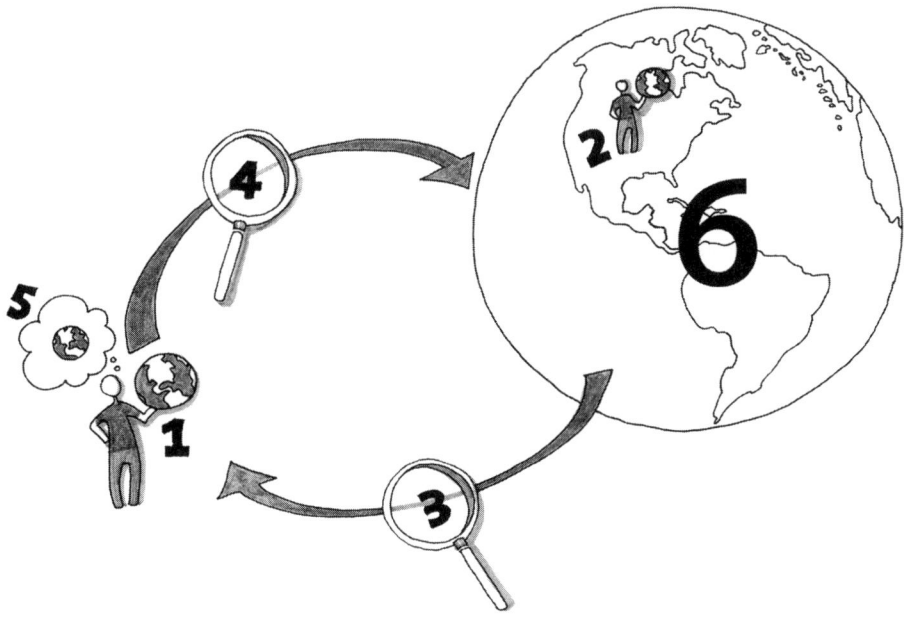

Figure 9.2   **Six senses of personal information combine to make a personal space of information (PSI). Illustration by Elizabeth Boling. Variation of a figure from Jones (2007)**

When all is added together, each of us has a unique personal space of information, or PSI, as depicted in Figure 9.2. We inhabit this space as surely as we inhabit a physical space. Our informational space affects the way we view and interact with the world(s) we inhabit. Our space of information also affects the way we are seen, categorized and treated by others.

KNOWING WHAT I KNOW; KNOWING WHAT I NEED TO KNOW

What about PKM? I described the transfer of knowledge as inevitably involving information in an intermediate stage. There is no such thing as a mind meld. The transfer is then in two parts with a different kind of knowledge management activity for each part:

1.   From knowledge to information via activities of knowledge elicitation

2.   From information to knowledge via activities of knowledge instillation

How do these activities become personal? It is not enough for these activities to be focused on an individual person. Knowledge management activities within organizations have long focused on individuals thought to have expertise that the organization as a whole could benefit from if only the knowledge could be transferred.

For activities of knowledge management to be personal, it would seem that these also need to be done by or at least initiated by the person and with the expectation that the person stands to benefit from the completion of these activities.

The self-interest in managing each of the six senses of personal information is evident as we go through the list from the first to the sixth sense of personal information. If information owned by us is not properly managed and we lose it (for example, in a disk crash) we could lose days, possibly years of work. If information about us (credit card numbers, for example) falls into the wrong hands, others could use this information to take money from us. And so on. For each sense, we can tell a story either of bad things that might happen if the information is poorly managed or the good things that might happen if the information is managed better.

Likewise, for each of the two kinds of knowledge management activity, we can ask a question that makes personal interest apparent:

*   *What do I know already?* The question has many aspects. What skills do I have? What can I 'do'? The question arises any time we look for a new job or a promotion. We do not want to over-sell our abilities

but too often we do the opposite. We under-sell our abilities not (not only) from a sense of modesty but also because much of our knowledge is deeply ingrained. To use the distinction discussed in the previous section, our knowledge is tacit and so not easily expressed for assessment.

- *What do I need to know? (What should I be learning?)* Again, using a work context, we look for the skills and know-how we should acquire either to get a better job or simply to keep the job we have. Where should we invest our time and effort? Answers depend partly on answers to the first question and partly on an assessment of the world out there. What are companies looking for? What jobs pay the best?

For purposes of illustration, these questions have been set against a backdrop of employment. But the scope of each question is broad. What do we know that might help us in social situations? What about deeply held beliefs and ways of viewing the world? How do we assess these to understand their impact in our daily lives? How do we change those that keep us from being happy? In this light, a range of insight or 'talking' therapies can be seen as a kind of PKM.

In the spirit of Mary Parker Follett's definition of management and to abbreviate a definition I have given elsewhere (Jones 2007) we can say that PIM is the artful use of information by a person to accomplish goals and fulfil roles in that person's life. PKM, in turn, would refer to a person's use of techniques of knowledge elicitation (assessment) and knowledge instillation (learning) to accomplish goals and fulfil roles in that person's life.

Techniques of PKM involve one or more forms of information. For example, journalling as a technique of personal assessment (personal knowledge elicitation) involves the journal as information (either in paper or digital form). The recital of a daily affirmation as a technique of personal change (knowledge instillation) may involve a book of affirmations as information.

Conclusion

If the term 'knowledge' is used excessively and indiscriminately when the term 'information' would do just as well, nevertheless, some useful distinctions between the terms can be drawn. One distinction says that 'knowledge' is what is in a person's head or what is embedded in a tool or a system. Knowledge is integrated and distributed. Knowledge is implicit, and difficult to articulate. It cannot be seen, 'touched' or directly manipulated.

Knowledge elicitation has been an important area of study in its own right, receiving special prominence in the 1980s with all the (mostly unmet) expectations concerning the promise of expert systems. Experts know a great deal but eliciting this knowledge in the form of rules that could be used by an expert system is not easy. This area morphed into the knowledge management movement of the 1990s with its focus on finding ways to capture, share and better leverage the knowledge embedded within corporations and other organizations (in key people, teams and processes).

By extension we can say that a key challenge of PKM is to make explicit – to elicit – the knowledge of a person. And a bigger challenge is to instil new knowledge that may give the person a better chance to meet their aims in life. The person involved is both the subject and the object of these activities. That is the 'P' in PKM. People practice activities of PKM upon themselves because they perceive a gain in doing so.

Knowledge management generates and consumes information. This is true whether the knowledge management is personal, that is, done by an individual on their behalf or corporate, that is, done by a group of people on behalf of an organization. Knowledge elicited is knowledge expressed; knowledge expressed is information. The expression may be oral or in written form. Written expression may be in plain text, if–then rules, or complicated diagrams of flow and choice points. In all cases, no matter the expression, we have information. Others may read and learn so that they acquire and internalize some reasonable facsimile of this knowledge. In this case we can say the knowledge has been transferred. But the vehicle of transfer is information.

No knowledge but through information.

References

Aftab, O. et al. (2001), *Information Theory and the Digital Age* (Cambridge: Massachusetts Institute of Technology).

Argyris, C. (1994), *Knowledge for Action* (San Francisco: Jossey-Bass).

Blair, D. (2002), 'Knowledge Management: Hype, Hope, or Help?', *Journal of the American Society for Information Science and Technology* 53:12, 1019–28.

Bloom, B. (1984), 'The 2 Sigma Problem: The Search for Methods of Group Instruction as Effective as One-To-One Tutoring', *Educational Researcher* 13:6, 4–16.

Bondarenko, O. and Janssen, R. (2005), 'Documents at Hand: Learning from Paper to Improve Digital Technologies', *CHI 2005: ACM SIGCHI Conference on Human Factors in Computing Systems, Portland* (New York: ACM Press).

Braman, S. (1989), 'Defining Information, an Approach for Policy Makers', *Telecommunications Policy* 13:3, 233–42.

Bransford, J. et al. (2000), *How People Learn: Brain, Mind, Experience, and School* (Washington: National Academies Press).

Broadbent, D. (1958), *Perception and Communication* (London: Pergamon Press).

Buckland, M. (1991), 'Information as Thing', *Journal of the American Society for Information Science* 42:5, 351–60.

—— (1997), 'What Is a Document?', *Journal of the American Society of Information Science* 48:9, 804–9.

Capurro, R and Hjørland, B. (2003), 'The Concept of Information', *Annual Review of Information Science and Technology* 37, 343–411.

Cornelius, I. (2002), 'Theorizing Information', *Annual Review of Information Science and Technology* 36, 393–425.

Daft, R. (1988), *Management*, 2nd edn (Orlando: Dryden).

DAMA International Foundation (2005), 'Model Curriculum Framework for Post Secondary Education Programs in Data Resource Management', *Proceedings of ISECON 2005, v22, Columbus OH.* http://www.dama.org/i4a/pages/index.cfm?pageid=1.

Duffy et al. (1993), *Designing Environments for Constructive Learning* (Berlin: Springer Verlag).

Grudin, J. (1988), 'Why CSCW Applications Fail: Problems in the Design and Evaluation of Organization of Organizational Interfaces', *Proceedings of the 1988 ACM Conference on Computer-supported Cooperative Work, 26–8 September, Portland* (New York: ACM Press). http://doi.acm.org/10.1145/62266.62273.

Hoffman, R. (1989), 'A Survey of Methods for Eliciting the Knowledge of Experts,' *SIGART Bulletin* 108, 19–27.

Hutchins, E. (1994), *Cognition in the Wild* (Cambridge: MIT Press).

Jones, W. (2004), 'Finders, Keepers? The Present and Future Perfect in Support of Personal Information Management', First Monday, http://www.firstmonday.dk/issues/issue9_3/jones/index.html

—— (2007), *Keeping Found Things Found: The Study and Practice of Personal Information Management* (San Francisco: Morgan Kaufmann Publishers).

Kelly, G. (1955), *The Psychology of Personal Constructs* (New York: Norton).

Lashley, K. (1950), 'In Search of the Engram', *Symposia of the Society for Experimental Biology* 4, 454–82.

Levinson, M. (2008), 'Knowledge Management Definitions and Solutions', CIO Magazine Tutorial http://www.cio.com/article/40343/Knowledge_Management_Definition_and_Solutions, accessed 31 January 2009.

Machlup, F. (1983), 'Semantic Quirks in Studies of Information', in F. Machlup and U. Mansfield (eds), *The Study of Information: Interdisciplinary Messages* (New York: Wiley).

McDonald, D. and Ackerman, M. (2000), 'Expertise Recommender: A Flexible Recommendation System and Architecture'. *CSCW '00: Proceedings of the 2000 ACM Conference on Computer Supported Cooperative Work, Philadelphia* (New York: ACM). http://doi.acm.org/10.1145/358916.358994.

Newell, A. and Simon, H. (1972), *Human Problem Solving* (Englewood Cliffs: Prentice-Hall).

Novak, J. (1998), *Learning, Creating, and Using Knowledge: Concept Maps as Facilitative Tools in Schools and Corporations* (Mahweh: Lawrence Erlbaum Associates).

O'Dell, C. et al. (1998), *If Only We Knew What We Know: The Transfer of Internal Knowledge and Best Practice* (New York: Free Press).

Polanyi, M. (1967), *The Tacit Dimension* (New York: Anchor Books).

Schwartz, D. and Bransford, J. (1998), 'A Time for Telling', *Cognition and Instruction* 16:4, 475–522.

Sellen, A. and Harper, R. (2002), *The Myth of the Paperless Office* (Cambridge: MIT Press).

Shannon, C. (1948), 'A Mathematical Theory of Communication', *The Bell System Technical Journal* 27, 379–423, 623–56.

Shannon, C. and Weaver, W. (1949), *The Mathematical Theory of Communication* (Urbana: University of Illinois Press).

Sims, R. (2008), '43 Knowledge Management Definitions – and Counting…', http://blog.simslearningconnections.com/?p=279, accessed 16 March 2008.

Snyder, W. and McDermott, R. (2002), *Cultivating Communities of Practice: A Guide to Managing Knowledge* (Boston: Harvard Business Press).

Zins, C. (2007), 'Conceptual Approaches for Defining Data, Information, and Knowledge', *Journal of the American Society for Information Science and Technology* 58:4, 479–93.

10

Personal Knowledge Management and Knowledge Worker Capabilities

Tom H. Davenport

Introduction

What is a knowledge worker?[1] There is no definitional consensus, but one definition might be as follows:

> *Knowledge workers have high degrees of expertise, education or experience, and the primary purpose of their jobs involves the creation, distribution or application of knowledge.*

Knowledge workers think for a living and live by their wits. They solve problems, they understand and meet the needs of customers, they make decisions and they collaborate and communicate extensively with other people in the course of doing their own work.

There are many examples of knowledge workers: physicians and physicists, scientists and science fiction writers, airplane pilots and airplane designers. They do not necessarily have to work in knowledge-intensive industries – managers of any company are knowledge workers, applying knowledge to make decisions in the best interests of their enterprises. Even the most industrial company has engineers, researchers, marketers and planners.

Most estimates from governments suggest that knowledge workers comprise between a quarter and a third of all workers. But regardless of

---

1   This chapter draws extensively from Davenport (2005).

the size of this category, it is a very important one. Knowledge workers are responsible for sparking innovation and growth in organizations. They invent new products and services, design marketing programmes and create new strategies. In the current economy, they are the horses that pull the plough of economic progress. If companies are going to be more profitable, if strategies are going to be successful, if societies are going to become more advanced – it will be because knowledge workers did their work in a more productive and effective manner.

There are many ways to improve the performance and productivity of knowledge workers. Simply measuring their performance is a good beginning. Their work can be viewed as a process, and improved like other processes. They can be managed more effectively. Even changes in their workspaces can lead to improvements in knowledge work. Most interventions to improve performance in business are at the organizational or process level, but it does not have to be that way. We can also improve individual capabilities. Ultimately, knowledge worker performance comes down to the behaviours of individual knowledge workers. If we improve their individual abilities to create, acquire, process and use knowledge, we are likely to improve the performance of the processes they work on, and the organizations they work for.

Finally, of course, technology can be applied to improving knowledge work. When most organizations think of technology for knowledge workers, they think either of personal information management, or of organizational knowledge management. Personal information management typically includes individual technology and communications tools, personal productivity applications such as calendaring and email, and applications to manage and locate online content. Knowledge management technologies and programmes are typically designed to improve organizational capabilities, not those of individual knowledge workers. They are built for entire organizations, or major components of them. They expect that all knowledge workers will require the same types of knowledge, and work with it in the same ways. Some emerging technologies for information and knowledge management, such as blogs and social tagging systems, blur the line between personal information management and organizational knowledge management.

A relatively unexplored approach is to apply knowledge technologies and knowledge management approaches to individual knowledge workers – what might be called personal knowledge management. This approach, the subject of this book, is focused on improving the individual-level performance of knowledge workers. It is designed to enable knowledge worker capabilities – to support their creation, distribution or application of knowledge – with individualized approaches and individual autonomy over implementation.

Of course, some organization-level knowledge management initiatives can also improve individual performance, so what is the difference? Personal knowledge management initiatives have two attributes. First, they are directly focused on improving the performance of knowledge worker employees as individuals, not as members of a larger group. A customer relationship management (CRM) programme for customer service workers does not qualify, because a number of people in that function would use it, and the system is not (or at least rarely) customized to individual needs. CRM applications are typically also more about improving transactions rather than capturing or sharing knowledge. Secondly, individual-oriented initiatives are targeted at improving some skill or capability, rather than implementing a new technology or instituting a new business process. Giving knowledge workers a new piece of hardware or software – say, a personal digital assistant or cellphone – would not qualify, but teaching them how to use these devices effectively would. Inevitably, however, personal technology applications involve both information and knowledge. My primary focus in this chapter is on content types that are relatively value added – for example, more knowledge-oriented – but in practice it is probably impossible to exclude personal information management from personal knowledge management, and most actual businesspeople do not seem to find the distinction very helpful. One's email inbox, for example, can be a repository of highly prosaic information (new cafeteria closing hours!) and deep knowledge in documents and social networks. When I address the topic of personal knowledge management below, then, I will also be referring to tools that enhance the processing of personal information.

The potential for improving knowledge worker capabilities at the personal level has been explored in a different context by the Software Engineering Institute (SEI) at Carnegie-Mellon. The SEI is well known for its Capability Maturity Model (CMM), an assessment tool for software engineering processes. It evaluates firms or business units on their overall approaches to software development. But Watts Humphrey, the developer of the CMM, had another key insight. He realized that it was taking too long for many organizations to move up through the five stages of the CMM, and began to consider what might accelerate the process. He concluded that if organizations were to develop team and individual-level capabilities in addition to those at the organizational level, they would probably improve much faster.

SEI's research has borne out this hypothesis. Companies that successfully employ the 'personal software process' and the 'team software process' (Humphrey 1996, 1999) have been known to move from the lowest to highest levels of software development maturity in about a year – versus an average of close to ten years for this journey using only organization-level approaches. Similarly, organizations that adopt personal knowledge management might advance much more quickly to higher stages of maturity in knowledge management, although to my knowledge this hypothesis has not been tested.

What Kinds of Capabilities Do Knowledge Workers Need?

Many individual knowledge worker capabilities are specific to the type of work or process being performed. In the personal software process, for example, software developers are taught and assessed on their ability to estimate, plan, measure, deal with data and handle defects. Similarly, a consultant wishing to improve the personal consulting process should focus on such capabilities as interviewing, presentation and analytical skills.

But there are also generic knowledge worker skills that almost everyone employs, and could benefit from improving. What do all knowledge workers do? They read and write, of course, and our educational systems do a reasonable job of inculcating these skills.

Knowledge workers also spend a lot of time in meetings. Most organizations, of course, do not do a very good job of helping their employees run meetings effectively. A few, like Xerox, have instituted organization-wide programmes focused on maintaining a high quality of meetings. However, there is plenty of written material and educational options for people who want to learn more about meeting management (Doyle and Strauss 1993), so I will not say anything more about it here.

Knowledge workers also (by definition) create, share and apply knowledge, and this set of capabilities is at the core of personal knowledge management. These activities have not been closely studied by management researchers, and organizations do not generally facilitate their development. Some of the component capabilities include:

- Capturing knowledge in such a way that others can benefit from it. This was classically the role of published articles and books, but only a small subset of employees typically published anything. Today, some view blogs as a way to capture personal knowledge (Ives and Watlington 2005), although if blogging is widespread, the volume of content may quickly become overwhelming.

- Making personal documents available for use by others. Some organizations (for example, law firms) require employees to use tagging approaches for personal documents so that they can be accessed by others, but this approach is not common. For example, the Microsoft Word feature that requests metadata on created documents is widely ignored or disabled. In a survey, only 16 per cent of managers said they store valuable data in a collaborative workplace, like an intranet portal (Accenture 2007). Social tagging is popular on the Internet, but is not widely used for documents on personal computers.

- Searching for knowledge created by oneself or others. Search, of course, has been made increasingly easy by technologies such as Google, though many knowledge workers can find content more easily on the Internet than on their own hard drives or intranets. Although search is an important capability for any knowledge worker, few are actually trained in search techniques. Perhaps as a result, one large survey suggests that 36 per cent of searches by knowledge workers do not yield the intended content (Outsell 2009). Another survey of 1000 middle managers at large companies in the UK and US found that they spent more than a quarter of their time at work searching for information, and more than half of the data they uncover has no value to them (Accenture 2007).

- Networking and sharing knowledge with other knowledge workers. One study (Cross et al. 2003) found that the most productive knowledge workers across four organizations were those with extensive social networks. At that time, these individuals relied on human networks, rather than social networking tools. However, the Outsell study mentioned above found that more than 50 per cent of knowledge workers use some type of social network tool for professional and personal purposes.

The problematic nature of these capabilities suggests that there is much opportunity for improved personal knowledge management.

Research on Personal Knowledge Management

Earlier in this decade I participated in three research efforts to better understand this subject. Two were undertaken by a group of technology companies seeking to understand knowledge work; both corporate and individual-level research projects were undertaken by this group (Davenport and Conway 2004). I also conducted more detailed interviews with a small group of individuals who claim to be very effective in their own personal knowledge management.

One compelling reason for attempting to improve personal knowledge management is that knowledge workers in one of these studies spent large amounts of time (more than three hours per day in our data) in messaging, creating documents, searching for information and knowledge and other information-intensive activities. Despite this large time commitment, thus far knowledge workers have been mostly left to their own devices, so to speak, with little help from their organizations on how to perform key information and knowledge tasks effectively and efficiently. And those devices, or the technologies used for personal information and knowledge, have been largely separate and unintegrated. Thus far our desktop PCs, laptops, wireline and mobile phones, PDAs, hand-held communicators and other assorted technologies – not to mention the paper-based tools many individuals still employ – have been largely unconnected. At the same time that we face increasing technological challenges in managing personal information and knowledge, few individuals can be said to be well-educated and well-informed on how to use the tools to perform their jobs in an optimum fashion.

Working with these devices to manage personal work-related information and knowledge, however, is increasingly how people spend their time within and outside of organizations. It is not hard to believe that with better technology, better education and better management, the key tasks that knowledge workers perform within organizations could be done with greater speed and quality, and at lower cost. Technology, information and knowledge have become so closely integrated with work that better use of them can easily create more effective and efficient organizations.

In a 2003 study of personal knowledge management from the corporate perspective, the Information Work Productivity Council (I was the academic director, and collaborated with several company representatives) interviewed 21 managers of information and knowledge in large companies and two government agencies who were interested in the issue. The particular managers whom we interviewed were typically knowledge managers, managers of new technologies and IT managers who dealt with personal productivity tools for their organizations.

The second study, also conducted in 2003, focused on how individuals were dealing with personal information and knowledge, and involved just over 500 US-based information and technology users. These individuals volunteered to complete a web-based survey. We then reduced this sample to 439 qualified respondents, all of whom had access to a computer and email at work, spent some time during the week processing work-related information, and used email at least weekly.

The third study, which I conducted on my own, involved hour-long interviews with ten individuals who reported that they were highly effective managers of their personal information and knowledge environments. While ten may seem a small number, my informal surveys suggest that less than one per cent of IT and knowledge-oriented individuals would put themselves into the 'highly effective' category.

Corporate-level Findings

Corporate information and knowledge managers showed considerable variation in their orientation to personal knowledge management, with some companies already treating it as an important issue worthy of considerable attention, some on the road to that status, and some unaware of the issue – in roughly equal proportions (while the percentage of adopters may have increased somewhat since 2003, I do not think there have been wholesale changes in the relative proportions of these groups).

The leading-edge companies – found in the information and knowledge-intensive information technology, pharmaceutical and financial services industries – exhibited a variety of traits suggesting that they were focused on personal information and knowledge issues. Some were already actively dealing with specific initiatives to address productivity through the use of technology. Cisco Systems had begun, for example, a Change the Way We Work initiative for employees, which involved a recommended set of personal information and knowledge technologies, education in how to use them and a set of recommended behaviour changes for optimum information processing effectiveness. Capital One, the financial services firm, had a broad initiative underway to improve individual-level productivity with technology. Other companies in this category had similar programmes underway, either for all employees or a particular subset.

One of the earliest adopters of these approaches is Intel, which has created an eWorkforce initiative composed of three previous separate groups addressing knowledge management, collaboration and personal productivity. The eWorkforce group determined that better use of these technologies was a pressing problem for Intel, since its workers are aggressive users and spend large amounts of time using personal IT. Analyses revealed that 63 per cent of Intel employees participated in more than three project teams; 62 per cent routinely collaborated with people from different sites or regions; 40 per cent regularly worked with people who use different collaboration technologies and tools, and more than half worked with people who use different work processes. In 2005 employees conducted 8,300 web-based collaboration meetings and dialled in to roughly 19,000 audio conferences every week. The eWorkforce group supported knowledge worker use of PCs, laptops, cell phones and PDAs, and developed integrated solutions for 'generic' knowledge worker processes – tasks such as arranging and conducting an asynchronous meeting, running an ongoing team or managing a project. Deliverables from the eWorkforce project included a consolidated collaboration platform, a standard project-management platform, next-generation meeting management, first-generation presence management (graphically indicating presence and availability) and instant messaging.

Intel also addressed the development of common processes and the use of best-known methods for collaboration and group work. To do so it segmented knowledge workers into the following categories:

- Functionalists – primarily manufacturing workers (but including some office workers) who use IT occasionally but do not rely heavily on 'office IT' to perform their job functions.

- Cube captains – spend the majority of their time in the office, are very mainstream in their office IT needs and are overall very happy with the tool sets they have.

- Nomads – heavy users of remote access and mobile IT, whether while travelling or working in remote offices.

- Global collaborators – interface often with people around the world; they resemble nomads but work across time zones and need access to collaboration tools, anywhere, any time.

- Tech individualists – want and adopt early the latest IT tools and are willing to take risks with them.

The leading-edge organizations such as Intel were making heavy use of emerging technologies, such as instant messaging, PDAs and hand-held communicators and shared document repositories. More recently, they have experimented with so called Enterprise 2.0 technologies including blogs, wikis, tagging and internal versions of Twitter. However, their focus was not just on technology, but also on its use and the human issues behind the success or failure of technologies. The companies were generally making some attempt to change user behaviours and cultures. The Informatics and Knowledge Management organization within Novartis' research group, for example, had created a Global Head of Knowledge Culture. Others were using technology itself to guide the changes in behaviour. The support groups for individual users at these firms, like Intel's, were not specialists by technology, but had a holistic focus.

Other companies we interviewed were facing challenges with personal information and knowledge and were aware of them, but had not yet formulated a holistic response. In some respects they were 'on the road' to a focus on personal information and knowledge management. They were using some of the same emerging technologies as the leading-edge organizations, but the usage was less monitored and managed. There was a strong orientation to technology products as a means of dealing with personal information (for example, 'Our major project is changing from Lotus Notes to Microsoft Outlook and SharePoint'), but less of a focus on the effective use of those tools. There was generally no holistic support group for personal information, but in several cases a community was beginning to emerge across the relevant functions. In several cases, some major technology or business issue seemed to be preventing a focus on individual productivity, but discussion of productivity at a broader level was taking place within the company.

A third group of companies were somewhat interested in the topic (or they would not have taken the time to participate in an interview), but had not really identified it as important enough to address with any seriousness. Some of these organizations were primarily focused on other issues – economic survival, for example. But they did not generally recognize individual productivity as a corporate issue. They had no formal group to support even the basics of knowledge management or individual information use. What support they did provide to individual users was very fragmented by technology type. Little training or education was offered to users, and what was offered was product-specific. These organizations made little use of emerging technologies for personal information and knowledge; several specifically banned instant messaging, for example. Several stated apologetically that 'we know we should be doing more in this area, but there is just too much else going on,' or made similar remarks.

The high degree of variance in awareness of personal information and knowledge issues suggests that there is still a lack of consensus on what personal knowledge management means. It also suggests that it will be many years before this set of topics is at the forefront of practice.

Changing Personal Knowledge Management Behaviours

As the leading-edge firms suggest, in order for firms to begin improving the management of personal knowledge, they also have to begin to change the behaviour of users. There was considerable variation, even among the early adopters of personal knowledge management, in ideas about how this behaviour change might best be created. As might be expected, for example, Microsoft's approach to behaviour change is generally to try to elicit needed behaviours through the software it sells in the marketplace. All aspects of collaboration among knowledge workers, for example, should be handled by Microsoft's SharePoint collaboration software. If more human interventions are necessary, some Microsoft people would view this as a failing of the software. Intel's eWorkforce group, however, was taking an approach centred on customized tools, process consulting and job aids. Cisco was primarily focused on training as a means of creating behaviour change. It is still too early to understand the implications of these differences and what might comprise 'best practice' in changing user behaviour. The approaches of these leading-edge organizations have been driven thus far more by the culture of the company and the experience of the offering group, rather than an empirical analysis of what really works.

There is also little consensus on how to segment information and knowledge workers for differential treatment. Most leading firms, however seemed to recognize that they cannot treat all their knowledge workers alike, and are beginning to create segmentation approaches like Intel's. At least three organizations had an implicit or explicit segmentation by role – identifying particular roles and jobs that were numerous or important enough to justify an aggressive effort to design an information and knowledge environment around the role. Some other organizations, including EMC and the engineering company MWH Global, are creating a taxonomy of roles within their organizations so that information and knowledge can be delivered on a role-specific basis with some precision. A third approach, employed by Xerox, for example, was to develop or recognize communities of practice, and to create information and knowledge environments that support those communities. As with behaviour change, segmentation is in the early stages, and it is not yet clear which approach works best.

Overall, corporate-level interviews confirmed that at least for some organizations, the problems and opportunities of personal knowledge management are real, and worthy of concerted management attention. Firms that make and sell technology, and those in industries where effective personal knowledge management is critical to success, are believers in the idea and are already addressing it with initiatives. Other firms are either moving in that direction, or not doing anything at all. No matter how advanced on the issue, almost all companies are encountering issues of behaviour change and user segmentation.

Knowledge Worker Survey Findings

Just as the corporate survey showed that companies vary widely in their approaches to personal knowledge management, the Web survey of knowledge workers also revealed a high degree of variance with regard to these issues. In this survey the intent was to discover the behaviours and attitudes of typical users of information and knowledge management tools at work, with particular emphasis on messaging and information distribution technologies. These activities are obviously of importance to individuals and firms, since the average person spent more than three hours on them each day – and it is likely that these numbers have only increased over time.

In this survey there was a consistent group of respondents – about 20 per cent on each of several questions – who saw a substantial problem with their personal information and knowledge management. This group felt overwhelmed by their information flow, saw too much use of email in their organizations, and viewed email and other technologies as hindering rather than helping their productivity. On each of these issues the remaining 80 per cent saw no real problem, although there were considerable differences in how much information they received and the media they used.

It may be surprising to see just how much information and technology was used by the respondents of our survey. The average user in the survey:

- spent three hours and 14 minutes a day using technologies to process work-related information – just over 40 per cent of an eight-hour work day,

- devoted 1.58 hours/day to email (49 per cent of the information processing [IP] time, and 20 per cent of an eight-hour day),

- spent 47 minutes, or 24 per cent of IP time on telephone and voicemail,

- received 44 emails daily (four people said they received 500 a day!),

- sent 17 emails daily,

- had more than three email accounts,

- received 16 instant or text messages a day (for respondents using this technology),

- received 18 calls, placed 15 calls, got 7.6 voicemail messages and

- participated in 2.75 conference calls a week (if any).

Since 2003, of course, the likelihood is that these volumes and times would have only increased, with a variety of new hardware and software tools becoming available, and greater usage throughout the work and non-work day. While it was probably difficult to extract and manage knowledge from these frequent and diverse transactions in 2003, it is probably even more difficult today. It is also likely that the level of stress resulting from such use has increased. For example, in a recent survey from the Pew International Internet and American Life project, 46 per cent of workers say that information technology makes them work more hours, 49 per cent find it difficult to disconnect from work, and 49 per cent feel the technology makes their jobs more stressful (Pew 2008).

Looking further at this group, those who were overwhelmed did not receive more emails than average and did not spend more time processing work-related information during the day. However, they felt they were less effective at managing information and knowledge, felt that email was less valuable to their work and were substantially less likely to believe that they received help from their organization in managing information and knowledge. Just under half of the sample, 49 per cent, felt in control of their personal information and knowledge management.

Despite their complaints about personal information and knowledge management, many believed they were better than average. Forty-one per cent of the sample felt that they were more effective at personal information and knowledge management than others they know; only 11 per cent felt they were less effective. This finding speaks not only to the self-confidence of users, but also to the invisibility of how we manage our own personal environments. We simply do not know how other people do it.

The overall lack of orientation of users to personal information management is suggested by an open-ended question in the online survey. Respondents were asked what one thing they would change in their personal information environments. The most common responses were 'nothing', with 16 per cent, and 'don't know', with 13 per cent. Among more substantive responses, 11 per cent would reduce spam or pop-up ads, and 7.5 per cent would limit the amount of email. Other answers were too idiosyncratic to report. The large number of uninformed responses suggests that most individuals have not thought very much about this issue thus far – and that they have probably underinvested in their own personal information environments – which other researchers have suggested (Davis et al. 1997).

The survey also asked respondents to what degree their organizations helped them manage their personal information. Forty-one per cent said that they received little or no help from their organizations in managing personal information; only 3 per cent felt that their organization had totally mastered the problem of personal information management. This suggests that most organizations have a long way to go before they have fully dealt with this set of issues.

Attitudes Toward Specific Media and Technologies

Email was reported to be one of the most frequently used media in the survey, and also one of the most problematic in terms of negative attitudes. Twenty-six per cent of the sample felt that email was overused by their organizations; 10 per cent felt it was underused, and 64 per cent believed it was being properly used. Fifteen per cent felt that email diminished their work productivity, while 53 per cent felt that it increased it. On balance, the responses of the users were positive about email, but less positive than for some other messaging and information distribution technologies. For the roughly 20 per cent that has a significant problem with email, the key question is whether they are ineffective at managing it, or they are just more conscious of its negative effects than others.

Survey questions involving the telephone – actual telephone calls, voicemail and conference calls – elicited somewhat fewer negative attitudes than about email, and somewhat more positive attitudes. Only 12 per cent (vs 21 per cent for email) felt overwhelmed by the amount of telephone calls and messages they received. Almost half, or 49 per cent, felt telephone information is very or extremely valuable to their work performance – 8 per cent more than for email. Among those who used instant and text messaging, 29 per cent felt that IMs and text messages were very or extremely valuable to their work performance – substantially less than for email or telephone-based technologies.

Perhaps the most popular technologies were those involving information and knowledge 'pull' rather than 'push'. These are corporate websites, information portals and document sharing systems. Those who used these tools reported low levels of being overwhelmed (4 per cent) and diminished productivity (4 per cent), and high levels of value (47 per cent very or extremely valuable for corporate websites, and 64 per cent for document-sharing systems) and productivity enhancement (4 per cent report diminished productivity, 50 per cent enhanced for websites, and 3 per cent diminished, 67 per cent enhanced for document-sharing systems). The positive reaction to document sharing was the highest for any technology in the study. This suggests that knowledge-oriented tools can be more satisfying for users than the more transactional information tools such as email. Although 'pull' sites tend to be used more for organizational knowledge management than personal knowledge, as the amount of information and knowledge in organizations continues to proliferate, these technologies are likely to become even more popular.

Strategies for Managing Information and Knowledge

The survey also included questions on how these information users were coping with the types and amounts of information and knowledge they received. The majority of respondents did not react passively to information overload, but reported specific approaches they used to limit or control their personal information. These varied by technology. The most popular strategies for managing voicemail, for example, were:

- 61 per cent responded to voicemails right after listening to them,

- 59 per cent checked voicemail frequently and

- 40 per cent skipped uninteresting messages in the first few seconds.

The most popular strategies for managing information on portals or corporate websites were:

- 58 per cent reviewed information on the site on a regular basis,

- 55 per cent bookmarked key pages and added shortcuts and

- 46 per cent used browser functionality to find what they need.

The most popular strategies for managing document sharing and shared network information were:

- 57 per cent reviewed and updated files on a regular basis,

- 54 per cent bookmarked key pages and saved folders as favourites and

- 38 per cent checked sites/files when they received notifications or alerts.

Clearly large numbers of users were not reacting passively to information and knowledge overload, but were taking active steps to reduce the amount of content they received, to organize their information and knowledge, and to integrate content processing activities into their daily work environments.

These were not particularly sophisticated coping mechanisms involving advanced technologies or highly evolved preferences, but they do suggest that people are not just letting information and knowledge roll over them.

Individuals Who Have Mastered the Problem

To address the issue of how the most advanced individuals manage their personal knowledge, I interviewed ten individuals who claim that they are highly effective in managing their own personal information and knowledge environments. As noted above, I believe the incidence of people who place themselves in this category is very low. I often ask audiences to whom I speak to raise their hands if they are highly effective at personal information management. Less than 1 per cent – even among corporate information and knowledge managers – place themselves in this category.

Of course, we know relatively little about how others manage their personal information and knowledge streams, so people could be more capable than they think. Although the ten individuals interviewed were fairly modest about their own proficiency, they uniformly said that others came to them for help in finding obscure information or for insights about how to use technology to manage information.

The ten individuals had a variety of jobs. They included a fundraiser for a private school, the administrator for the board of directors of an automobile company, a venture capitalist, a consultant/researcher in a large firm, an independent consultant, a technology manager for a non-profit organization, a director of member services for a nonprofit research organization, a knowledge manager, an editor and a professor.

These highly proficient personal information managers were not all alike, but they had some things in common. Several of their common attributes are described below.

They avoided gadgets

One – the technology manager – tended to try new tools (including a BlackBerry and a notebook computer) because it was part of his job, but dropped them quickly if they did not prove effective. The rest, however, found a few key tools – hardware and software – and stuck with them over time. Several were smartphone/PDA devotees. One did virtually everything within Lotus Notes. There were several heavy Microsoft Outlook users. But they were universally conservative in adopting new tools. Most of the tools were well-known, although the venture capitalist was a strong advocate of a piece of personal information organization software called The Brain, and a couple were experimenting with new tools for searching personal files.

They limited the number of separate devices

One did everything on his laptop, and had abandoned several home desktop computers. Another was very enthusiastic about his smartphone – in part because it reduced two devices (phone and PDA) to one.

They invested effort in organizing information

One came into the office every Sunday for a couple of hours to prioritize his 'to do' lists and organize his information. The venture capitalist had to participate in a large number of conference calls, and he used them to organize his files and folders.

They weren't missionaries

When people came to them for help, they provided it, but most did not feel sufficiently capable to broadly advertise their skills. There was one exception to this principle, however: an individual who constantly proselytized about the virtues of better information management within his office. Even he admitted that some people found this tiresome, and his supervisor felt even more strongly, telling us in a brief conversation that the person's activities were 'a waste of time'. Shortly afterward, he left the organization.

They got help

They did not attend a lot of courses, but they read manuals and called on support people for help. Several had gotten instruction in searching their own computers and the Internet. One individual asked a database manager to explain to him the structure of the key databases in the organization, so that he could access information more easily.

They used assistants – to some degree

Most of the people I interviewed have some degree of administrative support available to them – what used to be called a secretary. These individuals relied on their assistants to schedule and confirm meetings, make travel arrangements and handle some communications. Yet several in the group seemed reluctant to turn everything over to their assistants. None of this group, for example, relied on an assistant to read and answer emails; a few utilized their assistants to help with some voicemails. Perhaps email was too personal to entrust to someone else, or my respondents' ability to type (universal in this group) made them inclined to handle anything involving that task. In any case, the role of assistants would seem to be crucial in effective information management, but it seems to be declining in my small sample.

They weren't doctrinaire about paper vs electronic approaches

Though several of the people said they were trying to reduce the role of paper in their informational lives, nobody was fully electronic. Several said they still used paper calendars, or printed and carried around paper copies of electronic calendars.

They decided what information and knowledge was most important to them, and organized it particularly well

The professor had online folders for every article or book he had written, and used a program for capturing and organizing citations. The venture capitalist had an Excel spreadsheet that summarized the financial situations of all the companies he was involved with. The board administrator had Notes files for every issue that came before the board.

They use lists

Most were not slavish about it, but there was general agreement that lists can be freeing, as David Allen (2003) has suggested in a series of books and conferences. These individuals kept lists of appointments, things to do, contacts, books to read and so forth. Some used electronic lists, some used paper, and one individual wrote particularly important things to do on the back of his hand. 'Since I got my Palm Pilot, however', he commented, 'I rarely get all the way up my arm now'.

They adapt the use of tools and approaches to the work situation at a given time

A US-based researcher in a consulting firm, for example, had always believed that instant messaging was a waste of her time and attention. Her primary job was to conduct research and create research reports, and even though IM was becoming a culturally important aspect of her firm, she resisted its use. However, she moved to Prague for a six-month period, and during that time was working on a project with several consultants that required close collaboration and less solitary concentration. She adopted IM and used it extremely heavily during that period. She felt it was extremely useful not only in doing the collaborative task, but also for reminding people that she was around and available, even though geographically distant. When she returned to the US, she began to use IM more sparingly, and turned it off whenever she had a report to write or a research issue to think through. She also neglected email during these periods, even though her unavailability violated some unstated cultural norms in her firm.

Consistent with the data from the corporate and individual surveys I reported on earlier in this chapter, most of these people were not assisted substantially by their organizations. None of their companies or organizations had made personal knowledge management a general priority. None had any holistic interventions available to make people more effective at managing personal information and knowledge. Though there were coaches available to help with managing personal information and knowledge,[2] the participants in this small survey had largely figured it out on their own.

Going Forward with Personal Knowledge Management

It would seem likely that the topic of personal knowledge management is poised to take off. Companies and individual employees are beginning to focus on it, new technologies are increasingly being introduced to address it, and the business case for improving personal productivity is becoming increasingly clear.

But this is clearly a field in transition, with considerable variation in awareness and behaviour. Some companies and individuals are clearly wrestling with the issue and taking action on it. Several companies have specific initiatives to improve the ways their employees manage their information and knowledge. Moreover a good proportion of individuals are concerned about the effect of

---

2   Kevin Lynn of California is such a coach. See www.officecoach.com.

technology, information and knowledge on their personal productivity, and are taking active steps to manage personal knowledge so they do not become overwhelmed.

A second group sees the problem, but is not taking concerted action. It is probably only a matter of time before they overcome their inertia and begin to respond. At the corporate or organizational level, this would mean going beyond a focus on technology products for personal knowledge management, and addressing how people use them. It would also mean uniting previously fragmented approaches to supporting individual-level technology, information and knowledge users. At the individual level, it would mean investing personal time and energy in improving one's own information and knowledge environment, and seeking help both inside and outside your organization.

A third group of organizations and individuals clearly do not get it yet. These companies and government agencies and individual users are not discussing or debating personal knowledge management, so they are not likely to do anything about the problem any time soon. The organizations with this attitude may be composed of a lot of individuals who do not care about the issue, and hence do not put any pressure on their companies. Perhaps when more consultants and vendors and authors begin to address the issue, they will start moving on it.

Those individuals who do come to realize the importance of personal knowledge management can employ a two-pronged strategy. They can both lobby for assistance from their organizations, and pursue actions on their own. The needed organizational actions could include segmentation programmes for different types of knowledge workers, development of tools and templates, creation of holistic support groups across technologies, better educational offerings, and others along the lines of those adopted by Intel and Cisco. Activities that can be pursued at the individual level include:

- Identifying what types of information and knowledge are particularly important to the individual's career and life, and focusing on the management of them.

- Pursuing knowledge or instruction in critical personal knowledge skills and behaviours, such as search.

- Creating a set of personal taxonomies and file structures that make it possible to easily store and retrieve important knowledge, both online and offline.

- Developing behaviours and routines (for example use of email, browsing, back-up) that accomplish key goals relative to knowledge and that fit with the individual's job and objectives.

- Mastering relevant new technologies for personal use as they become available, while resisting seduction by each new gadget.

Since knowledge work often takes place in teams, small groups of individuals can also collaborate to discover how they can best manage individual knowledge in ways that benefit the group. Naming and filing conventions for personal files, for example, can benefit sharing across group members. Group-defined personal information and knowledge behaviours, such as agreed-upon times and formats for communication, can facilitate the productivity of team-level processes. Again, coordinated behaviour in small groups can take place whether or not the larger organization embraces personal knowledge management and knowledge work productivity.

Of course, personal approaches to improving knowledge management are only one solution to the problem of knowledge worker performance. The only way we can truly go astray with the technologies and methods of personal knowledge management is to adopt them without attending to the other factors that can improve knowledge worker performance, including new behaviours, processes and relationships.

References

Accenture (2007), 'Managers say the Majority of Information Obtained for Their Work is Useless, Accenture Survey Finds', press release, 4 January, http://newsroom.accenture.com/article_display.cfm?article_id=4484, accessed 31 August 2009.

Allen, D. (2003), *Getting Things Done: The Art of Stress-Free Productivity* (New York: Penguin).

Cross, R. et al. (2003), 'The Social Side of Performance', *MIT Sloan Management Review*, 45:1, 20–22.

Davenport, T. (2005), *Thinking for a Living: How to Get Better Performance and Results from Knowledge Workers* (Boston: Harvard Business School Press).

Davenport, T. and Conway, S. (2004), 'Decoding Information Worker Productivity', *Optimize Magazine*, http://linuxriot.com/article/showArticle. jhtml?articleId=18600441&pgno=1, accessed 25 August 2009.

Davis, G. et al. (1997), *Personal Productivity with Information Technology* (New York: McGraw-Hill/Irwin).

Doyle, M. and Straus, D. (1993), *How to Make Meetings Work* (New York: Berkley).

Humphrey, W. (1996), *Introduction to the Personal Software Process* (Reading: Addison Wesley).

—— (1999), *Introduction to the Team Software Process* (Reading: Addison Wesley)

Ives, B. and Watlington, A. (2005), *Business Blogs: A Practical Guide* (Boston: Maranda Group).

Outsell (2009), 'Perfect Match? Not by a Long Shot: Outsell Finds 36 Percent of Professionals' Internet Searches Fall Short', http://www.outsellinc.com/press/press_releases/end_user_update, accessed 27 August 2009.

Pew (2008), 'Networked Workers', Pew Internet and American Life Project, September, http://www.pewinternet.org/Reports/2008/Networked-Workers. aspx?r=1, accessed 27 August 2009.

11

Exploring the Linkages between Personal Knowledge Management and Organizational Learning

Ricky K. F. Cheong and Eric Tsui

Introduction

In the area of knowledge management, existing and past research has tended to focus on the enterprise level. By comparison, Personal Knowledge Management (PKM) and peer-to-peer knowledge management have very much been under-explored (Tsui 2002). The competency and proficiency of Individual Knowledge Workers (IKW), among other factors, underpin the success of an organization's KM journey. Individual learning is closely linked with organizational learning in knowledge management. Ahmed et al. (2002) mentioned that KM involves individuals combining and sharing their experience, skills, intuition, ideas, judgements, context, motivations and interpretations. One of the KM strategies proposed by Wiig (1997) is personal knowledge responsibility. It means to focus on individual responsibility for knowledge-related investments, innovations and also on the competitive side, renewal, effective use and availability to others of the knowledge assets within each employee's area of accountability. It also entails being able to apply the most competitive knowledge to the enterprise's work. Wiig (2004) defined knowledge management (KM) as the systematic and deliberate creation, renewal, application and leveraging of knowledge and other intellectual capital (IC) assets to maximize the individual's and the enterprise's knowledge-related effectiveness and returns. KM involves the combination of people-focused and enterprise-focused knowledge.

Organizations need to align individual learning with corporate objectives to avoid inconsistencies. New knowledge always begins with the individual.

Making personal knowledge available to others is the central activity of a knowledge-creating company (Nonaka 1991). Learning starts from individuals and a learning organization is founded on the learning process of individuals in the organization (Wang and Ahmed 2003). Mainstream thinking on organizational learning considers individuals as 'agents' for an organization to learn (Argyris and Schon 1978). However, Ikehara (1999) argued that individual learning does not necessarily lead to organizational learning. It is the task of the learning organization to integrate individual learning into an organization's learning processes. Hyland and Matlay (1997) claimed that a learning organization can be defined or measured in terms of the sum total of accumulated individual and collective learning. However, Field (1997) also argued that individual learning does not always yield benefits or make any contribution to the organization, because employees may learn to improve themselves rather than benefit the organization.

Apparently, a learning organization requires the contributions of the individual knowledge workers. These workers need certain techniques to manage their own knowledge processes and to share their learning with others. To do this, it is necessary for IKWs to practice PKM and have a 'KM-friendly' learning environment.

This chapter contains a description of the definition of PKM and the PKM framework by Frand and Hixon (1999) and Avery et al. (2001), and the roles of PKM in the KM life cycle. We then disucss the role of PKM in an organization. The gaps between individual learning and organizational learning will also be discussed as well as how to bridge these gaps. Finally, a framework to implement the PKM strategy at both individual and organization levels is outlined.

Personal Knowledge Management

Frand and Hixon (1999) defined Personal Knowledge Management (PKM) as a system designed by individuals for their own personal use. It is a conceptual framework for organizing and integrating information that we, as individuals, feel is important, so that it becomes part of our personal knowledge base. It provides a strategy for transforming what might be random pieces of information into something that can be systematically applied and that expands our personal knowledge. Avery and colleagues (2001) mentioned that PKM is an overall structured process for intentionally managing information and turning it into useful knowledge. Efimova (2005) argued that PKM is an interactive process between individuals, other people and ideas. This is an approach which focuses on supporting knowledge worker productivity by taking an active perspective in studying their work. Wright (2005) mentioned that while PKM was primarily an unconscious process and occurred naturally, it was more than personal. Martin (2008) argued that PKM is knowing what knowledge we have and how we can organize it, mobilize it and use it to accomplish our goal and how we can continue to create knowledge.

Irrespective of how personal knowledge management is defined by different scholars, the key purpose of PKM is to provide a framework for IKWs to manage new information, integrate it and enrich each individual knowledge database in an effective manner. Doing this successfully will empower each individual to easily apply their own personal knowledge to deal with new and old problems, to learn from new experience and to create new knowledge. It is a continuous and interactive process which is not independent of other knowledge management processes.

PKM FRAMEWORK

Frand and Hixon (1999) mentioned that as we are living in a sea of data, our challenge is knowledge and its management: everyone must sift through a great deal of noise in order to retrieve the few bits of information that are of value to them. Some problems appear to be intrinsic to knowledge management, whether it is being performed using a word processor, a formal language-based tool or pencil and paper. These problems include (1) categorizing or classifying; (2) naming things and making distinctions between them; and (3) evaluating and assessing.

Frand and Hixon (1999) outlined five PKM techniques:

1. searching/finding,

2. categorizing/classifying,

3. naming things/making distinctions,

4. evaluating/assessing and

5. integrating/relating.

Individuals attempt to utilize the computer to help them manage the information explosion in a meaningful way.

Avery et al. (2001) proposed a PKM framework with seven skills. The skills are, in one sense, problem solving rather than problem definition skills, and focus on

1.   retrieving information,

2.   evaluating information,

3.   organizing information,

4.   collaborating around information,

5.   analysing information,

6.   presenting information and

7.   securing information.

The details of the skills proposed by Avery et al. (2001) are:

- *Retrieving information.* The challenge here is to identify those nuggets of information from the large information environment that can help to create new knowledge (Avery et al. 2001). It is necessary to be familiar with the search subject and keywords, to understand the usefulness of different information sources, to know how to use the search tools effectively and to be familiar with the concept of widening and narrowing the scope of the search.

- *Evaluation of information.* The challenge here is to be effective in evaluating the quality and relevance of information from a large amount of data (Dorsey 2001). This skill requires full understanding of the subject matter and sensitivity to the value of the available information.

- *Organizing information.* The skill of being able to organize information is the core personal knowledge management skill identified by Frand and Hixon (1999). The challenge here is to develop approaches that enable individual knowledge workers to develop strategies that are consistent with the nature of their work, with their learning styles and with the nature of the collaborative relationships they may have (Dorsey 2001). It requires considerable skill to connect new information to old information using the mental process of pattern matching or recognition. Skills are also required to use technologies, for example relational databases, websites, personal information software and so on, to store the information in a structural way (for example, chronological, functional and role-based approaches) and so on.

•   *Collaborating around information.* The challenge here, as it relates to technology, is to identify how information technology can support the process of working smarter, rather than merely harder, and to overcome obstacles in the absence of social cues for appropriate behaviour (Dorsey 2001). It requires the use of different technologies, for example email, instant messaging, conferencing systems, groupware and so on. These enable individual knowledge workers to acquire new knowledge and thus help the organization to achieve its business goals.

•   *Analysing information.* The challenge is to extract meaningful information from data. This is the fundamental process of converting information to knowledge (Avery et al. 2001). Information technology provides tools, for example spreadsheets and statistical software, to perform data analysis but the human element is the most important factor in the analysing process. It is the ability to process the information and make sense using human experience and knowledge. This ability is related to the intelligence of individuals, and sometimes intuition and specific tools, for example data mining tools, also play a key role in performing an analysis.

•   *Presenting information.* It is important to have a clear understanding of the purpose of the presentation as it relates to the audience (Dorsey 2001). This is the art of composition and speaking. It is not enough just to prepare a professional looking PowerPoint slide or a colourful chart. The presenter has to understand the characteristics of the audience: who they are, what information they require, from what perspective they will interpret the information and how they will make use of the information presented. The challenge is to ensure the audience can pick up the information or knowledge in the context that the presenter has selected.

- *Securing information.* This is frequently neglected as an information skill (Dorsey 2001). However, it is becoming more and more important, especially with the rapid development of the Internet. The importance of keeping information secure is built on the concept of intellectual property. A business will suffer if its trade secrets are stolen by competitors. The care of intellectual property, copyright and patents is important and it should be the concern of everyone, beginning with the individual, to improve the state of information security awareness, for example password management, safeguarding of information sources and so on.

BEYOND INFORMATION MANAGEMENT

Personal knowledge management goes beyond personal information management. Ackoff (1989) argued that knowledge needs to be understood to become wisdom. PKM is beyond information processing from raw data. Knowledge needs to be applied in order to create wisdom. Personal knowledge management not only entails the seven PKM skills suggested by Avery and colleagues (2001) but also needs to be applied to solve real problems and to create new knowledge. Knowledge management is a cyclical process as mentioned by Schotte (2003), Alfs (2003) and Mertins et al. (2003). Seufert et al. (2003) argued that there are four generic knowledge processes that can be distinguished: locate/capture, share/transfer, create and apply. The framework in Figure 11.1 illustrates the integration of PKM into the KM life cycle in an iterative fashion.

The Role of Personal Knowledge Management in an Organization

Personal knowledge management provides a framework which individuals can use to enable them to manage their information and to create knowledge. An organization can make use of its employees' PKM to improve its competitive advantages and overall performance. Mendelson and Ziegler (1999) defined five key factors to measure the smartness of an organization:

1.   external information awareness,

2.   internal knowledge dissemination,

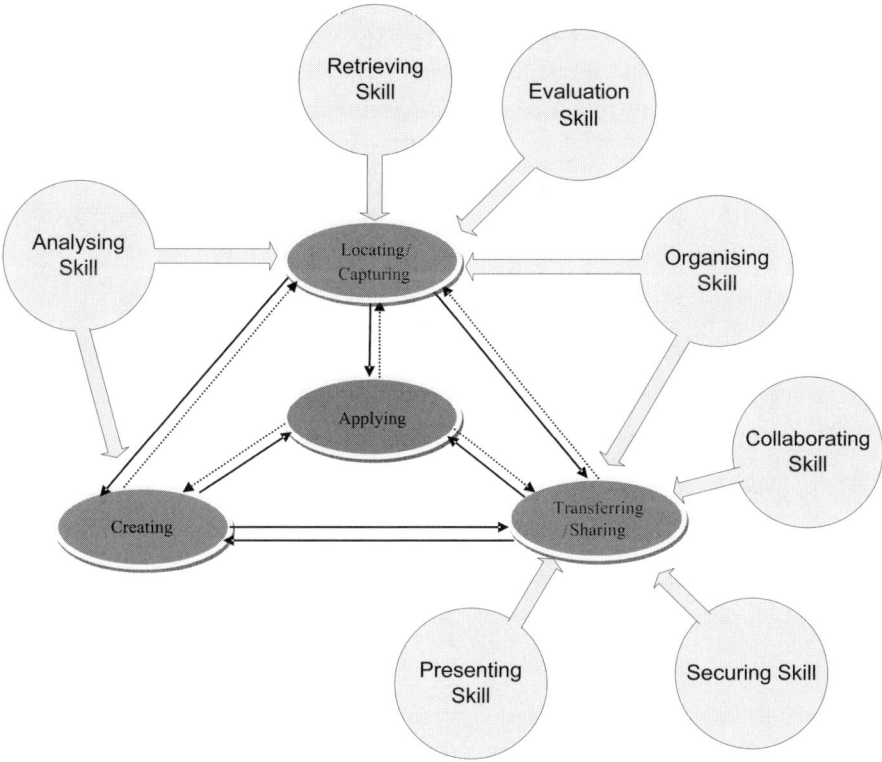

Figure 11.1   PKM integrated into the KM life cycle

3.   effective decision architecture,

4.   organizational focus and

5.   information-age business network.

Ziegler (2008) has since improved the framework by replacing the fifth factor with continuous innovation. These five key factors have been proven in research to have a positive correlation to a firm's performance (Mendelson and Ziegler 1999; Ziegler 2008). To understand the roles of PKM in an organization, we next explore the values of PKM that improve the above five key factors. The roles of PKM in an organization are summarized in Table 11.1.

Table 11.1   The roles of PKM in an organization

	Personal knowledge management skills						
	Retrieving	Evaluating	Analysing	Organizing	Collaborating	Presenting	Securing
External information awareness	Empower to obtain useful information from customers, partners and competitors about customer requirements, technology trends and business opportunities etc.						
Internal knowledge dissemination		Empower to improve the effectiveness of information flow, only the relevant and meaningful information to be communicated		Empower to flow the information effectively not only vertically but also horizontally in both formal and informal ways			
Effective decision-making		Empower decision-maker to have accurate and relevant information, to improve decision quality and decision-making time			Empower effective communication to shorten the decision-making time and express effectively the relevant information for decision-making		
Organization focus	Empower the individual to understand the core business information, e.g. technology, process and policy etc.				Empower effective sharing of core business information		Empower protection of business information
Continuous innovation	Empower individual to manage the information for generation of new ideas effectively			Empower effective sharing of innovation and information for new idea generation			Empower protection of innovation ideas

EXTERNAL INFORMATION AWARENESS

Individual knowledge workers, by using information retrieving and evaluation skills, can obtain useful information from customers, partners and competitors about customer requirements, technology trends, business opportunities and so on. When this useful external information is fed back to the organization, it will help the management to align the business strategies for product and marketing development. PKM can improve external information awareness in terms of customer dynamics, opportunities from technology change and competitiveness.

INTERNAL KNOWLEDGE DISSEMINATION

Good information evaluation and analysing skills can enable the individual knowledge worker to improve the effectiveness of information flow. Such skills can ensure that only relevant and meaningful information is communicated and thus the burden of evaluating and analysing excessive amounts of information in the next level of communication can be reduced. Organizing and collaborating skills can facilitate the effective flow of information not only vertically within the organization but also horizontally and in both formal and informal ways. Such skills reduce communication barriers and provide an effective flow of knowledge information in cross-functional and cross-hierarchical ways.

EFFECTIVE DECISION-MAKING

The effectiveness of decision-making has two aspects: one is decision quality and the other is decision time. The decision quality relies greatly on the quality of the information available to the decision-maker. It is about the relevance of information which is related to judgements about the accuracy of the information. Decision time depends on the time required for evaluating and analysing the information, and on the effectiveness of information-sharing within the organization in both horizontal and vertical directions. Good evaluating, organizing and analysing skills enable the decision-maker to improve decision quality while good presentation and collaborating skills can facilitate effective communication and shorten the time needed for making decisions.

ORGANIZATION FOCUS

The organization should focus on its strengths and core competencies. Individual knowledge workers within the organization should fully understand their core business information and this information should be widely shared within the organization. However, core business information should be well protected as should intellectual property, for example patents and copyrights which are assets of the business. The retrieval, evaluation and analytical skills help IKWs to understand their core business information. Collaboration and security are key to core business knowledge-sharing and protection of intellectual property.

CONTINUOUS INNOVATION

Continuous innovation is important for an organization in the areas of product development and quality improvement. Creativity and a full understanding of the current situation or problem area are needed if innovation is to take place. All seven PKM skills are needed by individuals who wish to contribute to this area. In order to generate new ideas for improvement, the use of retrieving, evaluating and analysing skills is crucial. Good organizing ability can enable IKWs to access and share information easily. Collaboration and presentation skills enable IKWs to express their ideas and information effectively while securing skills are important to protect innovative plans and ideas.

Gaps Between Individual Learning and Organizational Learning

Forcheri and colleagues (2000) defined individual learning as the capacity to build knowledge through individual reflection about external stimuli and sources, and through the personal re-elaboration of individual knowledge and experience in the light of interaction with others and with the environment. A learning organization should primarily focus on valuing, managing and enhancing the individual development of its employees (Scarbrough et al. 1998). The relationship between individual and organizational learning is a very important aspect (Kim 1993; Matlay 2000). It is important because all organizations are composed of individuals: an organization can learn independently of any specific individual but not independently of all individuals (Kim 1993). Individuals' learning activities can be facilitated or inhibited by the organization's learning system (Argyris and Schon 1978). The model of organizational learning will either obscure the actual learning process by ignoring the role of the individual or become a simplistic extension of individual learning by glossing over organizational complexities (Kim 1993).

Learning is commonly viewed as a process through which to acquire skills and knowledge, for example Jarvis (1987) defined learning as a process of transforming experience into knowledge, skills and attitudes. Both organizations and individuals have learning objectives which provide the motivation which drives the learning process. There are many factors affecting learning outcomes and these can be external or internal. To better understand the gaps between individual and organizational learning, it is important to know the effect of the three aspects of learning objectives, learning factors and the learning process, on individual learning and on organizational learning.

LEARNING OBJECTIVES

The learning objectives of an individual and of an organization are very different. Individuals focus mainly on their personal achievement while an organization focuses mostly on the firm's performance.

Individual learning objectives

Individual learning in an organization can be explained by adult learning theories (Su 2006). Many scholars have tried to explain why adults strive to learn (for example, Houle 1961; Miller 1967; Lieb 1999; Cheng 2007; Wynne 2008). Houle (1961) stated that job-related reasons provide the key to the motivation to learn, while Miller (1967) believes that social pressure is the motivation to learn. Lieb (1999), Cheng (2007) and Wynne (2008) proposed different but similar learning motivation factors and provided a comprehensive overview to aid understanding the individual learning objectives. As illustrated in Figure 11.2, this can be divided into three aspects: personal, job-related and social. In the view of the authors, the personal objectives are the primary expected achievements of an individual from learning, while job-related and social objectives are actually the reflection of personal achievements.

Personal learning objectives include personal growth/advancement which aims to:

1.   Improve personal skills and knowledge for job advancement (Cheng 2007; Lieb 1999; Wynne 2008).

2.   Contribute to the community (Lieb 1999; Wynne 2008).

3.   Bring about professional advancement (Lieb 1999; Wynne 2008) which serves to improve personal or professional status and gain public recognition, for example chartered accountant and lawyer status.

4.   Enhance cognitive interest (Lieb 1999; Wynne 2008) which is mainly to fulfil personal needs or gain satisfaction from learning and from having new knowledge which may not be job- or socially-related, but which serves solely to improve one's own life, for example music, golf, and so on.

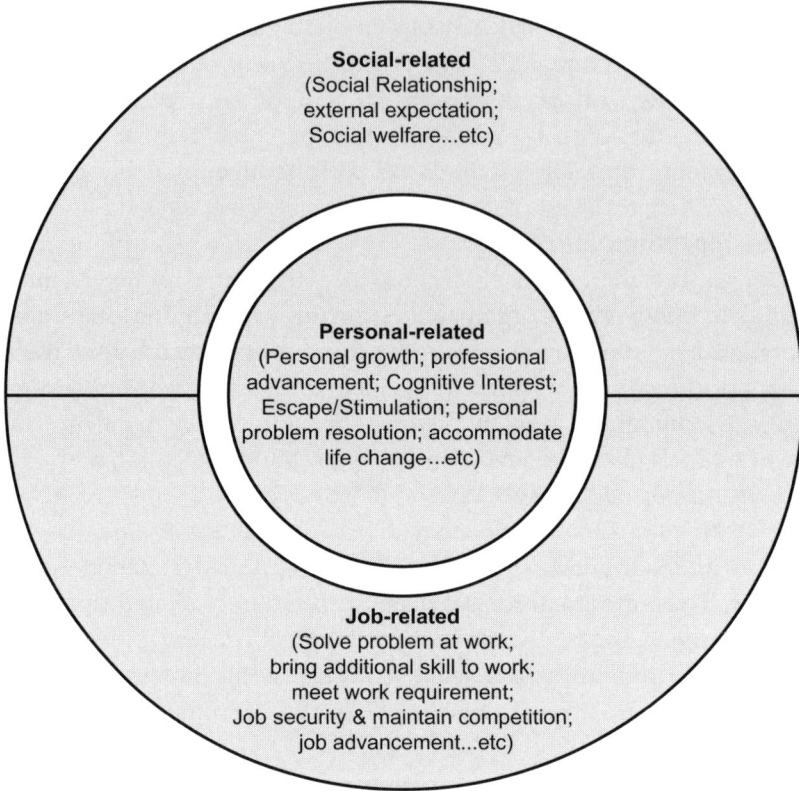

Figure 11.2   Types of individual learning objectives

5.   Allow the learner to escape or find stimulation (Lieb 1999; Wynne 2008) which helps individuals to find relief from boredom, provide a break from routine home or work life and discover a route to other exciting aspects of life.

6.   Enable the learner to resolve personal problems (Wynne 2008), for example developing the skills to handle personal conflict.

7.   Facilitate/accommodate life changes (Wynne 2008), for example retirement or parenting.

Job-related learning objectives include acquiring skills to solve problems at work; meet employment expectations or job requirements (Cheng 2007; Wynne 2008); stay abreast of competitors (Lieb 1999); bring additional skills to the workplace (Wynne 2008); advance in one's job (Lieb 1999; Wynne 2008); enjoy job security (Wynne 2008) and so on. Self-improvement is reflected in improvement in the working environment.

Social learning objectives include social relationships (Cheng 2007; Lieb 1999; Wynne 2008), for example making friends, to meet a need for association and friendship; external expectations (Lieb 1999), for example to fulfil the expectations or recommendations of someone with formal authority; and social welfare (Lieb 1999; Wynne 2008) which includes improving one's ability to serve mankind, prepare for service to the community and improve the ability to participate in community work. This is the reflection of self-improvement in the social environment.

Organizational learning objectives

Information and knowledge are created, stored and exchanged within the organization. These are the processes that improve the ability of the organization to survive and grow. Many scholars, for example Drucker (1993) and Nonaka (1991), are of the opinion that knowledge in the organization is the cornerstone of competitive advantage.

Common objectives for any learning organization are to improve the organization's effectiveness, responsiveness, efficiency, flexibility and ability to innovate. Paul James (2005) mentioned that effectiveness can be improved through better access to expertise and past learning experience; responsiveness can be improved through better and faster responses to customers if the organization has a more integrated knowledge of customers' preferences and needs; efficiency can be improved through reuse and transfer of knowledge; flexibility can be improved through better insight into customer and competitor trends; and innovation can be improved by the use of expert panels, cross-discipline teams and communities of practice.

As discussed earlier, Mendelson and Ziegler (1999) and Ziegler (2008) defined five key performance indicators for organizational competitive advantages: external information awareness, internal knowledge dissemination, effective decision architecture, organizational focus and continuous innovation. These factors have been proven in their research to have a positive correlation with the firm's performance.

Apart from competitive advantage, organizations may have learning objectives which are related to their corporate social responsibility. This is the voluntary contribution of finance, goods or services to community or governmental causes. It excludes activities directly related to organizational production and commerce, and excludes activity required under legislation or government direction (Rowe 2005). There is a new stream of thought which emphasizes the need for a more holistic approach to the study of firms and their role in society (Cavett-Goodwin 2007).

LEARNING FACTORS

The factors affecting individual learning are related to the individual's learning characteristics while factors affecting organizational learning are related to the environments inside the organization which may have a positive or a negative impact on learning.

Individual learning factors

Employees, being adult learners, are assumed to be capable of framing their own choices, reflecting on their options, and making responsible, informed decisions that serve their interest (Percival 1996). Individuals have different learning characteristics and as adult learners working in the organization, they are probably influenced by the andragogical assumptions defined by Malcolm Knowles, a champion of andragogy (the art and science of helping adults to learn). Knowles and his colleagues defined six crucial assumptions in their book, *The Adult Learner* (1998): the need to know, the learner's self-concept, the learner's experience, readiness to learn, orientation to learn and motivation to learn.

Cross (1978) researched the needs of the adult learner and reported three key characteristics of adult learners:

1. Adults prefer self-planned learning rather than enrolling in classes, as adults want to set their own learning pace and to use their own style of learning.

2. Adult learning is motivated primary by the desire to solve immediate and practical problems.

3. Adults have a reservoir of life experience and they desire to learn new knowledge-related to their own thoughts and experience. Their experience may hinder the learning and sometimes may need to be unlearned.

Cross (1981) also presented a model called Characteristics of Adults as Learners (CAL). It attempted to integrate other theoretical frameworks for adult learning such as andragogy, experiential learning and lifespan psychology (O'Brien 2008).

The CAL model consists of two variables: personal characteristics and situational characteristics. The personal characteristics consist of ageing, life phases and development stages (for example marriage, job changes and retirement). The situational characteristics consist of part-time versus full-time learning, and voluntary versus compulsory learning. Galicia-Castillo (2004) summarized the CAL model guidelines as shown in Table 11.2 and observed that the personal characteristics describe the learner while the situational characteristics describe the conditions where learning occurs.

Table 11.2   CAL model guidelines

Personal characteristics	Describes the learner • Related chronologic age • Physiological/ageing • Crystallized vs fluid • 'Wisdom' • Senses (vision/hearing) • Sociocultural/life phases • 'Readiness' for learning • Greatest opportunity for learning occur at transition points • Not related to chronologic age • Psychological/developmental phases • Challenge the learner to stimulate
Situational characteristics	Describes the conditions where learning occurs • Usually separates adult learning from child learning • Part-time learning vs full-time learning • Voluntary learning vs compulsory learning

Source: Galicia-Castillo (2004), based on Reigeluth (1999).

The CAL model is intended to provide guidelines for adult education programmes although there no research has been conducted to support the model (O'Brien 2008). This model is most helpful in setting up adult learning environments (Galicia-Castillo 2004). According to Cross (1981), the model is based on the following principles:

- Adult learning programmes should capitalize on the experience of participants.

- Adult learning programmes should be adapted to the age of the participants.

- Adults should be challenged to move to increasingly advanced stages of personal development.

- Adults should have as much choice as possible in the availability and organization of the learning programme.

Levine (2008) provided the following six characteristics of adult learners which confirmed the assumptions recommended by Knowles et al. (1998) and Cross (1981).

- An adult learner is primarily independent/self-directed in what they learn.

- The adult learner has considerable experience to draw upon.

- The adult learner is most apt to be interested in topics that relate to their current developmental stage of life.

- The adult learner is most interested in information and ideas that solve problems that they are presently faced with.

- The adult learner is most interested in information that can be immediately applied.

- The adult learner is self-motivated.

Based on the adult learning literature of Knowles et al. (1998), Cross (1981) and Levine (2008) the intrinsic factors affecting the adult learner can be summarized as personal characteristics, self-concept, orientation, readiness/ immediate needs and internal motivation.

Personal characteristics consist of, but are not limited to, age, gender, marriage, job rank, salary, experience, career professionalism and so on. These personal characteristics define individual learning styles and attitudes to learning. Knowles and colleagues (1998) mentioned that due to individual differences, any group of adults will be heterogeneous in terms of background, learning style, motivation, needs, interests and goals. Hence, in adult education, it is necessary to emphasize individualization of teaching, learning strategies and use of experiential techniques, for example group discussions, simulation exercises, problem-solving activity-based case methods and laboratory methods.

Knowles and colleagues (1998) argued that adults have a self-concept of being responsible for making their own decisions. Once they have arrived at that self-concept they develop a deep psychological need to be seen by others and treated by others as being capable of self-direction. As a person matures their self-concept moves from being a dependent personality toward being a self-directed human being (Smith 1999). Adults resent and resist situations in which they feel others are imposing their wills on them and adult educators should make every effort to create learning experiences in which adults are helped to make the transition from dependent learners to self-directing learners (Knowles et al. 1998).

Over the lifespan, people's readiness to learn becomes oriented increasingly to the developmental tasks of their social roles (Smith 1999). Adult learners become ready to learn those things they need to know and be able to do in order to cope effectively with their situation. The tasks associated with moving from one development stage to the next are a rich source of readiness to learn. It is not necessary to wait passively for people to become ready to learn; there are ways to induce readiness in adults through exposing them to models of superior performance, career counselling, simulation exercises and other techniques (Knowles et al. 1998).

Over time, a person's time perspective changes from one of postponed application of knowledge to immediacy of application, and accordingly their orientation toward learning shifts from one of subject-centredness to one of problem-centredness (Smith 1999). Adults are motivated to learn when they perceive that learning will help them perform tasks or deal with problems that they encounter in their life. The learning of new knowledge, skills, understanding, values and attitudes is more effective when adult learners are presented with learning topics in the context of application to their situation (Knowles et al. 1998).

As we age, our motivation to learn becomes internal (Smith 1999). Knowles and colleagues (1998) argued that adults are responsive to some external motivators (better jobs, promotion, higher salaries and so on), but the most potent motivators are internal pressures (the desire for increased job satisfaction, self-esteem, quality of life and so on). Knowles and colleagues (1998) quoted Tough's research (1979) that all normal adults are motivated to keep growing and developing, but this motivation is frequently blocked by barriers such as negative self-concept as a student, inaccessibility of opportunities or resources, time constraints and programmes that ignore the principles of adult learning.

Organization learning factors

Gold and colleagues (2001) argued that KM infrastructure capability, including an organization's structure, culture and technology, has a positive influence on organizational effectiveness. Alazmi and Zairi (2003) found that factors including culture, training, top management support, technology infrastructure, knowledge sharing and knowledge transfer and so on, are the important factors which help a KM programme to be successful. Other researchers suggested that culture, technology, systems and procedures, structure, tasks and incentives are the critical success factors for KM implementation (Davenport and Prusak 1998; Grover and Davenport 2001; Karlsen and Gottschalk 2004). The organization learning factors can be grouped into organizational structure, culture and technology infrastructure.

Traditionally, an organization is structured for some special technological process based on functional labour division and specialization. Such an organizational structure always opposes and limits the introduction of any new structure geared to creating a learning organization (Sakalas and Venskus 2007). There are three common dimensions of an organizational structure: complexity, formalization and centralization. Complexity is the degree of vertical, horizontal and spatial differentiation in an organization. Higher complexity makes it difficult to increase effectiveness of knowledge dissemination within the organization. Formalization is the degree to which jobs within the organization are standardized. A highly formalized structure will resist innovation within the organization (Liao 2007) and the workers have less freedom and motivation to create new knowledge. Centralization is the degree to which the formal authority to make decisions is concentrated in an individual, unit or level, thus permitting employees minimum input into their work. Liao (2007) argued that in highly centralized organizations, the knowledge is used by the person who created it and knowledge is shared mainly through direct person-to-person contacts.

However the organization is structured, to become an effective knowledge organization it should improve the processes for innovation, individual learning, collective learning and knowledge sharing (King 2008). The communication of information within the organization plays a key role in creating an effective knowledge-oriented organization.

Schein (1992, 1999) defined organizational culture as a pattern of shared basic assumptions that the group learned as it solved its problems of external adaptation and internal integration. This pattern worked well enough to be considered valid, and could therefore be taught to new members as the correct way to perceive, think and feel in relation to those problems. Park and colleagues (2004) defined organizational culture as the character or personality of an organization. It is the way things are done in an organization and among the organizational culture profile attributes modified by Harper (2000), Park and colleagues (2004) found that trust, sharing information freely and working closely with others (or developing friends at work) are the critical factors for the successful implementation of knowledge management technology.

Organizational culture plays a significant role in the process of learning within the organization. It is the main key to success (Tuggle and Shaw 2000). Senge (1990) encouraged learning organizations to share the same vision and foster team learning, which are organizational culture-related disciplines.

Technology is multifaceted. It is critical that the organization invests in a comprehensive infrastructure that supports various types of knowledge and types of communication (Gold et al. 2001). The technology dimension that is part of effective knowledge management includes business intelligence, collaboration, distributed learning, knowledge discovery, knowledge mapping, opportunity generation and security (Grant 1996; Leonard 1995). The role of information technology in a learning organization is to provide effective collection, storage, processing, distribution and utilization of information in the organization with a view to increasing the effectiveness and satisfaction of users (Rzevski and Prasad 1998). It should be able to support distributed decision-making, provide a teamwork environment, and handle knowledge rather than mere data, that is, creating organizational memory and intellectual capital.

However, Brynojolfsson and Hitt (1996, 1998) argued that there is a paradox in the business value of the investment in information technology (IT): not all of the benefit from the IT investment can be captured by the organization. Moreover, Tsui (2007) pointed out that much of the focus on knowledge management technologies is on enterprise-based KM systems, for example search engines, knowledge portals, electronic document management systems, content management and so on. These are top-down systems which are centrally controlled, rigidly governed and take months to deploy. Apart from enterprise-based KM systems, Tsui (2002) mentioned that there are also group-based and personal KM systems. The group-based KM systems are generally for both intra- and intercollaboration, while personal KM systems are adopted by individual knowledge workers and operate within the permissible bounds of the enterprise IT framework and security network. Group-based and personal KM systems will create conflict, for example with IT governance and duplication of functions, and so on. There is no straightforward solution for the co-existence of enterprise KM systems (Tsui 2002).

LEARNING PROCESS

The learning processes of individuals and of organizations are fundamentally different, not only because individual learning involves personal behaviour while an organization is a group of individuals, but also because the form of the knowledge is different. Individual knowledge is mainly in the form of tacit knowledge while organizational knowledge is mainly in the form of explicit knowledge.

Nonaka and Takeuchi (1995) mentioned that explicit knowledge is deeply ingrained in the traditions of Western management, from Frederick Taylor to Herbert Simon; it is in the form of words, numbers and can easily be communicated and shared in the form of hard data, scientific formulae, codified procedures, or universal principles. Polanyi (1996) described tacit knowledge as that which is based on the aphorism that 'we know more than we can tell'. It is not easily visible and expressible; it is highly personal and hard to formalize, making it difficult to communicate or to share with others. Subjective insights, intuitions and hunches are classified as tacit knowledge (Nonaka and Takeuchi 1995).

The individual learning process

The human learning process is complicated and many scholars have tried to explain their understanding of learning processes in different ways (Griffin 1987; Jarvis 1987; Kolb 1993). Griffin (1987, 210) defined the basic learning processes as

> *the inner happenings or experiences that the learner has when engaged in learning ... whether the learner is in a group, with a friend, or alone; when reading a book, listening to a lecture or reflecting on his or her own experience.*

Jarvis (1987) defined learning as a process of transforming experience into knowledge, skill and attitudes. Kolb (1993) followed the work of Dewey (1938), Lewin (1942) and Piaget (1970) and modelled the learning process as experiential learning which emphasizes that (1) the process of adaptation and learning is more important than content or outcomes; (2) knowledge is a transformation process, being continuously created and recreated, not an independent entity to be acquired or transmitted; (3) learning transforms experience in both its objective and subjective forms; and (4) to understand learning, we must understand the nature of knowledge, and vice versa.

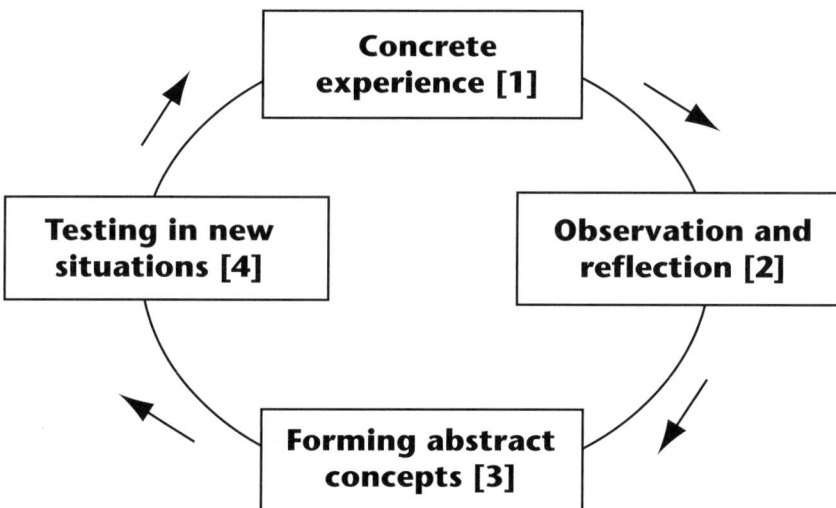

Figure 11.3   Experiential learning cycle

There are four stages in the experiential learning cycle: concrete experience, observation and reflection, forming abstract concepts and testing in new situations. Kolb (1993) provided a view of the experiential learning cycle integrated with the problem-solving process (Pounds 1965), the decision-making process (Simon 1947) and the creative process (Wallas 1926) as shown in Figure 11.4.

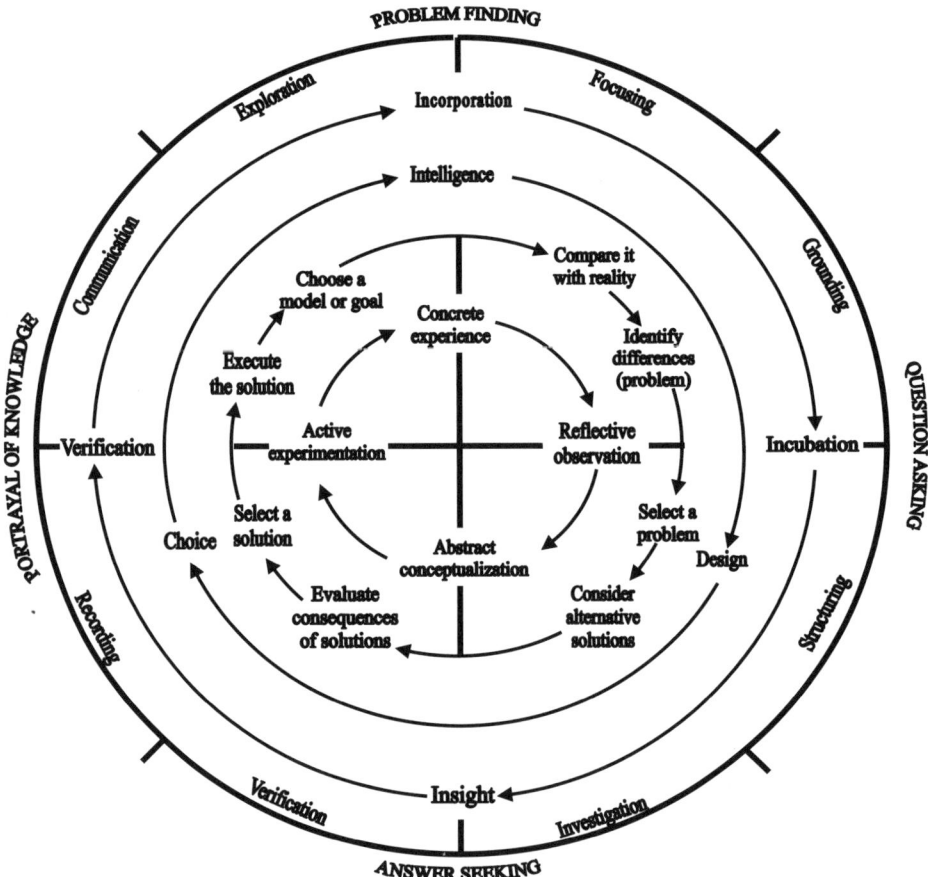

Figure 11.4   Similarities among conceptions of basic adaptive processes: inquiry/research, creativity, decision-making, problem-solving, learning (Kolb 1993, 151)

Organization learning process

Kim (1993, 40) argued that 'although the meaning of the term "learning" remains essentially the same as in the individual case, the learning process is fundamentally different at the organizational level'. Popper and Lipshitz (2000) mentioned that organizational learning occurs when the knowledge is disseminated among different individuals and organizational units, and processed at different levels of the organizational structure beyond the individual. Argyris and Schon (1978) stated that organizational learning involves detecting the mismatch of outcomes achieved by the organization and its expectations, and moving to correct the errors. This will permit the organization to carry on its present policies or to achieve its present objectives. There are three elements in the organizational learning process: governing variables, action strategies and consequences (Argyris and Schon 1974). Based on the responses to the errors, organizational learning can be seen as operating in either single-loop or double-loop mode.

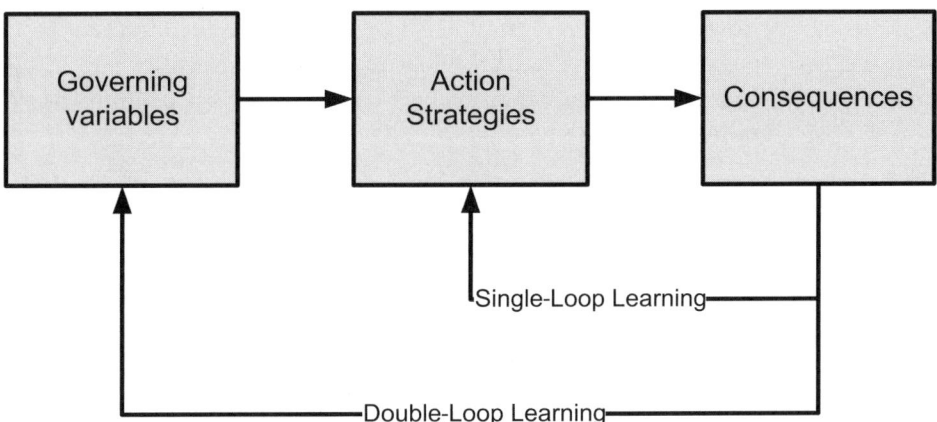

Figure 11.5   Single-loop and double-loop learning

Single-loop learning occurs when actions are adjusted to achieve the desired outcome without altering present policies, routines, norms and values. Double-loop learning occurs when the organization modifies its underlying norms, policies or objectives after errors have been detected and corrected (Argyris and Schon 1978).

Apart from Argyris and Schon, many scholars have tried to model the organizational learning process (Cangelosi and Drill 1965; March and Olsen 1975; Chakravarthy 1982; Daft and Weick 1984). Fiol and Lyles (1985) argued that organizational learning is basically viewed as the sum of cognitive and behavioural changes. It is the process by which knowledge about relationships between the organization and the environment is developed and is a process of putting cognitive theories into action (Argyris and Schon 1978; Hedberg 1981; Young et al. 1999). It is also a feedback system (Young et al. 1999) in which the organization will continually compare the perceived requirements against the outcome and will make adjustments based on the discrepancies found. Organizational learning is the aggregation of the individual and group learning which takes place during each task in the process (Young et al. 1999).

Bridging the Gaps Between Individual Learning and Organizational Learning

To bridge the gaps between individual learning and organizational learning, it is necessary to align the individual learning objectives to organizational learning objectives, fully understand the learning factors affecting individual and organizational learning, and then embed the individual learning process into the organizational learning process.

ALIGNING THE INDIVIDUAL AND ORGANIZATIONAL LEARNING OBJECTIVES

Organizational learning objectives are primarily for improving the organization's competitive advantages and social responsibility, while individual learning objectives are personal, job-related and social. Figure 11.6 illustrates the relationship between the individual and organizational learning objectives.

To better understand the relationship between the individual learning objectives and organizational learning objectives, try moving one of the gears in Figure 11.6. This will reveal the interactive relationships. For example, if you move the organizational competitive advantages wheel, the individual job-related wheel and the organizational social-related wheels will be directly affected. It also indirectly influences the individual personal objectives and individual social objectives. This means that by creating organizational learning objectives to improve the firm's competitive advantage, the individual's learning objectives and organizational social objectives can directly benefit and vice versa. It is a complicated interaction but the relationship is simple.

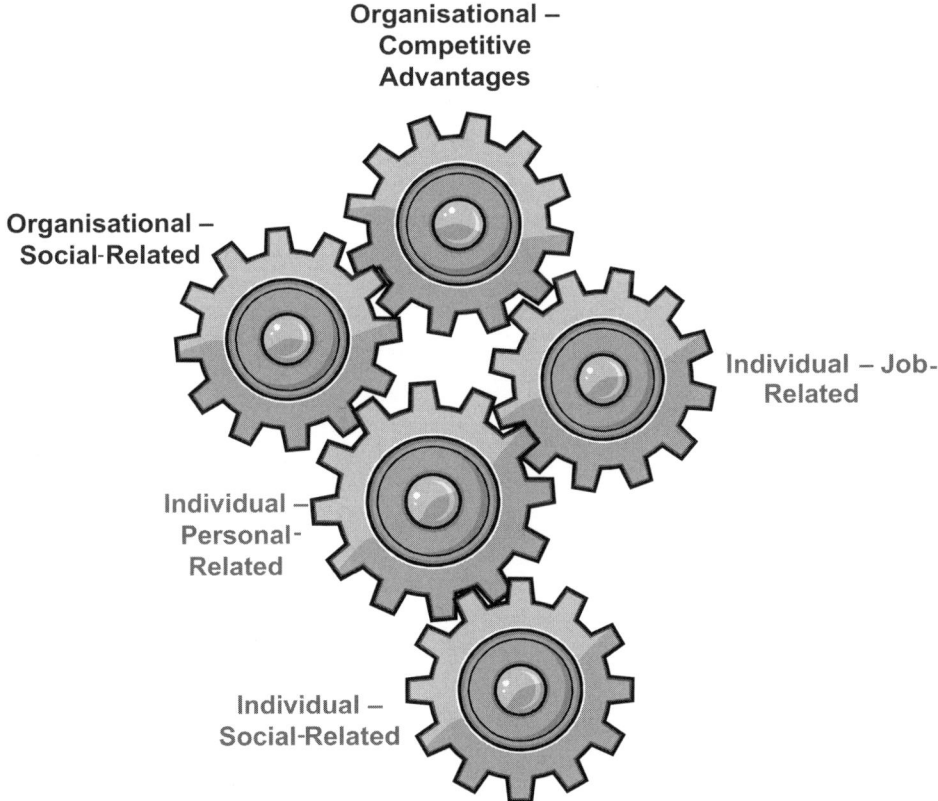

Figure 11.6   The relationship between individual and organizational learning objectives

When individuals align their own learning objectives to the organizational learning objectives, it will allow individuals to take advantage of the favourable environment provided by the organization to achieve their own learning objectives. The organization can focus its resources on individuals who can benefit the organization. Individuals need to understand the area of focus of their organizational learning objectives.

For example, Cisco has a resale channel programme for their partners. The partners are classified as Gold, Silver, Premier and Select based on their competence level (Cisco 2008). Gold is the highest level and requires at least four individuals at the company to be Cisco Certified Internetwork Experts (CCIE), the highest level of technical competence. By attaining Gold partner status, the partner can obtain better support from Cisco in both technical and financial terms. This will increase the competitive advantage of the partner against other partners. To become a CCIE, it is necessary for individuals to have studied by attending courses, but they also need to have had practical experience in solving different networking problems. By taking advantage of the company's objectives to become a Cisco Gold partner and studying in order to become a CCIE individuals will not only obtain better job security and job advancement in the company but can also increase their own market value in the industry.

By aligning learning objectives, the learning outcome is synergized; both individual and organization can achieve their learning objectives in a more effective way. It requires two-way communication of learning objectives and a full understanding of the opportunities to create learning synergy.

UNDERSTANDING THE INDIVIDUAL AND ORGANIZATIONAL LEARNING FACTORS

Individuals are the agents of organizational learning, which means the organization has to fully understand that individuals are different from each other and have different learning characteristics. Individuals should be aware of the organizational learning factors and play an active role in the learning environment to create maximum benefit for themselves and for the organization. Figure 11.7 provides an holistic view of the learning factors of the individual and of the organization.

From an organizational viewpoint, organizational structure defines the role of the individual learning agent and defines what kind of knowledge they should learn in order to perform their contractual duties. The organizational structure also influences individual readiness and orientation to learn, that is, any work-related topic they are required to learn. The organizational culture defines the terms of the psychological contract under which individuals will contribute their expertise. It also defines the learning orientation of the organization, that is, whether learning is within the range of the common norms and values of the individual or not. This contract will directly influence the individual's motivation to learn and their willingness to share their knowledge. The technology adopted in the organization provides a platform for individual learning agents to practice learning in their work. A good platform should help the learning process to capture and store the individual learning outcome. This can help build up a knowledge based environment and data-bank from which any other learning agent can retrieve information when necessary.

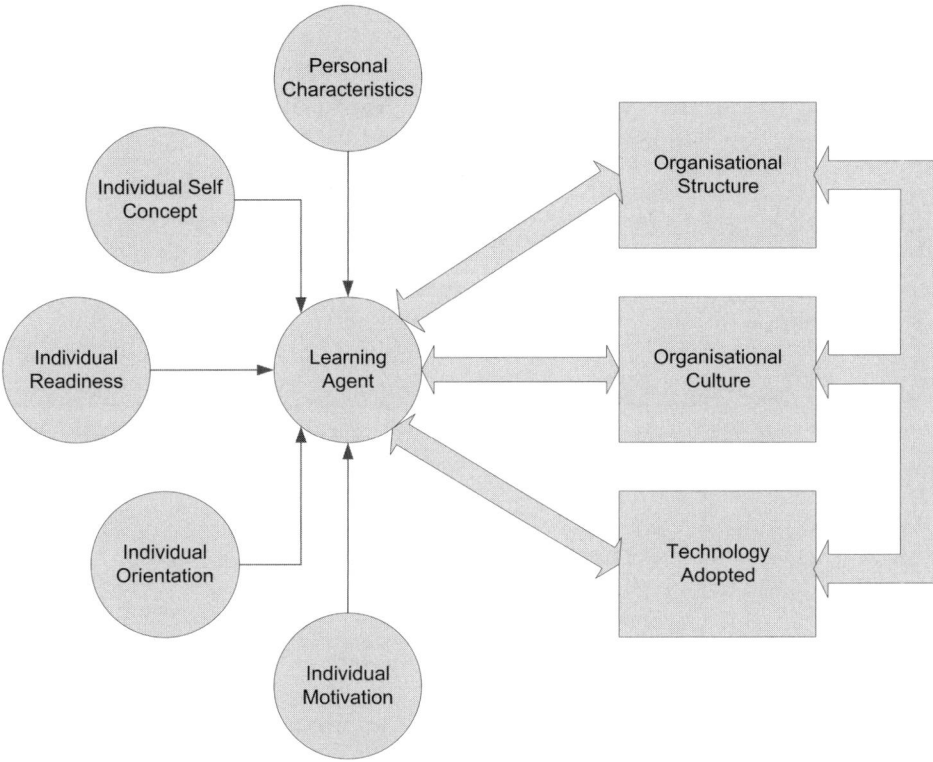

Figure 11.7   An holistic view of learning factors in an organization

The organization should fully understand the individual learning factors in order to determine what kind of resources and how many resources should be allocated to an individual learning agent. The resources should include, but not be limited to, the time and money for the training programme, rewards to motivate learning and for making a learning contribution, guidance from supervisors or peers, the technology platform available to individuals and so on. By providing such support, human capital will be created in the form of a wide range of individual expertise and also very importantly, the individuals will enhance their personal knowledge management skills.

EMBEDDING THE INDIVIDUAL LEARNING PROCESS INTO THE ORGANIZATIONAL LEARNING PROCESS

The individual learning process is different from the organizational learning process but it is not independent. In fact, it is closely related and should be embedded into the organizational learning process. The organizational learning process is a feedback system which requires the individual to feed back the learned experience, in the form of consequences, to the organization and to change the action strategy (in single-loop mode) and even the governance variables (in double-loop mode). The action strategy in the organization will provide a new situation for the individual to test, and one in which to continue in the individual learning cycle and feed back to the organization via observation and reflection. In Figure 11.8, the embedding of the experience learning process of the individual into the single-/double-loop learning process is illustrated.

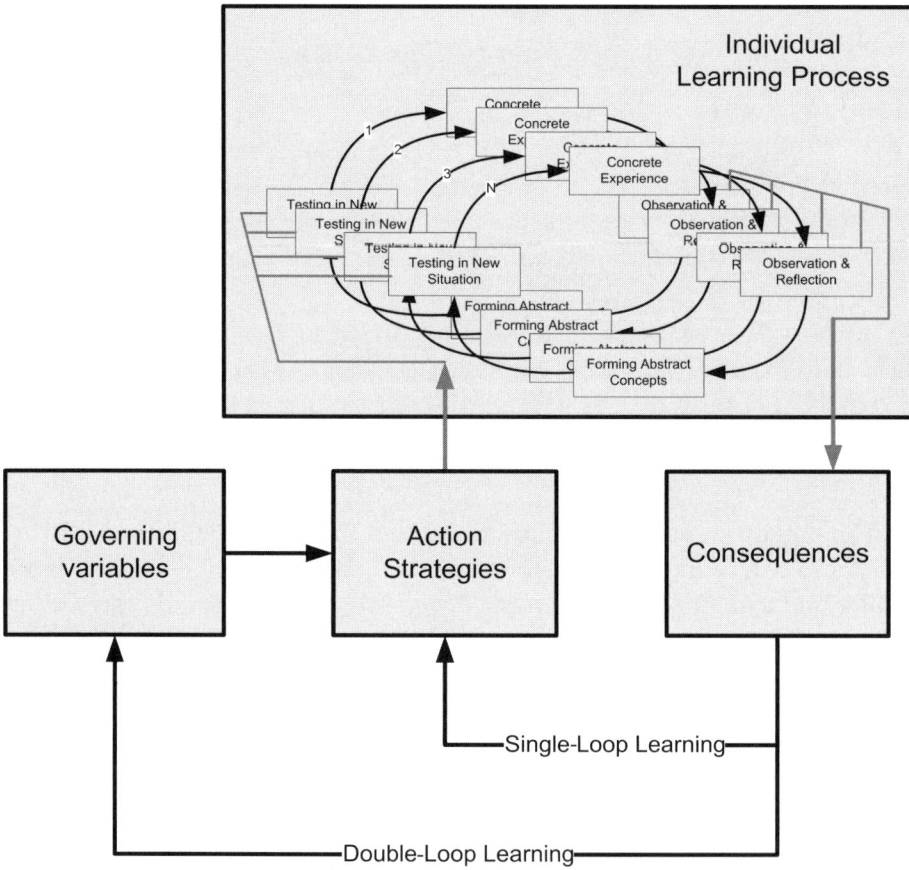

Figure 11.8   Embedding the individual learning process into the organizational learning process

Personal Knowledge Management Strategy

It is not easy to bridge the gaps between individual learning and organizational learning effectively. Nevertheless, the authors believe that it can be achieved by implementing a PKM strategy at both the individual and the organizational level. The role of a PKM strategy is to provide a platform for individuals and for the organization to align their learning objectives, cater for individual and organizational learning factors and embed the individual learning process into the organizational learning process.

INDIVIDUAL PKM STRATEGY

The roles of PKM in the KM life cycle and in an organization have been discussed already. Individuals should have a PKM strategy if they are to work smart in their knowledge work. An individual PKM strategy provides a framework for the individual to improve their PKM skills, to acquire their own knowledge and to transfer the knowledge to others. McGee (2005) argued that there are three essential elements of a personal knowledge management strategy: maintain your portfolio, manage your learning and master your toolkit. The authors' view is that the general PKM strategy should focus on the value of PKM skills, the PKM skills that are necessary to meet learning objectives, information source management, organizing the information for easy retrieval, development of a collaboration network and smart use of PKM tools. The following framework provides general guidelines for defining and implementing a PKM strategy.

Treat PKM skills as a valuable asset for self development

Individuals should develop, practise and demonstrate their PKM skills whenever possible in their daily life and working environment. Smart use of PKM skills is the key to success.

Develop the PKM skills which are required to meet individual learning objectives and are aligned to organizational learning objectives

Individuals should understand what PKM skills are required in order to meet their individual learning objectives which are aligned to their organizational learning objectives. Financial analysts may focus on developing their analysis skills while sales managers may focus on developing presentation skills, for example learning a new language to develop a new market.

Build your own information source and evaluate its trustworthiness

Individuals should build their own information source and evaluate its trustworthiness. This can be achieved by simply developing an information directory manually or by means of the PKM tools. Individuals should realize that information sources, especially information available on the Internet, needs to be evaluated very carefully.

Develop a consistent approach to organizing information

A consistent approach to managing information is important. It can help individuals to retrieve information quickly. A consistent approach can be achieved by systemically classifying the information by the source of information, type of information or by chronological order. The key is consistency in terms of how to classify the information and its location.

Build your own collaboration network

PKM is not an individual task and it should include peer-to-peer knowledge sharing. It is important for individuals to develop their own collaboration network by identifying what and how they can learn from their collaboration group members. It is not necessarily a formal collaboration structure but you should enjoy and know the benefits of your collaboration activities.

Smart use of PKM tools

There are many PKM toolkits available, for example email, instant messaging, web logs (blogs), search engines and so on. Individuals should be able to choose the appropriate PKM tools to fit their own learning objectives whether they are personal, social or job-related. Tsui (2002) classified PKM tools by their function as index/search; meta-search; associative links; information capturing and sharing; email management, analysis and unified messaging; voice recognition; collaboration and synchronization; and learning. The role of PKM tools in the knowledge process is summarized in Table 11.3.

Table 11.3   Alignment of PKM tool categories with knowledge processes

PKM tools category	Knowledge process				
	Creation	Codification/ representation	Classification/ indexing	Search and filter	Share/ distribution
Index/search			x	x	x
Meta-search			x	x	x
Associative links	x	x	x		
Information capturing and sharing	x	x	x		x
Concept/mind mapping		x	x	x	x
Email management, analysis and unified messaging		x	x	x	x
Voice recognition		x			
Collaboration and synchronization		x			x
Learning	x		x		

Source: Tsui (2002, p. 10).

ORGANIZATIONAL PKM STRATEGY

Organizational learning is not only the effort of individuals; the organization should provide a positive learning environment to yield a positive outcome from individual learning (Starbuck and Hedberg 2001). Kessels and Poell (2004) stated that knowledge productivity requires personal involvement and individual learning in a favourable social context. This work environment should be transformed into a conducive learning environment to encourage employees to become self-directed learners, to pursue their interests, to find personal meaning, and to adapt to and, if necessary, change their life circumstances. Therefore, an organization should have a strategy to facilitate implementation of PKM. The following is a general framework to guide an organization in its task of implementing their organizational PKM strategy.

Treat PKM skills as an asset for the organization

The organization should value individual PKM skills as an asset for business development. Organizations should help individuals to maintain and improve their PKM skills to meet organizational learning objectives. To manage individuals' PKM skills, it is necessary for the organization itself to develop a battery of skills and the means for measuring them.

Develop a PKM skills inventory as part of human capital management

Human capital is the productive wealth embodied in labour, skills and knowledge (OECD 2001). The PKM skills inventory should be an element of human capital management such that the organization can easily know the learning capability of every individual, knowing their strengths and weaknesses and matching the PKM skills to different job profiles. The PKM skills inventory should cover all seven skills of retrieving, evaluating, organizing, analysing, presenting, securing and collaborating around information.

PKM skills are part of the performance measurement and reward system

The PKM skills should be measured regularly as part of performance evaluation and as a factor when rewarding individuals. It will ensure that individuals are aware of the importance of maintaining and improving their PKM skills. It is important that different job profiles have different requirements regarding PKM skills. The organization should evaluate the PKM skills of individuals based on their own job profiles.

Develop an individual learning plan to improve PKM skills

Having the PKM skills inventory and performance evaluation in place, the organization should work with individuals to develop their learning plan to improve their PKM skills. This will help the individual to achieve the required PKM skills for the next level of work and also will help the organization to achieve the organizational learning objectives via the individual learning agents.

Make use of IT-based PKM tools to embed individual learning processes into the organizational learning process

The organization can make use of IT technology to facilitate the implementation of the PKM strategy. Tsui (2002) argued that the PKM technologies should be bottom-up, easy to install and powerful, search, information extraction and categorization tools. It is equally important that these tools are aligned to support the tasks that are commonly performed by individuals. This means that the PKM tools should enable the embedding of the individual's learning process into the organizational learning process. By using the PKM tools, the individual user is acting as a learning agent to provide feedback to the organizational learning process while at the same time they can gain knowledge from it and contribute to the knowledge creation process. The knowledge can be captured by the PKM tools and thus will be available for future retrieval. Good IT-based PKM toolkits can both motivate individuals to practise PKM and improve their work performance.

Conclusion

Personal knowledge management is not just the task of individuals. Collaboration is needed in order to share knowledge with each other. PKM plays a significant role in the KM life cycle and in organizational learning and is important to the success of KM implementation. The values fostered by PKM can benefit both individuals and the organization. PKM is an enabler for individuals to achieve their individual learning objectives whether personal, social- or job-related. For an organization, PKM will enable the achievement of competitive advantage and also the fulfilment of social obligations. Even though individual and organizational learning are different, linkages between them can be found in their learning objectives, factors and processes. PKM provides a platform to bridge the gap between the efforts of individuals and of the organization. The organization should embed the individual learning process into the organizational learning process. The new experiences of individuals should be fed back into the organizational learning to create a new action strategy. The governance variables within the organization should also be reviewed and modified to fit new situations, in what is called double-loop learning mode. When implementing the PKM strategy, individual learning factors should be addressed and should be considered together with the organizational learning factors, that is, the organizational structure, organizational culture and technology. It is a complex activity but the authors believe that PKM is an enabler for effectively managing individual learning and organizational learning. Further research in this area is required to help scholars and managers to deepen their understanding of its ramifications.

References

Ackoff, R. (1989), 'From Data to Wisdom', *Journal of Applied Systems Analysis* 16, 3–9.

Ahmed, P. et al. (2002), *Learning through Knowledge Management* (Oxford: Butterworth-Heinemann).

Alazmi, M. and Zairi, M. (2003), 'Knowledge Management Critical Success Factors', *Total Quality Management* 14:2, 199–204.

Alfs, S. (2003), 'Accenture's New Operating Model', in A. Beerli et al. (eds), *Knowledge Management and Networked Environments* (New York: Accenture LLP).

Argyris, C. and Schon, D. (1974), *Theory in Practice: Increasing Professional Effectiveness* (San Francisco: Jossey-Bass).

—— (1978), *Organizational Learning: A Theory of Action Perspective* (New York: Addison-Wesley).

Avery, S. et al. (2001), 'Personal Knowledge Management: Framework for Integration and Partnerships', in P. Smith (ed.), *Annual Conference of the Association of Small Computer Users in Education (ASCUE)* (Myrtle Beach: ASCUE).

Brynojolfsson, E. and Hitt, L. (1996), 'Productivity, Business Profitability, and Consumer Surplus: Three Different Measures of Information Technology Value', *MIS Quarterly* 20:2, 121–42.

—— (1998), 'Beyond the Productivity Paradox', *Communications of ACM* 48:8, 49–55.

Cangelosi, V. and Dill, W. (1965), 'Organizational Learning: Observations towards a Theory', *Administrative Science Quarterly* 10:2, 175–203.

Cavett-Goodwin, D. (2007), 'Making the Case for Corporate Social Responsibility', http://culturalshifts.com/archives/181, accessed 19 October 2008.

Chakravarthy, B. (1982), 'Adaption: A Promising Metaphor for Strategic Management', *Academy of Management Review* 7:1, 35–45.

Cheng, C. (2007), 'A Research Study of Frederick Herzberg's Motivator-Hygiene Theory on Continuing Education Participants in Taiwan', *Journal of American Academy of Business* 12:1, 186–92.

Cisco (2008), *Certified Partner – Overview*, http://www.cisco.com/web/partners/pr11/pr8/partners_pgm_category_page.html, accessed 20 October 2008.

Cross, K. (1978), 'The Adult Learner', presented at American Association for Higher Education National Conference, Washington.

—— (1981), *Adults as Learners* (San Francisco: Jossey-Bass).

Daft, R. and Weick, K. (1984), 'Toward a Model of Organizations as Interpretation Systems', *Academy of Management Review* 9:2, 284–95.

Davenport, T. and Prusak, L. (1998), *Working Knowledge: How Organizations Manage What They Know* (Boston: Harvard Business School Press.).

Dewey, J. (1938), *Experience and Education* (New York: Macmillan).

Dorsey, P. (2001), 'Personal Knowledge Management: Educational Framework for Global Business', http://www.millikin.edu/pkm/pkm_istanbul.html, accessed 24 September 2008.

Drucker, P. (1993), *Post Capitalist Society* (New York: Harper Business).

Efimova, L. (2005), 'Understanding Personal Knowledge Management: A Weblog Case', https://doc.telin.nl/dsweb/Get/Document-44969/pkm_weblogs_final.pdf, accessed 12 March 2008.

Field, L. (1997), 'Impediments to Empowerment and Learning within Organisations', *The Learning Organisation* 4:4, 149–58.

Fiol, C. and Lyles, M. (1985), 'Organizational Learning', *Academy of Management Review* 10:4, 803–13.

Forcheri, P. et al. (2000), 'ICT Driven Individual Learning: New Opportunities and Perspectives', *Educational Technology & Society* 3:1, 51–61.

Frand, J. and Hixon, C. (1999), 'Personal Knowledge Management: Who, What, Why, When, Where, How'?, http://www.anderson.ucla.edu/faculty/jason.frand/researcher/speeches/PKM.htm, accessed 18 January 2008.

Galicia-Castillo, M. (2004), 'Adult Learning Theory', http://www.odu.edu/educ/roverbau/Class_Websites/761_Spring_04/Assets/course_docs/ID_Theory_Reps_Sp04/Cross-Galicia-Castillo.pdf, accessed August 1 2008.

Gold, A. et al. (2001), 'Knowledge Management: An Organizational Capabilities Perspective', *Journal of Management Information Systems* 18:1, 185–214.

Grant, R. (1996), 'Toward a Knowledge Based Theory of the Firm', *Strategic Management Journal* 17 (Winter Special Issue), 109–22.

Griffin, V. (1987), 'Naming the Processes', in D. Bound and V. Griffin (eds), *Appreciating Adults Learning* (London: Kogan Page).

Grover, V. and Davenport, T. (2001), 'General Perspectives on Knowledge Management: Fostering a Research Agenda', *Journal of Management Information Systems* 18:1, 5–21.

Harper, G. (2000), 'Assessing Information Technology Success as a Function of Organizational Culture', Ph.D. dissertation, University of Alabama.

Hedberg, B. (1981), 'How Organisations Learn and Unlearn', in P. Nystrom and W. Starbuck (eds) , *Handbook of Organisational Design* (London: Routledge)..

Houle, C. (1961), *The Inquiring Mind* (Madison: University of Wisconsin Press).

Hyland, T. and Matlay, H. (1997), 'Small Businesses, Training Needs and VET Provision', *Journal of Education and Work* 10:2, 129–39.

Ikehara, H. (1999), 'Implications of Gestalt Theory and Practice for the Learning Organisation', *The Learning Organisation* 6:2, 63–9.

James, P. (2005), 'Knowledge Asset Management: The Strategic Management and Knowledge Management Nexus', DBA Thesis, Southern Cross University, Lismore.

Jarvis, P. (1987), *Adult Learning in Social Context* (London: Croom Helm).

Karlsen, J. and Gottschalk, P. (2004), 'Factors Affecting Knowledge Transfer in IT Projects', *Engineering Management Journal* 16:1, 3–10.

Kessels, J. and Poell, R. (2004), 'Andragogy and Social Capital Theory: The Implications for Human Resource Development', *Advances in Developing Human Resources* 6:2, 146–57.

Khoo, C. et al. (eds) (2006), *Proceedings of Asia-Pacific Conference on Library & Information Education & Practice 2006 (A-LIEP 2006)* (Singapore: School of Communication & Information, Nanyang Technological University).

Kim, D. (1993), 'The Link between Individual and Organisational Learning', *Sloan Management Review* Fall, 37–50.

King, W. (2008), 'An Integrated Architecture for an Effective Knowledge Organisation', *Journal of Knowledge Management* 12: 2, 29–41.

Knowles, M. et al. (1998), *The Adult Learner* (Houston: Gulf Publishing).

Kolb, D. (1993), 'The Process of Experiential Learning', in Thorpe et al. (eds), *Culture and Process of Adult Learning: A Reader* (London: Routledge).

Leonard, D. (1995), *Wellsrpings of Knowledge: Building and Sustaining the Source of Innovation* (Boston: Harvard Business School Press).

Levine, S. (2008), 'The Challenge of Helping Adults Learn: Characteristics of Adult Learners and Implications for Teaching Technical Information', http://www.learnerassociates.net/workshop/adltlrn1.pdf, accessed 4 August 2008.

Lewin, K. (1942), 'Field Theory and Learning', in D. Cartwright (ed.), *Field Theory in Social Science: Selected Theoretical Papers* (London: Social Science Paperbacks).

Liao, Y-S. (2007), 'The Effects of Knowledge Management Strategy and Organisation Structure on Innovation', *International Journal of Management* 24:1 53–60.

Lieb, S. (1999), 'Principles of Adult Learning', http://honolulu.hawaii.edu/intranet/committees/FacDevCom/guidebk/teachtip/adults-2.htm, accessed 1 August 2008.

March, J. and Olsen, J. (1975), 'The Uncertainty of the Past: Organizational Learning Under Ambiguity', *European Journal of Political Research* 3, 147–71.

Martin, J. (2008), 'Personal Knowledge Management: The Basis of Corporate and Institutional Knowledge Management', http://www.spottedcowpress.ca/KnowledgeManagement/pdfs/06MartinJ.pdf, accessed 18 September 2008.

Matlay, H. (2000), 'Organisational Learning in Small Learning Organisations', *Education + Training* 42:4/5, 202–10.

McGee, J. (2005), 'Why You Need a Personal Knowledge Management Strategy', Enterprise Systems, http://www.esj.com/enterprise/article.aspx?EditorialsID=1393, accessed 20 October 2008.

Mendelson, H. and Ziegler, J. (1999), *Survival of the Smartest* (New York: John Wiley & Sons).

Mertins, K. et al. (2003), *Knowledge Management: Concepts and Best Practices*, 2nd edn (New York: Springer).

Miller, H. (1967), *Participation of Adults in Education: A Force-Field Analysis* (Boston: Center for the Study of Liberal Education for Adults, Boston University).

Nonaka, I. (1991), 'The Knowledge-Creating Company', *Havard Business Review* 69: Nov/Dec, 96–104.

Nonaka, I. and Takeuchi, H. (1995), *The Knowledge-Creating Company: How Japanese Companies Create the Dynamics of Innovation* (Oxford: Oxford University Press).

O'Brien, G. (2008), 'What are the Principles of Adult Learning'?, http://www.southernhealth.com.au/cpme/articles/adult_learning.htm, accessed 1 August 2008.

OECD (2001), 'Human Capital', http://stats.oecd.org/glossary/detail.asp?ID=1264, accessed 20 October 2008.

Park, H. et al. (2004), 'Critical Attributes of Organizational Culture that Promote Knowledge Management Implementation Success', *Journal of Knowledge Management* 8:3, 106–17.

Percival, A. (1996), 'Invited Reaction: An Adult Educator Responds', *Human Resource Development Quarterly* 7:2, 131–39.

Piaget, J. (1970), *Genetic Epistemology* (New York: Columbia University Press).

Polanyi, M. (1996), *The Tacit Dimension* (London: Doubleday).

Popper, M. and Lipshitz, R. (2000), 'Organisational Learning: Mechanisms, Culture, and Feasibility', *Management Learning* 32:2, 181–96.

Pounds, W. (1965), 'On Problem Finding', *Sloan School Working Paper No. 145-65* (Cambridge: MIT Sloan School of Management).

Reigeluth, C. (ed.) (1999), *Instructional Design Theories and Models: A New Paradigm of Instructional Theory, Vol. 2* (Mahwah: Lawrence Erlbaum).

Rowe, J. (2005), 'Corporate Social Responsibility as Business Strategy', University of California, Santa Cruz, http://repositories.cdlib.org/cgirs/reprint/CGIRS-Reprint-2005-08/, accessed 19 October 2008.

Rzevski, G. and Prasad, K. (1998), 'The Synergy of Learning Organisations and Flexible Information Technology', *AI & Society*, 12, 98–106.

Sakalas, A. and Venskus, R. (2007), 'Interaction of Learning Organization and Organizational Structure', *Engineering Economics* 3:53, 65–70.

Scarbrough, H. et al. (1998), *Knowledge Management: A Literature Review* (London: Institute of Personnel and Development).

Schein, E. (1992), *Organizational Culture and Leadership* (San Francisco: Jossey-Bass).

—— (1999), *The Corporate Culture Survival Guide* (San Francisco: Jossey-Bass).

Schotte, T. (2003), 'Customer Knowledge Management: How Does my Customer Look and Feel?' in Beerli, A. et al. (eds), *Knowledge Management and Networked Environments* (New York: Accenture LLP).

Senge, P. (1990), *The Fifth Discipline: The Art and Practice of the Learning Organization* (New York: Doubleday).

Seufert, A. et al. (2003), 'Unleashing the Power of Networks for Knowledge Management', in A. Beerli et al. (eds), *Knowledge Management and Networked Environments* (New York: Accenture LLP).

Simon, H. (1947), *Administrative Behaviour* (New York: Macmillan).

Smith, M. (1999), 'Andragogy', http://www.infed.org/lifelonglearning/b-andra.htm, accessed 19 July 2008.

Starbuck, W. and Hedberg, B. (2001), 'How Organizations Learn From Success and Failure', in Dierkes, et al. (eds), *Handbook of Organizational Learning and Knowledge* (New York: Oxford University Press).

Su, S. (2006), 'Individual Learning and Organisational Learning in Academic Libraries', in C. Khoo, et al. (eds), *Proceedings of Asia-Pacific Conference on Library & Information Education & Practice 2006 (A-LIEP 2006)* (Singapore: School of Communication & Information, Nanyang Technological University)..

Thorpe, M. et al. (eds) (1993), *Culture and Process of Adult Learning: A Reader* (London: Routledge).

Tough, A. (1979), *The Adult's Learning Projects* 2nd edn (Austin: Learning Concepts).

Tsui, E. (2002), 'Technologies for Personal and Peer-to-peer (P2P) Knowledge Management', *CSC Leading Edge Forum (LEF) Technology Grant Report* (Melbourne: Computer Sciences Corporation).

—— (2007), 'Exploring the Robustness of Rapid Deployment Collaboration Tools – Experiences from Several KM Technology Workshops', *International Journal of Knowledge and Systems Sciences* 4:3, 42–52.

Tuggle, F. and Shaw, N. (2000), 'The Effect of Organizational Culture on the Implementation of Knowledge Management', presented at Florida Artifical Intelligence Research Symposium (FLAIRS) (Orlando: AAAI Press).

Wallas, G. (1926), *The Art of Thought* (New York: Harcourt Brace).

Wang, C. and Ahmed, P. (2003), 'Organizational Learning: A Critical Review', *The Learning Organization* 10:1, 8–17.

Wiig, K. (1997), 'Knowledge Management: An Introduction and Perspective', *The Journal of Knowledge Management* 1:1, 6–14.

——(2004), *People-Focused Knowledge Management* (Oxford: Elsevier Butterworth-Heinemann).

Wright, K. (2005), 'Personal Knowledge Management: Supporting Individual Knowledge Worker Performance', *Knowledge Management Research and Practice* 3:3, 156.

Wynne, R. (2008), 'Motivating Factors in Adult Learning', http://www.assetproject.info/learner_methodologies/before/motivating.htm, accessed 9 August 2008.

Young, S. et al. (1999), 'Organizational Learning as a Feedback System: A Conceptual Framework', *The 17th International Conference of the System Dynamics Society and the 5th Australian & New Zealand Systems Conference*, 20–23 July, Wellington, New Zealand.

Ziegler, J. (2008), 'What are the Key Principles of Organizational IQ?', http://www.synesis.com/synesis/OrganizationalIQ.html#IQ, accessed 19 March 2008.

12

The Importance of Personal Knowledge Management in the Knowledge Society

Karl Martin Wiig[1]

Introduction

The knowledge society is global. Broadly, it realizes that people need to be literate and competent in many areas to participate equitably in the global society as individuals, as supporters of the economy, and as effective citizens. It has progressed from the nineteenth and twentieth centuries' scientific management and industrial economy that focused on observable and quantifiable behaviours, information and work to deliver goods and services efficiently and reliably. The new economic focus is broader and driven by needs to make people more knowable and satisfy expanded requirements like incorporating intellectual capital (IC) in customer-specific deliverables. In a smoothly performing society, people everywhere – in their personal lives and as part of the workforce and society – need to operate effectively. Hence, it has become important to understand how people reason and how to ascertain that they have the best available knowledge for whatever function they need to perform. Consequently, the need to manage knowledge and knowledge-related processes throughout society – personal knowledge management (PKM) – has become a central issue with three objectives:[2]

1. From the personal perspective – the objective is personal fulfillment and quality of life (QoL).

---

1   The chapter is based on a book manuscript on the importance of personal IC in the society, currently under preparation.
2   These are similar to categories suggested by Mashayekh (2007).

2.   From society's economic and business perspectives – the objective
      is workforce competence.

3.   From society's operational and functional perspectives – the
      objective is citizenship capabilities and societal behaviour.

Making people more knowledgeable and operations smarter have been
goals pursued formally and informally for millennia. Structured and deliberate
KM with people and broader IC focus is pursued to varying degrees in many
enterprises and nations worldwide. The broader objective of KM anywhere is
to initiate effective approaches to improve knowledge-related performance in
the short and long term. As practised by competent enterprises, KM is:

> *the systematic, explicit, and deliberate management and operation of*
> *intellectual capital (IC) assets and knowledge-related processes – be*
> *they people-, technology-, management- or resource-focused. KM, in*
> *addition to short-term operational considerations, includes the longer-*
> *term strategic and tactical initiatives to create, build, renew, utilize, and*
> *safeguard IC assets and knowledge. Its overall objective is to maximize*
> *the enterprise's IC-related effectiveness and returns in all its forms.*
>
>   *Wiig (2008, 2)*

The root objective of PKM is the desire to make citizens highly
knowledgeable. They should function competently and effectively in their daily
lives, as part of the workforce and as public citizens. In a society with broad
personal competences, decision-making everywhere will maximize personal
goals, provide effective public agencies and governance, make commerce
and industry competitive, and ensure that personal and family decisions and
actions will improve societal functions and QoL.

Many organizations rely on deliberate and systematic KM to strengthen the
organization's strategic directions and to make its tactics and daily operations
more effective. Many also adopt multidisciplinary capabilities to make KM
more effective in support of the enterprise. That has led to pursuit of advanced
technologies and integration with management, cognitive, social and library
sciences, to name a few.

Enterprises of all kinds are challenged to be successful and viable by
servicing their stakeholders competitively and effectively. Nowhere are these
challenges more important than in helping people to understand their work

and their functions as private citizens and family members. For personal, enterprise and societal success, people everywhere must have requisite knowledge matched by reliable information to make good decisions. They must execute decisions to implement actions that support the chosen goals. In enterprises, challenges come from economic, political and social changes that affect strategies, tactical steps and daily operations. Challenges also come from advances in business practices, better knowledge, increased IC assets and in business-related technology.

Distributed competences are increasingly important since local conditions and the world at large are constantly changing and the rate of change is increasing. Old judgements, practices and knowledge are often of less value, so new knowledge and perspectives are required.

Knowledge-related Globalization Pressures

The globalized knowledge economy of the twenty-first century presents new demands that change how we govern countries and cities, manage businesses and pursue our personal lives as private citizens and as part of the workforce. Worldwide markets increasingly require sophisticated goods and services. Competitors create new pressure by providing highly desirable products. These changes are so extensive that our past understandings and judgements of national, commercial and personal requirements, opportunities and threats often are invalidated, thus requiring development of new perspectives and considerations. Personal, enterprise, regional and national survival and viability rests on effective and competitive performance. The rules have changed.

There are many dimensions to this new world. Several are influenced by how societies deal with knowledge – how they build, renew, utilize and safeguard personal, enterprise and societal IC assets. For example, nations need to consider how and for what purposes they educate their citizens. More broadly, they must also foster and support other knowledge-related initiatives, practices and processes, including lifelong learning (LLL). They need to be clear about which objectives and priorities they decide to pursue to ensure that these are pursued and that the KM initiatives are implemented successfully.

The public sector is similarly affected. Comprehensive information and communication technologies (ICT) such as Web 2.0 provide new capabilities and practices that change much of the nature of public service and interactions with the public at large. As citizens learn from television, the Internet and other sources about what happens in the rest of the world, they become more discriminating in their demands for better public services. The new work requires greater knowledge – narrow and targeted task knowledge, broader enterprise and world knowledge – to understand the breadth of operations and navigational knowledge needed to network effectively.

The global knowledge society does not only affect countries, regions and larger enterprises. It also affects smaller enterprises that need to be more effective and innovative to compete – often in local markets invaded by external competitors that may be more efficient and provide a wide range of sophisticated goods and services. On a global scale this is progress. Locally, this is an unwelcome intrusion that leads to unwanted changes and may even threaten or destroy the livelihood of those who are unprepared.

Societal Goals

Societies throughout the world work to improve international relations, global competitiveness, domestic prosperity and growth, and the quality of life for their citizens. In particular, nations work to ascertain that effective IC assets are available to government and public operations, to commerce and industry and to the general public with focus on personal IC everywhere. For instance, a major goal for most societies is stability and Figure 12.1 provides examples of eight societal stability factors.

Societal stability and crime is largely influenced by the gap between the rich and poor – and in some nations, the shrinking of the middle class. The potentially destabilizing effect of the QoL gap is implicit in the Economy and financial system factor shown in Figure 12.1.

Achieving societal stability requires that citizens are sufficiently knowledgeable to participate intelligently in public affairs and government – that is, being competent by having broad perspectives, independent and well-considered opinions, instead of being uncritical pawns influenced by capricious political movements and misinformation and propaganda. In addition, people need sufficient knowledge, skills and expertise to form a competent workforce, to be able to provide for themselves and their families, and to conduct themselves with social responsibility. Once a society determines which knowledge-related

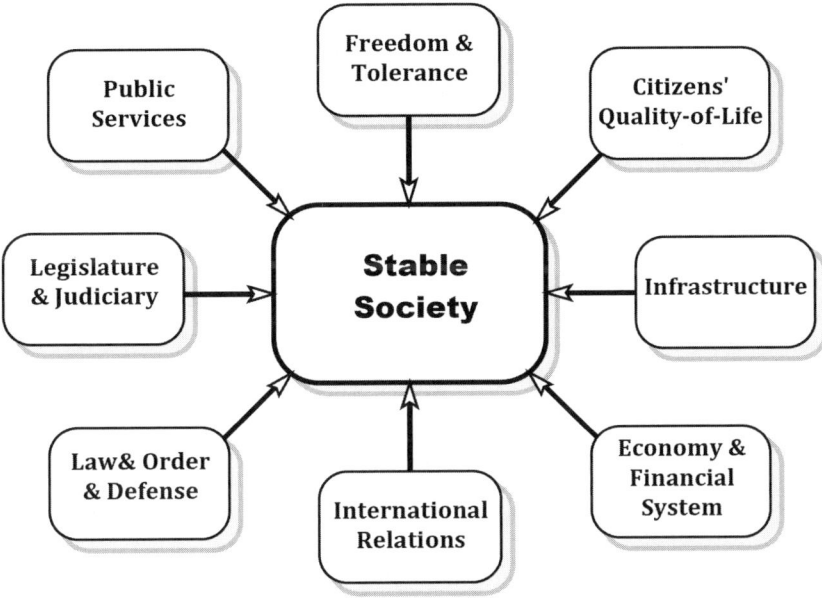

Figure 12.1   **Examples of societal stability factors. Copyright © 2007 by Knowledge Research Institute, Inc. Reproduced with permission**

factors will affect its goals and intents, it can set priorities for its societal KM and determine which initiatives will be effective in pursuing its objectives.

SOCIETAL COMPETENCE IS VITAL

Societies need competence to deal appropriately with chaordic challenges and to function well. Ideally, they need to be competent in all eight areas indicated in Figure 12.2. Competence in every one of these areas relies on the competence of people – the knowledge they possess and the IC available to them whenever needed.

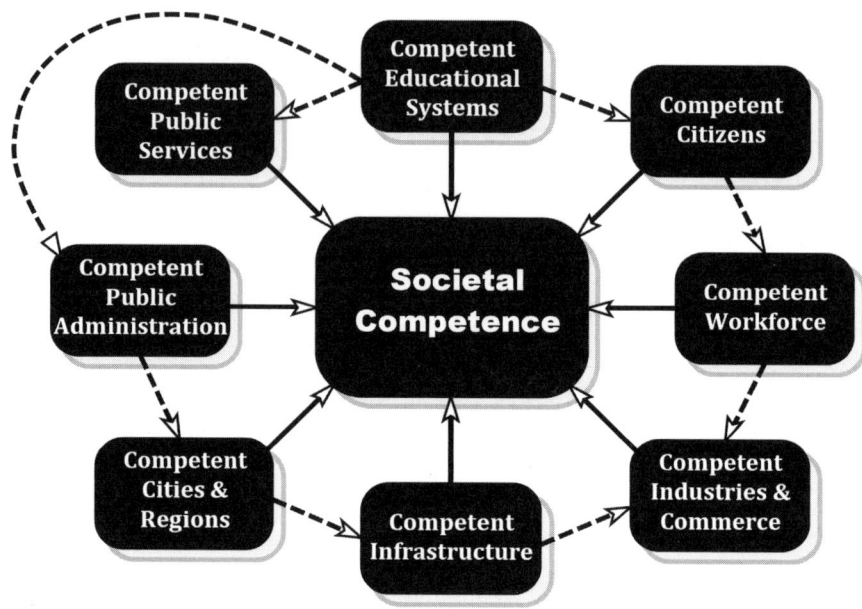

Figure 12.2   Examples of societal stability factors. Copyright © 2007 by
Knowledge Research Institute, Inc. Reproduced with permission

Society is Chaordic

The advent of the globalized knowledge and information society has brought powerful capabilities with fast changes. Examples include the speed of transactions of all kinds, commercial contracts, political and social movements, competitive goods and services and scientific knowledge. There are constant improvements and progress – conditions that lead to changes in goods and services, in work, in organizational relationships and in the daily life of private citizens. Over time, every organization will meet challenging operating conditions with conflicting objectives. However, as changes occur and new directions need to be pursued, the result is friction between business as usual and the new requirements.

All these changes lead to conflicting requirements between providing stable environments for normal living and delivering today's work – and at the same time accommodating creation and effective implementation of desired changes. The result is that work complexity covers the full range from basic routine tasks to chaotic challenges. Environments are 'chaordic' (Hock 1997) and require strong capabilities to deal effectively with chaotic effects of external and strategic changes while at the same time providing the orderly and stable conditions needed to provide desirable operating conditions for daily work.

The Individual is Important!

The performance of any society and enterprise results from people's actions in response to situations given their contexts, intents and goals. People's actions are voluntary[3] and based on situation-specific knowledge that is modified by deeply internalized tacit values, beliefs, judgements and understandings. For better performance. people must be provided with resources and opportunities to do their best. They need knowledge and understanding as well as motivation and supportive attitudes.

The overall performance and viability of societies and enterprises result from innumerable small actions by individuals, as illustrated in Figure 12.3. Small personal 'nano actions' combine with larger departmental actions that combine to create consolidated enterprise actions that result in the performance of the whole organization. The quality and extent of knowledge possessed by people – their competence – and structural IC assets available to them determine the realized enterprise performance.

Cognitive science research continues to provide better understanding of the mental functions of people when they engage in work (see for example Gazzaniga et al. 2008). For example, there is increasing understanding of the complexity, utility and business value of how proficient workers apply the knowledge they possess to analyse and interpret situations, to make decisions, and deliver quality knowledge work and other activities. This is the case in higher levels of work by managers and professionals. However, it is also the case for 'simpler work' in factories and small businesses. In operational work, the variety of challenges and needs for knowledge and judgement are important for reliable delivery of quality work products undeterred by difficulties and irregularities – be they unanticipated changes in requirements, correction of errors, or other problems. There is increased understanding of how to strengthen working people's cognition by providing them with just-in-time collaboration, automated decision support systems (DSSs) and access to other IC assets. Support capabilities also reduce the need to educate or train workers to handle rarely encountered tasks.

---

3   Voluntary here means that given a particular situation, its opportunities, risks, pressures and constraints, the action that is voluntarily pursued will be that with the smallest psychological cost.

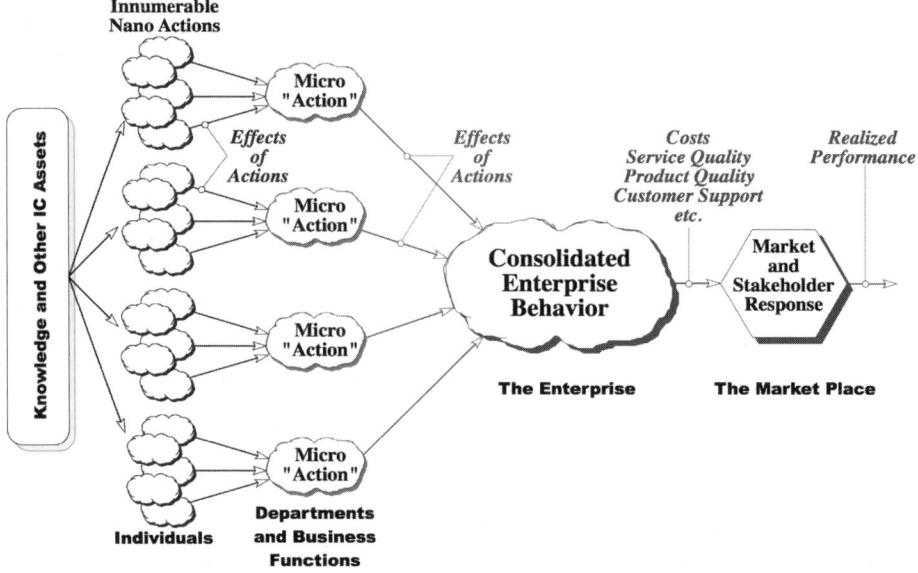

Figure 12.3   Personal actions accumulate to enterprise performance.
Copyright © 2000 by Knowledge Research Institute, Inc.
Reproduced with permission

The importance of personally possessed knowledge in order for people to behave and work effectively has become clearer. Early on, managerial emphasis on work procedures and methods was placed on observable processes and work. Likewise, the appropriateness of personal behaviours in society, in family settings and everywhere else were judged by observable and describable traits with less understanding of the motivators and backgrounds that lead to individual behaviours.

Focus has now expanded to include less observable cognition and knowledge. Whereas it has been understood that know-how and expertise influence quality of behaviour, the knowledge economy has brought new emphasis on individual education and training. There is understanding of unobservable aspects of behaviours and work, particularly about how people think and utilize knowledge when performing tasks ranging from simple to complex. As a result, effectiveness in the workplace is improved when people are provided with understanding of the broader contexts in which they find themselves.

Competence of the individual is particularly important in small- to medium-sized enterprises (SMEs) where variability of work requires workers to be more agile than in larger enterprises. SMEs as job creators are also important, as Samawati and Stumph (2006) concluded: 'enterprises with fewer than 500 employees, have been the dominant force in the area of job creation'. Furthermore, in most societies, the total workforce of SMEs is greater than in larger enterprises. For example, in the USA, the total number of workers in firms exceeds 134 million. Of these, 78 million or 58 per cent work in SMEs with fewer than 500 employees and 22 million (17 per cent) work in firms with one to four employees. SMEs represent 99.7 per cent of all firms, they create more than half of the private non-farm gross domestic product, and they create 60 to 80 per cent of the net new jobs.

SPONTANEOUS ORDER

According to Wikipedia, '"Spontaneous order" is the spontaneous emergence of order out of seeming chaos; the emergence of various kinds of social order from a combination of self-interested individuals who are not intentionally trying to create order'.[4] Society and enterprises rely on competent decision-making by individuals for managing themselves in crowded traffic, in organizing the workday, in executing work tasks appropriately, in arranging and managing personal life and as participating citizens in society. All these – and many more – individual and group challenges are complex and require individual competence for effective performance. Again, the individual's knowledge becomes centrally important.

The Importance of Knowledge[5]

A basic premise in the knowledge society is that improved access and application of better personal knowledge will result in better and quicker situation-handling, increased innovation and greater ability to achieve goals. Knowledge, it is realized, is the dominant factor that fuels people's intellects, makes effective performance possible, generates judgements and leads to creation of new knowledge. From a broader perspective, knowledge is the driver of economic growth and progress – in people, in organizations and in society. Without knowledge, intelligent and effective behaviour – the ability to interpret, understand, judge, assess, innovate, decide, act and monitor –

---

4   http://en.wikipedia.org/wiki/Spontaneous_order.
5   Discussion of different kinds of knowledge is presented in Wiig (2004).

will not be possible even if the best information is made available and the best personal attitudes are fostered.

Hence, deliberate and systematic PKM is required to make available the best IC to provide intellectual growth and renewal required for personal, enterprise and societal viability and success. PKM makes the enterprise more effective in internal operations, customer understanding and service, marketplace success, financial performance and general stakeholder relations – all measures of enterprise performance.

However, as stated by Quinn et al. (1996, 71), 'surprisingly little attention has been given to managing professional intellect' and the focus is still often on observable aspects of IC – such as documented or verbally communicated personal knowledge, the kinds of structural knowledge and supporting information incorporated in technology-based systems. At the same time, less attention is placed on IC assets like the personal tacit knowledge embedded in organizational systems and procedures, or less discoverable, in practices and traditions.

Workers at all levels – bureaucrats, line workers, clerks, supervisors and managers – must understand the contexts and requirements for their work to be effective. In the knowledge society, greater adaptation to context requires autonomy and flexibility that demand broad and deep knowledge covering the primary work domain as well as methodology, enterprise navigation and broad world domains.

Knowledge, Intellectual Capital and Information

Knowledge that is needed by workers and citizens in all walks of life can be separated into five topic areas, each of which can be personally possessed – or, when needed, obtained from experts, colleagues or provided by ICT support systems. Knowledge also occurs at different levels of concreteness and conceptual comprehension. People possess much knowledge in the form of mental models (see Johnson-Laird 2006) at different levels of depth: as rudimentary understanding, 'how-to' operational understanding, deeper 'script' understanding and good general and schematic understanding of the area. As people delve into a knowledge area, they also develop metaknowledge of that area (see Kuhn 2000; Wiig 2004, 86 and 36). From a business perspective, the six topic areas considered here are:

1. *Task-specific knowledge*: includes knowledge of how to perform work tasks and how these relate to the operational area and the enterprise – be it profit-making corporations, societal bureaucracies or private family units. This topic area also includes understanding of appropriate behaviour.

2. *Enterprise knowledge*: includes understanding of the enterprise's practices and policies, structure, operation, strategy, intents and direction. It includes knowledge of products, services, customers and suppliers. The area also includes understanding of the enterprise's resources, its strengths and weaknesses.

3. *Relationship knowledge*: Includes understanding of navigational knowledge and understanding relationships within the enterprise and to external entities, relationships to exchange information and to obtain assistance. This topic area also includes knowledge of stakeholders ranging from suppliers, customers, co-workers, family and friends and how to behave.

4. *Context knowledge*: includes understanding of the context in which the industry operates, its role in society, the competitive environment and its future prospects.

5. *Broad world knowledge*: includes knowledge of the state and trends of economics, geography, social and political aspects, science and technology.

6. *Methodological knowledge*: includes knowledge such as of critical thinking, mathematics, statistics, investigative methods, planning systems, personnel handling approaches and so on.

Existing knowledge reflects cumulated experiences, understanding and judgements. It also includes new insights based on past work challenges and expectations for new opportunities and contexts. Existing knowledge in its most tangible forms is explicit – often in stories, documents, organized into knowledge bases (KBs), embedded in automated systems and in manual systems and procedures. It can also be embedded implicitly in products and services, in work practices and in understanding of what works and what does not. However, the greater part of existing knowledge is tacit and possessed by people in their minds in ways that they cannot readily make explicit.

However, they can access tacit knowledge mentally (often through priming memory) while conducting real work and solving problems and may then be able to share parts with others (Wiig 2004). The mechanisms by which tacit knowledge is built in the mind and made available are better understood from recent cognitive science research in ways that assist practical PKM (Fauconnier and Turner 2003).

INTELLECTUAL CAPITAL

When considering the role of KM, the broader aspects of IC need to be considered to ascertain that KM is pursued to best advantage. As shown in Figure 12.4, IC is one of the two building blocks of corporate capital. The other building block is physical capital. The concept of IC was elaborated in the 1990s and is still the subject of extensive analysis and debate (Roos et al. 1998; Stewart 1991, 1997). However, the version in Figure 12.4 is generally accepted.

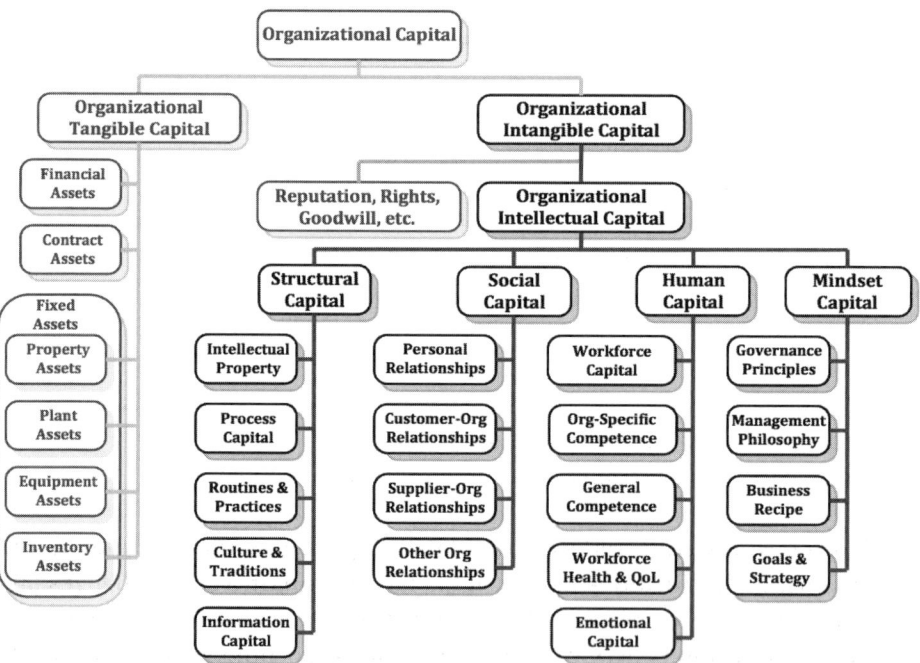

Figure 12.4   **Intellectual capital components within corporate capital. Copyright © 2002 by Knowledge Research Institute, Inc. Reproduced with permission**

In general, IC accounts for current assets – those which are in existence now. That differs from the scope of KM, which also must pursue tactical and strategic initiatives to develop future capabilities. 'HR and workforce' directly affects KM by including explicit, embedded and implicit personal knowledge possessed by people at all levels of the enterprise. KM must also focus on embedded IC in structural capital.

KNOWLEDGE AND INFORMATION ARE DIFFERENT

The *purpose of knowledge* is to understand observations and situations, to determine options for actions and to implement them effectively by providing people (or intelligent agents) with capabilities with which to reason and act. In part, knowledge also consists of understanding of how to juxtapose and integrate seemingly isolated information items to develop new meanings – to create new insights with which to approach effective handling of target situations (particularly by conceptual blending as discussed by Fauconnier and Turner 2003). Knowledge is used to explore, evaluate and handle situations, assess, decide, solve problems, plan, act and monitor. It is important to establish that for the most part, knowledge cannot be managed directly, only indirectly by managing and supporting knowledge-related processes.

The *purpose of information* is to describe and specify conditions, things and concepts – any kind of describable situation or concrete or abstract object. Information consists of data organized to characterize a particular situation, condition, context, challenge or opportunity. Information is mostly explicit, readily examined and its management requires conscientious and detailed attention to logical manipulation, storage, presentation and distribution.

INFORMATION IS DIFFERENT FROM AND SUBORDINATE TO KNOWLEDGE

The different roles of knowledge and information in business work are indicated in Figure 12.5 which illustrates why KM and information management (IM) are both separate and necessary. For knowledge to be fully effective, it must have access to information that matches its needs in timeliness, granularity and all other dimensions of concern. That makes information subordinate to knowledge. Hence, management of knowledge (KM) is fundamentally different from management of information (IM) and KM and IM should be managed independently by separate disciplines.

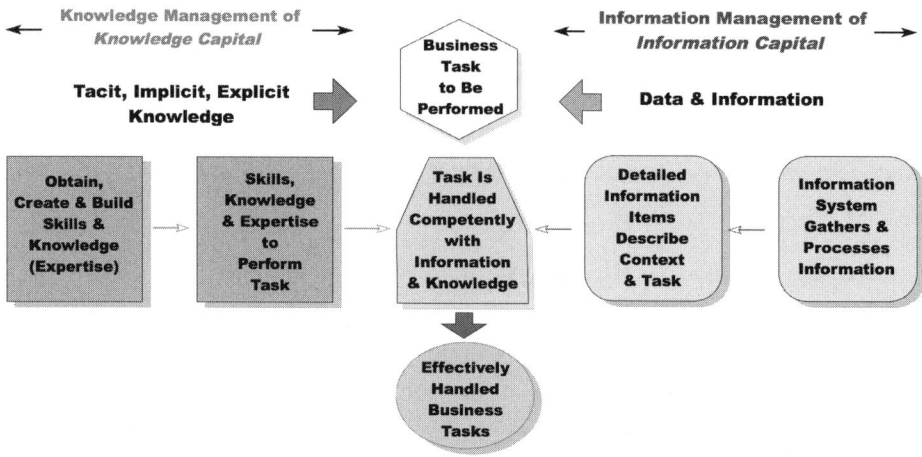

Figure 12.5   Different functions and management of knowledge and information. Copyright © 2003 by Knowledge Research Institute, Inc. Reproduced with permission

The Value of Knowledge

The societal value of knowledge is vast and broadly important. The importance of knowledgeable and effective work is readily understood for governance of society, for industry and commerce and generally for the future prospects of the society and its economy. What has been emphasized less is the value of knowledge for regular citizens and in the daily life of people everywhere.

People become more effective citizens when they understand societal functions and dynamics – how best to participate in societal processes such as elections, obtaining permits, securing titles for property and how to plan for their future. Similarly, knowledgeable citizens are more effective when pursuing education and preparing for their future. One important aspect is the need for widespread understanding of personal opportunities – for family, prosperity and quality of life factors like freedoms. These understandings are built on knowledge of educational options, how to qualify and afford different options and what the future prospects are. In societies without such widespread understanding, people may be ignorant about how to improve themselves, are often less motivated and continue life as before.

Most successful enterprises are proactive and agile to adapt to the dynamic global environment. They actively explore and innovate to improve products and services, make operations more effective, improve relationships with customers, suppliers and other stakeholders, and pursue flexible strategies that will provide the best performance. Their behaviours and culture require savvy understanding and judgement, knowledgeable situation handling and extensive, pertinent and reliable information. Proactive organizations expect that people at every level make good decisions and rely upon distributed competence – knowledge – to understand enterprise direction and for decisions and actions to reflect this understanding. In these enterprises, operating, tactical and strategic functions are dynamic with frequent changes that often are significant in both extent and value. They aim to pursue new opportunities, correct problems and in some cases, avert disasters.

There are great needs for PKM since shared understanding of enterprise strategy and direction is missing in most enterprises as Peterson and Nielson (2009) report:

- 56 per cent of workers do not clearly understand their company's most important goals,

- 73 per cent of workers do not think their company's goals are translated into specific work they can execute, and

- 70 per cent of workers do not routinely plan how to support agreed-upon goals and tasks in their workgroups.

THE VALUE OF LITERACY

The lack of literacy severely affects societal success. The economic impact of illiteracy is large, and low literacy hampers many nations in their efforts to provide for citizens and participate equitably in the global economy. Over 100 countries are severely affected with great needs for improved literacy. Literacy throughout the world needs to be significantly improved and is inequitably distributed throughout the world as UNESCO (2001) reports:

- 26 per cent of the world's adult population is illiterate,

- 98 per cent of non-literates live in developing countries,

- in the least developed countries, the overall illiteracy rate is 49 per cent,

- 52 per cent of all non-literates live in India and China, which have one third of the world's population,

- less than 60 per cent of adults are literate in Africa and

- women make up two-thirds of all non-literates.

By increasing literacy with effective PKM, the potential economic return to a nation is large. Long-term effects of improved knowledge indicate that an increase of 1 per cent in a literacy score leads to a 2.5 per cent personal productivity increase and to a 1.5 per cent increase in GDP (Coulombe et al. 2004). Average personal annual income and national literacy rates are related as indicated in Figure 12.6 for representative nations.

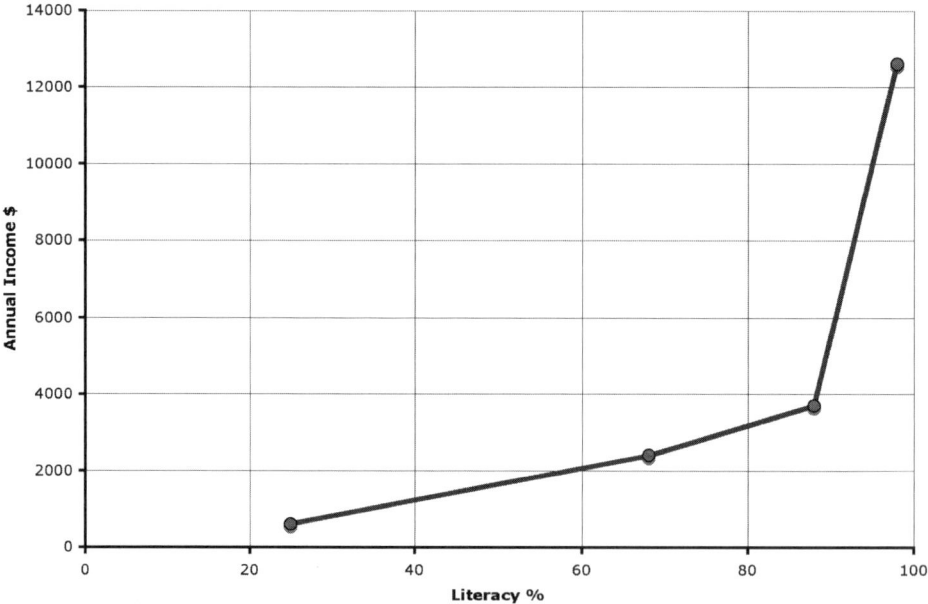

Figure 12.6   The relationship between literacy and personal annual income

Source: UNESCO 2001

Knowledge Workers

Whereas some consider personal knowledge primarily to be important for 'white collar' knowledge workers, in the knowledge economy, people at every working level must possess good personal knowledge and skills to deal competently with daily work. They must be flexible to deal with variations in tasks, handle computer systems and other advanced work-aids and be agile and adapt to different job requirements and take on different responsibilities.

As people gain understanding and experience, their competence increases and they progress from being unskilled at the beginning to higher levels of proficiency. Seven proficiency categories for workers are considered in terms of their knowledge and skill levels:

1. *Unskilled workers*: are unaware of specific job requirements, with limited understanding or judgement – can perform basic routine work with minimal training.

2. *Beginners – novices*: have beginning awareness of field – begin to build skills and real experience (amateurish).

3. *Advanced beginners – apprentices*: are aware and partially informed with the beginnings of a deeper understanding – are skilled in narrow areas.

4. *Competent performers – journeymen*: are competent and broadly skilled – are knowledgeable in selected areas.

5. *Proficient performers – craftsmen*: are highly proficient in particular areas – are generally knowledgeable.

6. *Expert performers – masters*: are highly experts in many areas and broadly knowledgeable.

7. *Elite performers – grand masters*: are world-class experts in all areas of the knowledge domain.

Understanding the working individual's knowledge functions and needs makes it possible to create more effective PKM initiatives. This has been pursued in industrial enterprises but is often overlooked in the broader society.

It is necessary to consider which knowledge workers in different positions must possess in their minds and how much additional knowledge might be obtained from KM systems and from collaborators and experts to ascertain that their work will be effective.

Knowledge Work

As the world becomes more sophisticated and integrated, work contexts change with increasing complications and complexity. Simple routine work is often automated, leaving people to deal with more demanding tasks. Successful enterprises adopt new, more demanding approaches that require greater worker competence. The changes are evident in the increasing productivity in areas ranging from manufacturing and agriculture to service industries. Knowledge work can be separated into regular operational work, tactical work and strategic work.

OPERATIONAL WORK

The daily activities of selling, producing and delivering goods and services are part of operational work which often is basic or routine work performed by workers without extensive training or education. More demanding work is conducted by apprentices and competent or proficient performers with extensive skills and knowledge. For operational work to be executed efficiently, reliably and accurately, workers must possess job-specific skills and knowledge. These IC assets must be renewed and expanded regularly to handle changes and new requirements. Intelligent automated systems must also have their embedded IC updated to be current and appropriate. Established systems and procedures must be built to reflect the best available knowledge, which by its nature will be embedded implicitly and must be updated.

The job-specific IC assets are often well suited for PKM and KM system support. Some operational work needs broader world and methodological knowledge, particularly to deal with irregularities and problem situations. An example is the broad knowledge required by logistics dispatchers to handle logistics problems.

TACTICAL WORK

Tactical work deals with planning operational work and ascertaining that operational resources are available. It supports enterprise strategy by interpreting operational requirements and securing resources needed for strategy implementation. Tactical work also supports operations by ascertaining that operational capabilities are renewed and maintained. It must ensure that tactical and operational innovations are utilized to improve products and services and make operations effective. Tactical work is more complicated and complex than operational work and on an individual workday's basis, is more valuable than operational work.

Tactical work requires relatively broad world and industry knowledge and excellent enterprise and methodological knowledge. These knowledge areas are good candidates for PKM and KM system support, particularly for less dynamic IC assets. Situations where knowledge changes quickly or needs to be developed to address novel situations can be candidates for PKM approaches such as creative communities of practice (CoPs) and collaboration.

STRATEGIC WORK

Strategic work deals with determining the enterprise's direction. Most strategic work cannot be well defined and deals with re-determining the enterprise's direction and intents as external and internal conditions and contexts change. Strategic work is always complicated and complex and often involves developing an understanding of changes and new scenarios, what their consequences might be and what should be done. Strategic tasks must also address internal issues to shape the enterprise's capabilities such as personnel changes and training, development of new relations and markets, new product and service lines and organizational structure.

Strategic work requires broad knowledge covering general world knowledge, specific industry knowledge and knowledge of the enterprise's strengths, weaknesses and general characteristics. It requires extensive methodological knowledge – the best defined knowledge that can usefully be supported by PKM.

SITUATION-HANDLING

People handle work tasks and challenges – situations – by observing, giving them attention, identifying what they are about, exploring and making decisions about how to handle them appropriately, implementing the decisions – the selected actions – and monitoring what is happening, explicitly or tacitly. Considering situation-handling from this perspective leads to four primary tasks: sense-making, decision-making/problem solving, implementation and monitoring (Wiig 2004).

Figure 12.7 provides a simplified overview of the four tasks and their relationships. The functional capabilities needed to operationalize each primary task are: situational awareness; action space and innovation capability; execution capability; and governance competence and perspectives. These capabilities are dependent on the extent and quality of knowledge that people possess or have available to tackle the tasks. If functional capacity knowledge is limited it will become a constraint that reduces the effectiveness of the situation-handling.

Work Complexity

Work situations vary widely. Some, such as assembly line tasks, may be fast, reliable and relatively error-free. Tasks may be well-known and require skills that are routine, even automatized and deeply internalized in a person's mind. Most daily tasks are routine and much routine work is automated with ICT. Other situations, such as project work to solve stubborn operating problems, are complicated and require extensive, at times abstract, methodological knowledge and metaknowledge. Even in well-known routine cases, effective situation-handling can involve many steps and iterations and may require specialized knowledge. Consider seven categories of knowledge work complexity:

1. *Basic routine work*: simple, repetitive and well understood work that in the aggregate is important to the enterprise. This work can be scheduled with confidence. Some can be performed by unskilled workers and novices.

2. *Near routine work*: logical and common variations of daily routine work that can be planned with certainty. In the aggregate this often is the bulk of important daily work. Some can be performed by

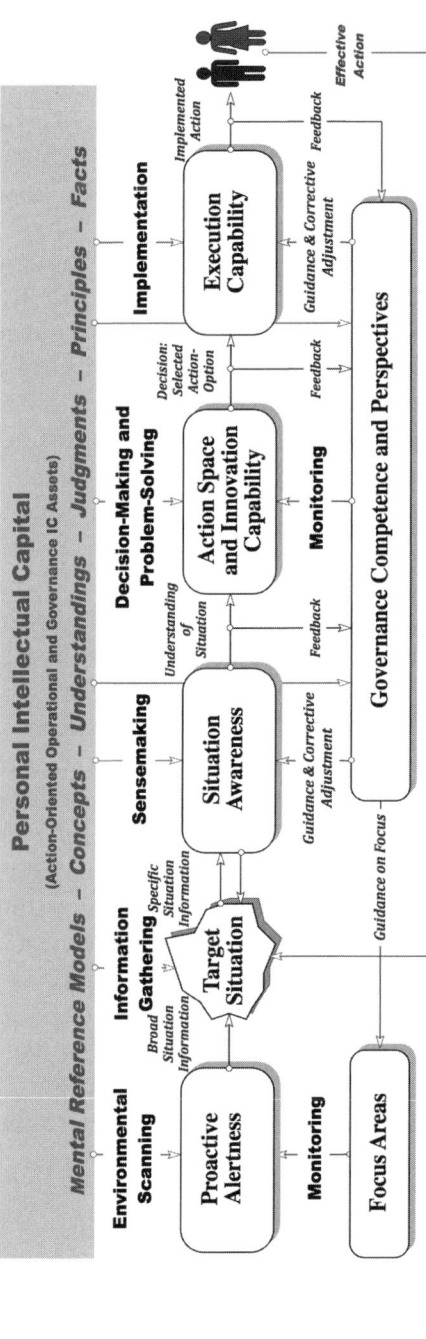

Figure 12.7   The personal situation-handling model. Copyright © 2003 by Knowledge Research Institute, Inc. Reproduced with permission

apprentices while competent and proficient performers provide most of the work.

3. *Regular complicated work*: complicated extensions of routine work which are required for high-quality results and regularly require competent performers for good execution. In the aggregate, this work is important and can be forecasted and planned with some certainty. Operational planning often falls into this category.

4. *Uncommon complicated work*: uncommon and unexpected less-known variations of routine work that can only be planned with uncertainty and forecasted as contingencies. This work is important for daily and future operations. It is often needed to avert problems and typically requires proficient performers for successful completion. Planning for organizational and operational changes falls into this category.

5. *Complex work*: whereas this work may be partially understood by specialists, it often includes resolution of conflicts between competing objectives. Complex work typically requires systems perspectives and integration of knowledge areas. Complex work requires experts and elite performers and is very important for enterprise viability. Part of it can be planned whereas other situations are uncertain. Determination of strategic directions, enterprise organization and strategic partners fall into this category.

6. *Chaotic work challenges*: difficult, not understood and ill-defined situations that cannot be expected with any certainty. They are unusual 'wicked' problem situations outside expected work scopes that require expert and elite performers and are of great enterprise importance. Unexpected market and technological challenges fall into this category.

7. *'Black swan' events* (Taleb 2007): these challenges cannot be foreseen and are totally unexpected, without precedence and can have monumental or catastrophic impact – and can in some instances provide unexpected opportunities. They must be dealt with by the best expert and elite performers available. Unexpected terrorist attacks, social unrest and economic crashes fall into this category.

Personal Knowledge Management in Society (Wiig 2004, 2007)

Enduring societal competence and viability require effective functioning of individuals, family units, enterprises, financial and other systems, government entities and infrastructure. The needs are for broad IC management perspectives and efforts that span short-term initiatives and long-term considerations. A competent workforce must be developed, maintained and renewed focusing on adults and young people and extend into lifelong learning. Infrastructure must be created and maintained for support of education, work, industry and commerce, sociopolitical and socio-economic functions and quality of life.

The largest area of deliberate and systematic KM is by necessity people-focused to support people as they participate in all aspects of society and explicit PKM addresses cognitive support for people. Its perspective is broader than conventional KM and comes from cognitive and social sciences and emphasizes how single individuals, teams and whole organizations can be strengthened with better and targeted IC. However, PKM also includes conventional KM approaches like the learning organization (LO) and knowledge-sharing methods like communities of practice (CoP) (Wenger 1998) within the enterprise and networks of practice (NoP) (Brown and Duguid 2000) among people with similar interests in different, at times competing, enterprises. As indicated in the introduction, PKM must support all three societal levels:

1. From the personal perspective – the objective is personal fulfilment and quality of life.

2. From society's economic and business perspectives – the objective is workforce competence.

3. From society's operational and functional perspectives – the objective is citizenship capabilities and societal behaviour.

Understanding how people and organizations handle situations, including decision-making and problem-solving tasks, is important for conducting PKM successfully. That requires insights into areas as diverse as situation-handling practices, cognitive sciences, knowledge transfer methods, microeconomics, management principles and supporting information technology. These insights are required to diagnose knowledge-related operations where knowledge-intensive work is often tacit and knowledge bottlenecks may be difficult to identify. They are also needed to conceptualize and implement KM initiatives and monitor utilization of knowledge-related resources.

If future work was a simple continuation of today's work, existing knowledge would be all one needed for effective KM. However, today's world is chaordic and much, often the most important work, must deal competently with internal and external changes, unanticipated opportunities and challenges. Hence, effective PKM must specifically address ways to prepare personal competence at every societal level to meet these demands, which generally are largely unknown and therefore require deep and broad knowledge.

When people retire, change positions, are promoted or leave, most organizations are faced with problems caused by lack of people with the requisite competence. In many nations and districts there are also undersupplies of qualified people. The USA has shortages of engineers, medical doctors and nurses – as does Germany. Also, well-educated people may be available with good general subject knowledge but lack the job-specific skills needed. Consequently, there are constant needs for PKM nearly everywhere to build knowledge and improve IC assets.

Determining KM Strategy and Initiatives

Theoretically, many KM alternatives are possible – even potentially beneficial. However, in practice some choices are more attractive than others. From a practical perspective many factors determine the attractiveness and feasibility of alternatives. These include the organization's and individuals' needs, available professional capabilities and IC resources and prevailing culture and practices. In addition, it must be determined what is possible within the context, how it will work in practice, and particularly, how changes introduced by the alternatives will improve performance. Examples of the aspects of PKM that include strategic and tactical requirements are indicated in Figure 12.8.

OPERATIONAL KM CONSIDERATIONS

Operational KM focuses on creating and fostering general KM practices and initiating and managing individual knowledge processes. Examples include: implementing lifelong learning programmes and expert networks to make decision-makers more competent to handle specific tasks in public agencies, social services, enterprises or people in their daily lives. Operational KM objectives emphasize collecting, organizing, transferring and utilizing knowledge while also creating and operating KM systems, establishing external KM connections and partnering.

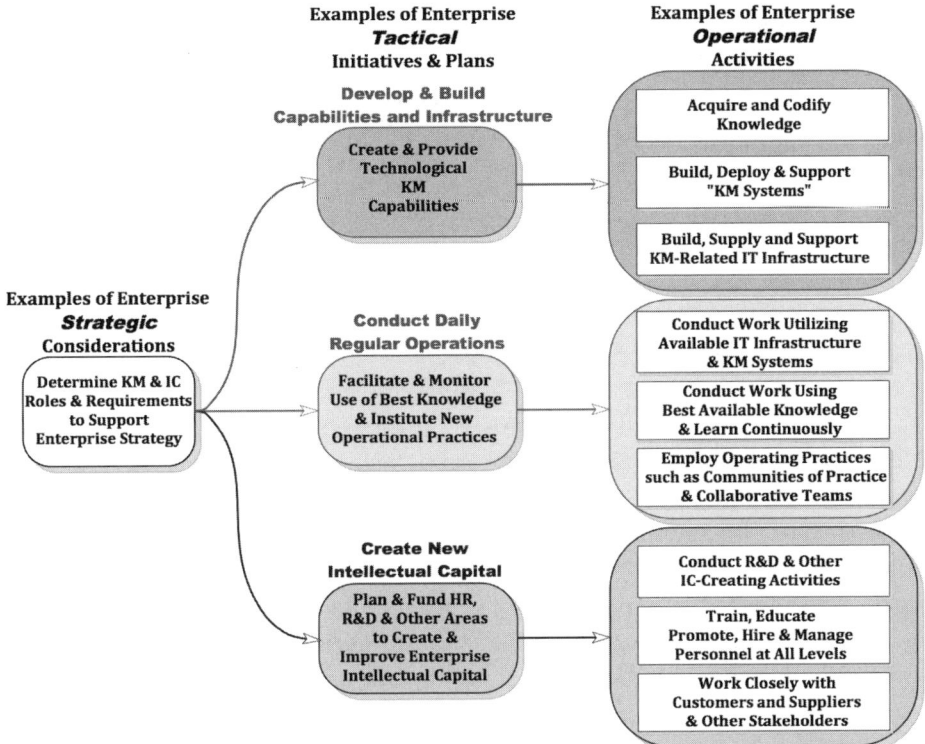

Figure 12.8 Strategic, tactical and operational knowledge management-related activities. Copyright © 2007 by Knowledge Research Institute, Inc. Reproduced with permission

TACTICAL KM CONSIDERATIONS

Tactical KM focuses on devising knowledge processes to achieve more effective operations. For example, PKM-supported innovation increases personal competence for authority delegation, thereby reducing unnecessary bureaucratic procedures, time required to provide service and employee turnover. Tactical KM objectives are to facilitate operational KM by creating KM infrastructure, build KM staff capabilities, establish KM practices and monitor KM efforts everywhere.

STRATEGIC KM CONSIDERATIONS

Strategic KM perspectives focus on creating and expanding relationships with customers, suppliers, strategic partners and other stakeholders to meet enterprise goals. An example is to use PKM to increase employee expertise to deliver new customer services. Strategic KM objectives are: (a) to assist enterprise strategy creation by providing insights into how KM can support, improve or expand enterprise strategy; and (b) to determine the direction for KM itself based on how it should support and implement enterprise strategy, tactical efforts and daily regular operations.

KM support of operational work is relatively straightforward since it is often possible to define and describe normal tasks and their situation-handling concisely and concretely. Also, knowledge for operational work can be less dynamic than for tactical and strategic work and therefore may lend itself better for explication and inclusion in knowledge bases (KBs) and decision-support systems (DSSs). However, most operational work will also have special situations: (a) irregularities – problem situations where things go wrong or are difficult; and (b) infrequent tasks that require specialized knowledge for on-site decision-making and fast actions to avert greater problems – or just to expedite work by lessening operational friction.

Tactical, and particularly strategic, work is more challenging than operational work. However, the value of this work tends to be high. The nature of KM for tactical and strategic work falls into different areas such as creating ICT supported knowledge-based modelling for complicated 'what-if' analysis, knowledge mining in unstructured natural language KBs, social software for collaboration and CoP support and general infrastructure capabilities. However, the major challenges result from the broad range of tasks that these functions must address – many of which deal with novel situations which need creative solutions based on new knowledge.

Knowledge Pathways and Options

Some PKM pathways in society are formal and publicly or enterprise managed. Others are informal, and it is generally agreed that over a lifetime, informal learning provides most of a person's knowledge from experiences, learning-while-doing and networking. Figure 12.9 provides examples of typical educational pathways as normally found in every country. Most of these pathways are formal while some, like most LLL options, are informal.

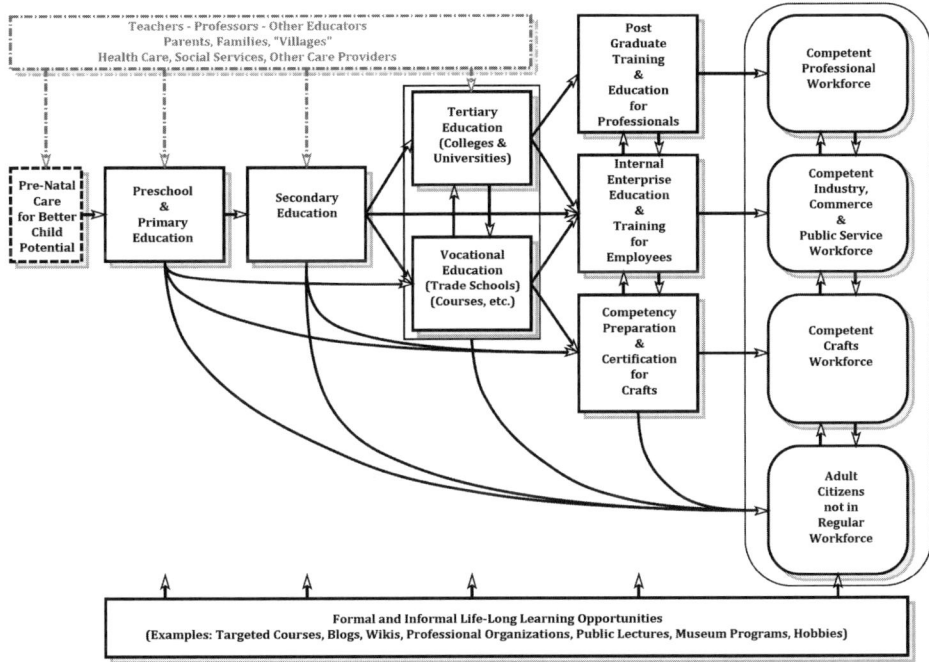

**Figure 12.9   Simplified model of educational pathways in society.
Copyright © 2008 by Knowledge Research Institute, Inc.
Reproduced with permission**

In most enterprises, most operational KM deals with transferring knowledge from subject matter experts (knowledge holders – KHs) to knowledge workers (KWs), either directly or via pathways like training classes or automated systems. In societies, similar transfers take place. Figure 12.10 presents examples of knowledge transfer pathways from experts and KHs to KWs and automated business systems. Some paths are largely technology-based and result in the creation of knowledge-based systems. Others are people-based with KHs and KWs in direct or indirect contact and increasingly supported by technology capabilities of many kinds. The examples of technology-based paths result in creation and use of many kinds of automated business systems (ABSs), decision support systems and knowledge bases. DSS and KB capabilities are used directly by KWs while ABSs are mainstays of information management (IM) in the enterprise and generally perform their tasks without human interaction. The examples in Figure 12.10 distinguish between *explicit* and *tacit knowledge*, which as indicated above are significant elements of IC. In addition (not shown) is the *embedded knowledge* in automated systems.

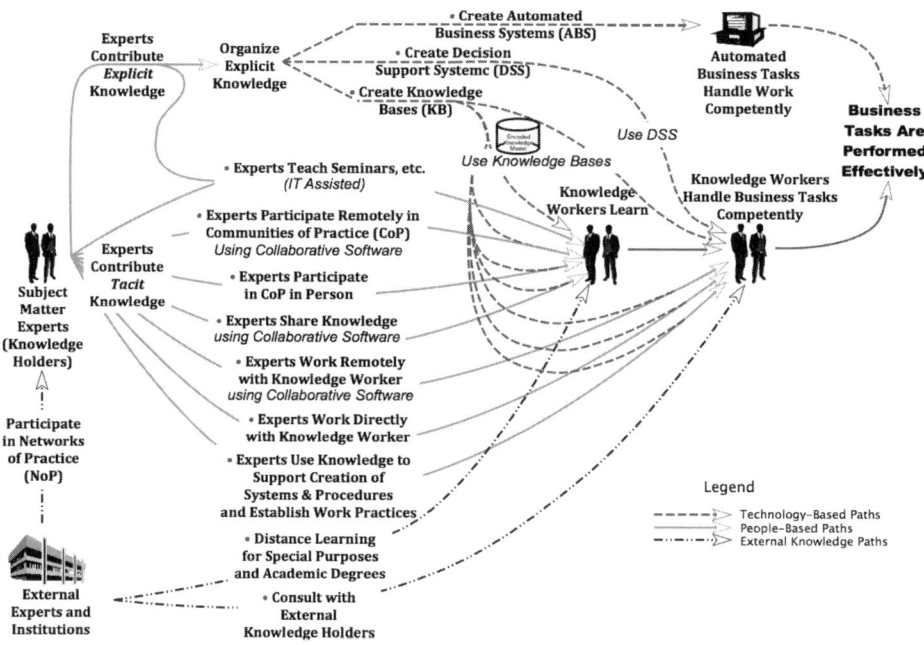

Figure 12.10   Pathways from knowledge sources to knowledge workers
and automated systems. Copyright © 2008 by Knowledge
Research Institute, Inc. Reproduced with permission

Explicit knowledge transfers require that KHs contribute what they can explain or demonstrate to capture and document pertinent knowledge. Explicit knowledge may be provided as narrative, videos, graphics, text, equations, ontologies, computer code and so on. Transferring explicit knowledge into successfully useable forms requires considerable resources and expertise in several fields beyond the target subject and conventional KM. Disciplines needed for this work include advanced computer sciences and artificial intelligence (AI), cognitive sciences and ergonomics, branches of philosophy and management sciences. Specifically, expertise is required to elicit knowledge competently, organize knowledge into structures such as ontologies, and systems that facilitate effective use, create efficient technical systems and create powerful man–machine interfaces including sophisticated search features that facilitate efficient execution of business tasks. In addition, human interfaces must match the cognitive approaches that KWs engage in during knowledge work.

Other knowledge pathways include knowledge from external sources like research organizations, universities, consultancies and other knowledge holders. In some instances, that also includes collaboration and outsourcing knowledge building through targeted R&D projects. Yet other pathways involve the gradual inclusion of *implicit knowledge* into routines, practices, culture and traditions that result from all-present people efforts to improve organizational and work processes.

Some Personal Knowledge Management Approaches

Table 12.1 provides a few examples of PKM formal and informal options for a range of societal purposes. These are operational PKM examples – and the number of options is large. As indicated earlier, there is also a need to identify and pursue tactical and strategic options.

Table 12.1   Examples of formal and informal PKM options

	General knowledge-building purposes	Societal purpose knowledge-building	Enterprise purpose knowledge-building	Personal purpose knowledge-building
Knowledge-building objective	Build general levels of IC in the population as basis for further development.	Build specialized IC for public service competence and public participation by citizens.	Build specialized business and industry IC for workforce competence.	Build specific IC in support of individual interests, daily life management, and improved QoL.
Formal education and knowledge transfer	• Preschools • Primary education • Secondary education • Tertiary education	• Secondary education • Tertiary education (social and political science, etc.)	• Tertiary education • Vocational education • Corporate universities • Targeted courses	• Preschools • Primary, secondary, vocational and tertiary education
Informal knowledge creation and transfer and education	• Museums • Community programmes • Topic-specific websites • Web 2.0, blogs, wikis	• Community programmes • Topic-specific websites, blogs, wikis (economic, societal and political issues, etc.)	• Learning on the job • KB decision support systems • Collaboration, teamwork, CoPs, NoPs	• Museums • Community programmes • Topic-specific websites, blogs, wikis (health, finance, legal)

Societal Infrastructure Support for Personal Knowledge Management

Infrastructure to support PKM includes capabilities for collaboration, structural IC, knowledge transfer and personal IC management. Within these areas are technical facilities such as video conferencing facilities, document morgues, email and wikis, social software, ontologies, search engines, knowledge-base structures and websites. However, PKM infrastructure also includes KM-related policies such as established enterprise approaches for capturing and reusing lessons learned, accessing experts, structured collaboration project team practices, sharing in intellectual property such as inventions and many others.

KNOWLEDGE MANAGEMENT AND SOCIAL SOFTWARE

Social software covers a wide range of support applications. Among these are collaborative software and groupware, instant messaging and wikis for conducting exploratory multi-logs and knowledge-sharing. Effective collaborative software and groupware are sophisticated Internet or intranet applications that may support multiple windows for participant video and voice communications, for video displays, PowerPoint and other presentations, for sharing text and graphics and for private notes and documents. Collaborative software has become important for informal work sessions, CoPs, team collaboration and for briefings, distance education and other multiple-party functions in the enterprise, in NoPs and in society as a whole.

One area of importance here is the use of wikis. From one perspective, wikis let people work together online similarly to how they work face-to-face by having threaded discussions to explore ideas or deepen understanding of a knowledge area. Another use of wikis is the enterprise-dedicated creation and continually updating of KBs by any approved participant which are on websites, such as is happening with Wikipedia.

KNOWLEDGE MANAGEMENT AND ADVANCED SEARCH – SEMANTIC SEARCH

Advanced search procedures have great value to knowledge workers who are engaged in intellectual and conceptual work. These procedures may rely on pre-indexed information that may be organized by semantic principles. They may also – and with increasing importance – operate using natural language processing (NLP) of unstructured materials such as reports and document text in archival databases or in the public domain. The latter search procedures may use dictionaries of synonyms and phrase relationships or powerful NLP to perform semantic and even concept-based searches.

Final Observations – A Societal Challenge

Developed nations have been able to create and sell highly prized goods and services in part as a result of higher educational levels in their professional and crafts workforces. Historically, developing nations have provided goods with less knowledge-intensiveness at relatively low cost, goods produced by workforces with less education – and by people who receive much lower salaries and lead a reduced QoL. Consequently, developed nations have bought a wide range of goods (and to a smaller extent, services) from developing nations at lower costs than they themselves could deliver – often with the sacrifice of people with less economic and political clout.

Increased reliance on knowledge and understanding and their influence will lead to many changes and shifts in local economies and trading between nations. For example, as the global playing field is flattened, opportunities for industrialized developed nations (in North America, Europe, Japan, and so on) to obtain low-cost goods and services from lower-cost nations (for example, India, China and much of Latin America and Africa) will be diminished. This change has already started as people in some nations improve their competencies and start to demand an improved QoL – therefore becoming more costly.

The educational gap between many nations is in the process of being reduced. For example, in 2008, India has a greater number of people with doctorates in engineering and science than any other nation – although there still is significant illiteracy. Educational levels in the USA and parts of Europe seem to be stagnant or even deteriorating – in absolute terms and compared with those in many up-and-coming nations. Successful outsourcing of knowledge-intensive and sophisticated work to developing nations is common. Immediately, the issues surface: 'which advanced and knowledge-intensive products will the developed world be able to create and deliver to maintain its current living standards if it falls behind in educating its workforce?' 'What will the world look like if we all become equally knowledgeable and empowered?' and 'Who will perform what now is labour-intensive low-paying work like sewing garments or harvesting produce?'

From a societal perspective, applying deliberate and systematic PKM that emphasizes societal performance appears to be both desirable and appropriate – for now. More effective personal and societal behaviours will certainly provide increased societal value according to current objectives. However, it is not clear that current objectives are appropriate for long-term societal stability and balance (Malone and Yohe 2002; Stavely 2002). Nations may adopt new goals – they may decide to collaborate instead of compete – and to depend upon each other since they have to co-exist on our limited-sized planet.

As we consider the progress of our efforts to manage knowledge to make societies more effective, the question arises: 'What is the purpose of these endeavours?' The objectives for the directly affected societies for the next year and the next decade are quite clear. Narrowly, they have to do with national or regional survival, success and QoL for citizens and other stakeholders directly affected by the society's operations and functions. It is not so clear what the broader and longer-term objectives are – or should be – and which implications may ensue. From myopic and self-serving societal perspectives, the long-term objectives may be for strong nations to prosper at the expense of weaker nations. From global perspectives, issues such as equality among nations and 'the gap in wealth and health that separates rich and poor' start to emerge (Landes 1999). Malone and Yohe (2002, 368) state it clearly: 'Continued exponential and asymmetrical growth in both population and individual economic productivity would propel world society along a path that is environmentally unsustainable, economically inequitable, and hence socially unstable'.

Potentially, we may use the building and application of knowledge and understanding – worldwide – as the tool by which we level the global playing field. This, we believe, is the real challenge for deliberate and systematic societal knowledge management.

It is clear that unless a society focuses on improving people's competence and ability to work effectively, it will be at a global disadvantage. That will be the case if the enterprise is a company, a non-governmental organization (NGO), a government department or a whole nation. The required people-focus must address several aspects – and they must be balanced. The aspects cover knowledge empowerment of employees, their decision autonomy, their need to understand societal policies, directions, strategies and obligations to stakeholders and lastly – but absolutely importantly – their accountability. Many organizations have gone overboard in one direction or another by emphasizing a single aspect, such as the political, social or economic sector –

and only that one. However, as Mintzberg (Stavely 2002) argues, that does not work. As elsewhere in life – a balanced approach is required here and can only be achieved when public servants and the general population are knowledgeable and receive reliable and truthful information.

References

Brown, J. and Duguid, P. (2000), *The Social Life of Information* (Boston: Harvard Business School Press).

Coulombe, S. et al. (2004), *International Adult Literacy Survey: Literacy Scores, Human Capital and Growth across Fourteen OECD Countries*. Statistics Canada, Catalogue no. 89-552-XPE, no. 11, http://www.nald.ca/fulltext/oecd/oecd. pdf, accessed 16 June 2009.

Fauconnier, G. and Turner, M. (2003), *The Way We Think: Conceptual Blending and the Mind's Hidden Complexities* (New York: Basic Books).

Gazzaniga, M. et al. (2008), *Cognitive Neuroscience*, 3rd edn. (New York: Norton).

Hock, D. (1997), *Birth of the Chaordic Age* (San Francisco: Berrett-Koehler).

Johnson-Laird, P. (2006), *How We Reason* (New York: Oxford University Press).

Kuhn, D. (2000), 'Metacognitive Development', *Current Directions in Psychological Science* 9:5, 178–81.

Landes, D. (1999), *The Wealth and Poverty of Nations: Why Some Are So Rich and Some So Poor* (New York: Norton).

Malone, T. and Yohe, G. (2002), 'Knowledge Partnerships for a Sustainable, Equitable, and Stable Society', *Journal of Knowledge Management* 6:4, 368–78.

Mashayekh, F. (2007), 'Lifelong Learning in Knowledge Society', http://cnx.org/content/m14754/latest/, accessed 16 June 2009.

Peterson, B. and Nielson, G. (2009), *Fake Work: Why People Are Working Harder than Ever but Accomplishing Less, and How to Fix the Problem* (New York: Simon & Schuster).

Quinn, J. et al. (1996), 'Managing Professional Intellect: Making the Most of the Best', *Harvard Business Review* 74:2, 71–80.

Roos, J. et al. (1998), *Managing Intellectual Capital in Practice: Navigating in the New Business Landscape* (Boston: Elsevier Butterworth-Heinemann).

Samawati, S. and Stumph, C. (2006), 'Private Enterprise Job Creation in the Midwest: Does Size Matter?' *Christian Brothers University Applied Business Review* 27 March, https://secure.cbu.edu/mt/abr/archives/2006/03/private_enterpr.html, accessed 16 June 2009.

Stavely, A. (2002), 'Oration honouring Dr. Henry Mintzberg', *Gazette*, 13 June, http://www.mun.ca/marcomm/gazette/2001-2002/june13/convo13.html, accessed 16 June 2009.

Stewart, T. (1991), 'Brainpower', *Fortune* 123:11, 44–60.

—— (1997), *Intellectual Capital: The New Wealth of Organizations* (New York: Currency Doubleday).

Taleb, N. (2007), *The Black Swan: The Impact of the Highly Improbable* (New York: Random House).

UNESCO (2001), 'International Literacy Day 2001', www.sil.org/literacy/LitFacts.htm, accessed 16 June 2009.

Wenger, E. (1998), *Communities of Practice: Learning, Meaning and Identity* (New York: Cambridge University Press).

Wiig, K.M. (2004), *People-Focused Knowledge Management: How Effective Decision Making Leads to Corporate Success* (Boston: Butterworth-Heinemann).

—— (2007), 'Effective Societal Knowledge Management', *Journal of Knowledge Management* 11:5, 141–56.

—— (2008), *Competent Enterprise Knowledge Management*, White Paper (Arlington: Knowledge Research Institute).

Index

References to illustrations are in **bold**.

If you have found this book useful you may be interested in other titles from Gower

Electronic Performance Support
Using Digital Technology to Enhance Human Ability
Edited by Philip Barker and Paul van Schaik
Hardback: 978-0-566-08884-1
e-book: 978-0-566-09239-8

Enterprise 2.0
How Social Software Will Change the Future of Work
Niall Cook
Hardback: 978-0-566-08800-1

Making Knowledge Visible
Communicating Knowledge Through Information Products
Elizabeth Orna
Hardback: 978-0-566-08562-8
Paperback: 978-0-566-08563-5

Visit **www.gowerpublishing.com** and

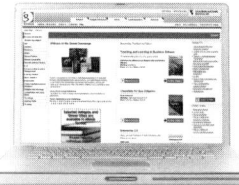

- search the entire catalogue of Gower books in print
- order titles online at 10% discount
- take advantage of special offers
- sign up for our monthly e-mail update service
- download free sample chapters from all recent titles
- download or order our catalogue

GOWER